DANA GILLESPIE

Weren't Born A Man

Dana Gillespie

with David Shasha

HAWKSMOOR
PUBLISHING

First published 2020 by Hawksmoor Publishing

Kemp House, 152-160 City Rd, London, EC1V 2NX

www.hawksmoorpublishing.com

ISBN: 9781838099046 [Hardback] | 9781838099053 [Softback]

Sir Elton John "Spending time with Dana was very special. She was magical, and helped me overcome my shyness. She knew my story before I did! All the memories I have of her are fond ones. So much laughter and kindness which helped me enormously. Those brilliant times will never be forgotten."

Sir Tim Rice "Dana Gillespie is larger and more fun than life, whether on land or sea, stage or skis. Simultaneously beautifully earthy and ethereal, and effortlessly able to wring both sadness and hope out of the blues, often in the same line. She's got everything she needs, she's an artist, she don't look back. Everything's all right, everything's fine. I can't wait to read your book."

Rick Wakeman "Having had the great pleasure of performing with Dana (in the musical sense of the word I hasten to add), I only wish I had played on more of her recordings. Introduced to me by her producer and mutual friend David Bowie, playing with her (again I mean musically so as to avoid any confusion) on the famous Trident Bechstein Grand was so enjoyable, and since then our paths have crossed more than a few times… including us both playing at the same blues festival in Ticino where her voice was truly amazing and better than ever. A real talent with everything she has ever done… I can't wait to read the book! A beautiful artistic lady in every sense of the word."

Angie Bowie "Dana Gillespie is a Goddess among Women, and in her element regaling, revealing, reliving all the stories, all the adventures, all the music: live and producing 70 albums, the songwriting, the shows attended and performed.

Dana has enjoyed a jam-packed, creative and professional life with time for artistry and attention paid to spirituality and her inner life. Dana has performed and travelled internationally to support the teachings of Sai Baba. She organized the talent and the details of the festival in Mustique for 20 years. And then there is the passion and Love, the boyfriends, the partnerships, the audiences, the travel, the recording, the backstage gossip and Feel the Heat!"

Julian Clary "From David Bowie to Alf Garnett… They say that variety is the spice of life, and Dana's life has seen more spice than most. What a life! What a woman! What a book!"

Tony Defries "When I met Dana half a century ago, we formed an instant bond of mutual adoration. In all those years, time has not tempered nor distanced nor dimmed *That Loving Feeling*. She is exotic, adorable, uninhibited, beautiful, funny, erudite and smart. Whether speaking or singing, her voice wraps around every note with ease, while shades of caramel, toffee, and chocolate come to mind. Her delivery and fabulous phrasing is effortless and relaxed, and she is one of the most honest, generous, unassuming and unaffected artists I have ever worked with."

Marc Almond "Dana is fearless. She treads all over PC preciousness with some of the most funny and scandalous anecdotes I've heard of a life outrageously lived. And if that wasn't enough, she sings the blues with a sauciness that's chilli hot and ripe with erotic innuendo that can only come from a lady of full experience. A treasure, a legend, the Queen of cleavage and the last Empress of Bohemia."

Cherry Vanilla "What an amazing career. You were there with David and Defries before any of us were around. It will be nice to hear about the early days when you and David first met. We never knew that David. Keep making music, writing, and being the sensual, beautiful woman that you are."

Phill Brown "Dana Gillespie, with her entourage and band, could be described with justification as the epitome of sex, drugs and rock 'n' roll. The sessions I worked on with Dana went to further extremes than any I worked on during the whole of the 1970s."

Aimi MacDonald "Such joyful memories of working with Dana in Pantomime; a very cool and focused, talented lady."

ACKNOWLEDGEMENTS

This is not the first time I have sat down to write my memoirs. About 10 years ago, with the support of my good friend Michael Leiner and his splendid secretary Jean Hardy, I even managed to complete an earlier version, which I called 'I Rest My Case'. It was never published, and was only seen by a few friends and relations, whose main comment was "Where's the hot sex?!"

Since then, I tried to revisit it on several occasions, but never seemed to find the time. Then, as I approached my 70th birthday, I felt that if I didn't do it now, I probably never would.

About a year-and-a-half ago, my 'partner in crime' in writing this book, David Shasha, was the latest in a long line of people to tell me that I should do it. The difference on this occasion was that he introduced me to his friend Greville Waterman, who in turn introduced me to James Lumsden-Cook at the publishing house Hawksmoor Publishing, who has patiently developed the book and worked tirelessly to bring the project to fruition. Without their support and belief in my story, you would not now be holding this book in your hands.

Armed with the original manuscript, several volumes of books of my press cuttings, and a disturbing ability to discover things about me that I had forgotten decades ago, Shasha (as I call him – I have known so many Davids!) spent many hours recording interviews with me at home. He was often 'assisted' by his pet dachshund Lola, who provided me with licks and cuddles throughout the process, particularly when rewarded with a treat. Working with the transcripts of those recordings, he produced a new draft from which we began the exercise of creating this book.

I doubt that many people would have had the patience to do this, so I consider Shasha to be an angel, especially as he is a total music freak, which really helped when talking about my past with so many musicians. I was getting to the point where I thought I should just give up with the book altogether, but he came into my life and saved it from extinction, and so to him I give more thanks than can ever be put down on paper.

Shasha's wife Zuzanna has allowed me to 'borrow' him for countless days, and his children Maciek and Nina, have helped with transcribing and proof-reading, as well as assisting both of us on the regular occasions when our (in)abilities with a computer brought work to a standstill.

So many others have contributed to this book, whom I should like to acknowledge here.

My sincere thanks to Elton John, Tim Rice, Angie Bowie, Julian Clary, Rick Wakeman, Tony Defries, Marc Almond, Cherry Vanilla, Aimi MacDonald, and Phill Brown for their kind words.

Many of the photographs were taken by Jorg Huber and Leslie Spitz who are sadly no longer with us, but whom I nevertheless wish to acknowledge. We had many great adventures together, and I miss them both. My good friend Gered Mankowitz gave me access to his wonderful vault of photographs, including the front cover images. Tony Zanetta managed to unearth many of my 'Pornaroids' from the Mainman era (though sadly not the one of Bowie and Jagger together, which has disappeared). Tony Defries had given me the polaroid camera and encouraged me to use it, and had he not done so, then many of the photographs in this book would not exist. He and his wife Marlene have been very kind in opening up the Mainman archive for me. My guitarist in The London Blues Band, Jake Zaitz, took the photograph of me and my heavily-stickered guitar case, and his wife Anastasiia the photo on the back cover. My dear friend Marcus Shields took the picture of Shasha and Lola, "the Hairy One". I should also mention David Exley who worked wonders on some of the old polaroids, making them look like they were taken yesterday rather than nearly 50 years ago.

I have tried to acknowledge all of the photographers whose images appear in this book, but if any have been inadvertently overlooked then please accept my apologies.

Other long-standing friends have provided me with support and encouragement, including Mike Hewitson (who took the photos of me with Elton and Kiki), Phill Brown, and David Charkham. Another friend from Lugano in Switzerland, Ed Bersier, helped with the earlier version, as did Belinda Wright. Thanks also to Pete

Sims & Andy Boyle, Charles Donovan, Tris Penna, and Dominic Cheetham.

I would also like to thank Milijana Novakovic, who does a wonderful job managing my Facebook page (www.Facebook.com/ DanaGillespieOfficial).

My thanks to all the members of The London Blues Band, both past and present, for their wonderful support over the years, and also Joachim Palden and his musicians, who have backed me so splendidly for the best part of four decades.

I have performed with countless musicians and actors over the years. Some are referred to in the text, but acknowledging all of them would require a second volume! There again, some people may be grateful not to have got a mention…

My apologies to all the people whom I haven't name-checked, but should have. Blame old age!

That excuse also applies if you find any mistakes. What is contained within these pages is my life as I remember it. If you remember anything differently, please tell me – so I can correct my mistakes in all the subsequent editions(!).

Dana.

www.dana-gillespie.com

DAVID SHASHA

David Shasha is a self-confessed music nut who, like many men of his age, first became aware of Dana when she released her "Weren't Born A Man" album in the early seventies. Many years later, after asking her why she had never written her life story, he soon found himself at her home in South Kensington reading her press cuttings and listening to her reminiscences. He lives across the park from Dana in London with his wife, two children – and Lola the dachshund. This is his first book.

CONTENTS

INTRODUCTION

When I look back, my immediate thought is, 'Holy Shit, I have had an incredible life!'

Where do I start?

- Being British junior waterski champion for four years
- Spending time with Bob Dylan, and hanging out in his hotel suite with The Beatles
- Having wild times with Keith Moon, Michael Caine, Sean Connery, Roman Polanski and the cream of 1960's rock royalty
- Recording with Jimmy Page and Elton John
- Going out with David Bowie, singing a song written for me by him, then living with David and his then-wife, Angie, in their New York hotel suite
- Living in Iggy Pop's old flat, and having my portrait done by Andy Warhol's Factory
- Performing as Mary Magdalene in the original London production of Jesus Christ Superstar, and as the Acid Queen in Tommy
- Singing the Blues with Mick Jagger, Ronnie Wood – and Princess Margaret – in Mustique
- Sharing a stage with Chuck Berry and Bo Diddley
- Appearing in movies with Peter Cook and Dudley Moore, Terry-Thomas, Kenneth Williams, Leslie Phillips, Spike Milligan, and many other British comedy greats
- Taking the lead in hit shows in the West End of London and at the Edinburgh Festival
- Acting in films directed by Nicholas Roeg, Ken Russell, and Mai Zetterling
- Launching and running the Mustique Blues Festival for 20 years
- Performing Shakespeare with Sir John Gielgud and Arthur Lowe
- TV appearances on Til Death Us Do Part, Little and Large, Seaside Special, Hazell, The Bill, and others

1

- Pantomiming with Jimmy Edwards and 'the lovely Aimi MacDonald' in Eastbourne
- Topping the pop charts across Europe
- Performing to an audience of one million people in India
- Being voted top of the Record Mirror poll for 'Top Pop Ladies', as well as 'Top British Female Blues Vocalist', and being inducted into the Blues Hall Of Fame
- Discovering myself through the teachings of Indian guru Sathya Sai Baba, and travelling the world to share His thoughts and principles

I have made over 70 albums, including folk, rock, musicals, Blues, and even recordings in Sanskrit called Bhajans. I have acted in 14 feature films, have appeared on television and radio around the world, and am still performing in Blues festivals and concerts across Europe.

I grew up in a house where both my mother and father lived with their 'significant others'. I survived an avalanche, drove Marc Bolan's minivan, burst out of my costume on film sets, was saved from drowning by a ghost, and introduced a gangster to royalty. I was making records before I was old enough to smoke or drink, and sang on David Bowie's breakthrough 'Ziggy Stardust' album.

Angie Bowie, a close friend to this day, wrote of me, 'Dana was a great singer, songwriter, actress, athlete, and beauty, and her accomplishments ranged from winning a place on the British water ski team to playing Mary Magdalene in the original West End production of Jesus Christ Superstar, to amassing a body of sexual expertise uncanny in one so young. She was something else; one look and you were an instant fan. David had said, "You two are really going to get along", and he was right. London was our oyster; all we had to do with reach out and touch it, and it would respond'.

We certainly had some pretty wild times together in the seventies.

People say that *you need to have lived before you can sing the Blues.* Well, I have certainly lived, and I adore the life I'm living now.

If anything, I suppose I'm glad to have survived, and to still be here to tell the tales. I hope you enjoy them.

Dana, London, September 2020

1: THE FIRST TEN YEARS

Let me start at the beginning.

I was born at 12.15 am on March 30th, 1949, in Woking Hospital, Surrey, to Anne (nee Buxton), and Dr. Henry Gillespie, and was named Richenda Antoinette de Winterstein Gillespie.

I sometimes wonder if we choose our parents, as there is no doubt that I was incredibly lucky with mine. My mother was gracious and kind to all, and my father was a fascinating, gregarious, and often womanising man. From these two wonderful liberal characters, I learned how to live my life without too much interference, and with virtually no restraints.

My mother's side of the family was traditionally English, with roots in Norfolk and a family heritage that includes the Gurney, Fry, and Buxton families, all quite tightly knitted. The Gurneys were an influential family of English Quakers who founded the eponymous bank, which merged with Barclays in the late nineteenth century. The Frys were also Quakers, and are perhaps best known for founding the famous Fry's confectionary business. Elizabeth Gurney married Joseph Fry in 1800. The Buxtons, meanwhile, were either in breweries, or they were bible thumpers, which meant converting natives in Darkest Africa, as it was always known in our part of the family.

The relations on my mother's side of the family were big on doing good. My mother's great-great-grandfather, Sir Thomas Fowell Buxton (1786-1845), campaigned with William Wilberforce to introduce the Slavery Abolition Act in 1833. He was a Member of Parliament at the age of 32, was the first Chairman of the Royal Society for the Prevention of Cruelty to Animals, and was the brother-in-law of prison reformer Elizabeth Fry (nee Gurney). In addition to her prison work, she also played a major role in improving the British hospital system, as well as the treatment of the insane. The faces of both Elizabeth and Sir Thomas appeared on the back of the old (2001-2016) British five-pound note. Elizabeth is on the right, with her signature underneath, whilst Sir Thomas stands on the far left of the note, easily recognisable by his long sideburns, though he got no name check.

When I was very young, I can remember many ancient great aunts and uncles returning from fascinating-sounding faraway places. A lot of the exotic things in their homes were brought back from countries in Africa and Asia. I still have a huge Chinese gong that was used to call people to lunch or dinner, which I enthusiastically used to bang at the age of five, much to the annoyance of the older folks. Anything exotic and Oriental, and I was hooked.

I haven't changed much in that respect.

One of my relations was called Lucy Bentinck, known in the family as Great Aunt Lucy, though I think she must have had several 'Greats' to her name as she always seemed really old to me. She once took me, aged nine, to meet Sir Edmund Hillary, but I can only remember shaking hands with Sherpa Tensing.

My mother, Anne Frances Roden Buxton, was born in 1920 and was one of four sisters and two brothers. The whole clan was very close, which meant that, at Christmas time, there would often be 30 or more people sitting down to eat, with cousins popping up from all over the world. The food was often stone cold by the time it got from the Aga to my plate.

Sunday meant going to church in the morning, and I'm afraid to say that I usually fell asleep on my mother's shoulder during the boring sermons. If I didn't go to sleep, I would often get terrible fits of giggles. Even to this day, when I have to go to a family wedding or funeral, this same urge to laugh gets to me, and I have to chew the inside of my gums to stop myself. My father always used to say that if one has the choice of going to a wedding or a funeral, pick the funeral… at least you'll know the outcome. He also used to say that if you had to choose between sex or food, choose food as at least you could eat three times a day. I was much thinner in my younger days!

Judging from early photographs, my mother was a large-busted, slim-legged, eye-catching woman. During the War, she was either on a bicycle with a tin bucket on her head for bomb protection, or she was driving ambulances in Holland. Somehow, in the middle of all this madness, she met my father. He was as different as you could get in those difficult days.

For a start, he was a very good-looking Austrian/German, which meant that my mother's father was horrified at the thought of his daughter marrying the 'enemy', especially as they had only known each other for about three weeks. I can only assume that the War made people do impetuous things, as it was rather out of character for my mother to do anything crazy like that. She was always the solid, sensible sort of woman; in her youth, she had been Head Girl at Westonbirt boarding school, and was a Girl Guide with lots of badges on her arms. Yet, here she was, falling for a highly unsuitable man, who was clearly far too attractive and charming to remain faithful for long. Mind you, she probably worked this out after I came into this world.

My father had been christened Hans Heinrich Winterstein when born in 1910, but he was always known as Henry, though later-on in life the close family members all called him Dadster. He officially changed his name to Gillespie, saying that it would be impossible to get work as a doctor with such a difficult name to pronounce as Winterstein. As he was studying medicine in Edinburgh, and had been sponsored by a Scottish doctor called Gillespie, it seemed as good a name as any.

It's also a good name to have in the Blues and Jazz world. If I had a pound for every time I was asked if Dizzy Gillespie was my father, I'd be rolling in it by now. It seems strange to me that anyone should think this, as Dizzy was quite a few shades darker than me, though I suppose I could have been an adopted daughter.

Not much is known about my father's past, but he was the seventh generation of medical men and was known to be extremely good at his job. He always said that his mother had been a beauty who had been 'generous with her affections' in order to survive the horrors of war. I can only remember her when she was quite old, living in London, in the White House near Regents Park. As I was very young at the time, my memories of her are from her feet upwards; she had big surgical looking shoes – sturdy and brown – and long voluminous skirts.

The White House consisted of small self-contained apartments in a large white block, and always smelt slightly of boiled cabbage; it must have been on many a menu. We often used to go with my grandmother to Schmidts, the only German food shop where one could buy decent leberwurst and sauerkraut. At Christmas time, they sold marvellous lebkuchen that hung on the festive tree next to the gelee royale, another of my father's favourites.

My grandmother was always known as Oma, in true Germanic style, and a lot of her time was spent making amazing clothes for my sister's dolls. I, myself, was never a doll person, much preferring teddy bears; even now, I linger longingly in a toy shop if it has a Steiff soft toy department.

My elder sister was three years old when I was born, and although christened Nicola we called her Nixi. As younger sisters often do, I followed her around and probably drove her mad, but she had to put up with me as we shared a nursery.

As mentioned, Christmas was a big event in our family, and there would always be presents under the tree from our godparents. One year, Nixi got a bicycle from her godfather, Count Ostheim, and I got a pony called Rusty from my godmother, Jean Buxton. My other godparents were Countess Margaret de Reneville, who was the daughter of the writer Claire Sheridan, and Sir Tommy Buxton. The only thing Sir Tommy ever gave me when I was growing up was a doll that I didn't like, but he did provide me with a wonderful story that my mother told years later.

It seems that Sir Tommy had been in Russia during the War, as he'd learnt the language at university and was using his talents in the Foreign Office. While there, he did the unthinkable by falling in love with a beautiful, slim Russian girl called Ina. Of course, this was strictly against spy rules and one time – when he was on leave in England – he was told by his superiors that Ina had been killed in a crash. Ina was also told, in Russia, that Tommy was dead, so they both got on with their lives, thinking that the other was gone. Tommy always carried a torch for her and, though he married once for a short while, he never forgot Ina.

About 40 years later, when Tommy was fiddling about with the radio, looking for the BBC World Service, he suddenly heard what he was convinced was Ina's voice. So sure was he that he rang the BBC to enquire further. It was indeed her! After some extensive searching, he even managed to track her down; one can only imagine the shock she felt hearing from him after such a long time.

Tommy wanted to meet her. She told him that she had been married, but that her husband had died of cancer. She also warned him that she didn't look the same as he would remember her. But that didn't deter Tommy, who organised for her to come to England for a visit. It was arranged that they should both come and stay at the home of my mother in Norfolk. True enough, Ina had changed. She had become *huge* – the way of many Russian women living on bread and potatoes – but that didn't get in the way of Tommy and Ina carrying on where they had left off many years earlier. She would come and visit him twice a year; sometimes, he would go to see her in Russia.

The poignant ending to all of this is that, on one occasion, Tommy went to collect Ina from Victoria station, but had a heart attack and died while waiting for her on the platform. When she arrived at the station and couldn't find him, she called my mother to ask why he wasn't there. Somehow my mother had already learned about Tommy's heart attack and had to pass on the sad news to Ina. She and my mother remained friends until Ina herself died a couple of years later.

For me, the story is extraordinary from the point of view of the uniqueness of the human voice. To recognise it and be so convinced someone is alive, even when you've been told many years earlier that they are dead, is amazing.

*

My father had an elder brother, known to me as Uncle Carl, who was considered one of the top shrinks in London at that time. I was told that he was an expert on male impotence, but that his clients were sometimes a little dismayed to be told to change their partners in order to resume successful sex lives!

Uncle Carl loved women from the shady world of theatre, and like my father, he married three times. Neither Uncle Carl, nor Oma, ever lost their thick Germanic styles of pronunciation, but my father spoke perfect English without a hint of an accent. He was a literary man with a marvellously full library, and was more correct with his English than a lot of the home-grown folks.

Oma and Opa (my paternal grandfather) got divorced long before I was born, and I only ever saw him once, when I was about six and we were on a family holiday in Germany. The main memory I have of him is that he was thin and resembled a hawk, but nevertheless looked like the eminent doctor that he was. In 1933, he had moved to Istanbul, or Constantinople as it was known then, having become a professor at the University of Istanbul. My father often talked of having drunk raki with Kemel Attaturk, and even now in Turkey there are pictures of Attaturk in many a cafe, so revered was he.

My father once told me a lovely story about his grandmother. When she was newly married, and travelling around India, she saw elephants working in the forest, lifting and moving tree trunks around. Thinking how well this would work if she brought an elephant back to Austria, she ordered one, together with its mahout (elephant trainer). She then forgot about the order and carried on with her journey around the world, only to receive a notification – six months later – that her elephant and mahout had arrived in Vienna. Not surprisingly, the climate did not suit the elephant, and it quickly became clear that the animal was a dead loss as a worker in the Austrian forests. Rather than lose face, she decided to ride it around the countryside, and sometimes even into Vienna. This strange and eccentric English woman, whose husband had died, leaving her in a foreign land, must have been quite a sight as she rode her elephant around the city centre.

While Uncle Carl was busy with his dysfunctional males and neurotic women after the War, my father was making his name as a radiologist. My parents moved to live in Woking, Surrey, before I was born, so all I ever knew for the first ten years of my life was a wonderful house called Fishers Hill. Built by Sir Edwin Lutyens in 1900, for the brother of the then-Prime Minister, Gerald Balfour, it was said that Sir Winston Churchill had stayed at the house on many occasions and that he had written many of his wartime speeches there while a guest of the Balfours. Jimmy Page, who will appear a little later in this book, is another aficionado of Lutyens, having owned at least two such houses.

Fishers Hill was a large dark house, but Lutyens had a way of designing with red brick, lead-edged windows, and wood beams, and the place felt very homely to me. It had, allegedly, been used for many séances over the years, as orientalism and the occult was the big thing then. In one of the books on Luytens' life, it was stated that "Fishers Hill was steeped in ectoplasm."

The house also had beautiful gardens laid out by Gertrude Jekyll, where I spent many happy hours playing. My mother would often pack a little picnic basket for me, and I would wander into the nearby woods and play quite contentedly for hours, safe from all the horrors that can happen to a small child nowadays. Most of my childhood memories are of that garden. There were plenty of rhododendrons, magnolia, and medlar trees to climb, and there was a part of the garden where my father bred snails. These were not just any old snails, though. This particular breed had been introduced to Britain by the Romans, and Nixi and I would accompany Dadster to Newlands Corner to hunt for them where they could be found in the wild. Any snails we'd find would be brought to the garden breeding area, to be lovingly cared for by my father.

As a child, we had two dachshunds in the house, plus a black cat called Tonykins who would sit on my father's stomach every Sunday after a heavy luncheon, slowly going up and down to the mittagsschlaf breathing of my father, as he lay on his back on the red velvet sofa.

Although Rusty the pony was a gift to me, Nixi rode her as she was a better and more experienced rider, so I was plonked on one of the two old nags that grazed near our land. It wasn't till I was 11 that I went through the real girly horse-mad phase, but I outgrew it pretty quickly when boys and music took over my life.

*

During the first ten years of my life at Fishers Hill, I was first sent to a local Rudolph Steiner school, then Nixi and I moved on to a good preparatory school called Halstead. We were dropped there most mornings by my father, who then went on to work as the top radiologist at St. Peter's Hospital, Chertsey. He would stop daily, en route, at a place that grew only carnations, where he'd buy a fresh red flower to put in his lapel, and I would go into ecstasies over the smell of the hundreds of flowers all together under one roof.

Dadster was always a sharp dresser. His suits were often of a cut where the leg was a little tighter than your average trousers, the lining of the jacket was invariably in scarlet or purple silk set off by a pink or purple tie, and he always wore suede shoes on his feet. Not so flash by today's standards, but definitely a little bit different for those conservative times.

Sometimes, my mother would drive us to school in the car, often singing hymns at the wheel; gentle renderings of "Jerusalem", "Lead, Kindly Light", and "For Those In Peril On The Sea", which had particular relevance to her because of her father's Navy years. However, the most memorable song she would sing to me went like this,

Cocaine Bill and Morphine Sue,

Were walking down the avenue,

Have a little sniff sniff on me, Have a little sniff on me.

Every time the word "sniff" came along, she would actually sniff, rather than using the word, and I sniffed along with her. I'm sure she didn't really understand the lyrics, and as a five-year-old, I definitely didn't, but years later – when I reminded her about her curious choice of song for a toddler – she said that this song was very 'in' then, and sung a lot during the War.

*

At night, Nixi and I would be tucked into bed with the occasional bedtime story. One time, when I must have been about seven, I remember asking my mother, as she came for the goodnight kiss, "What are we?"

The reply makes me smile even now, as she said, "We are Aristocrats."

I'm not sure that I quite understood what that meant then, but I felt it meant something special. Of course, it doesn't mean a thing to me now.

One has to be careful what you say to children, as they remember the strangest things. For example, my father was a Freemason, and he would regularly disappear into the evening carrying his little suitcase with the apron and other regalia in it. I was always told he was going to the Mau Mau, which was the family nickname for the Masons, only I didn't know it was a nickname. Some years later, at school, when we were being taught about the African uprising of the Mau Mau, I *insisted* to my teacher that my father was a member of the Mau Mau. Understandably, the teacher got furious with me as I wouldn't back down, so convinced was I of this fact.

Once a week, we went to ballet lessons, wearing pale green outfits and learning the Cecchetti style of classical dance. We also had weekly piano lessons, which I didn't enjoy at all as I just wanted to play what I felt, rather than learn scales. We had a grand piano in the drawing-room, and a piano stool with lion-clawed feet, and a tapestry on the seat. This showed my father's family crest: a stag's head rising out of a crown with the words 'Qui va piano va sano' underneath, which means 'What goes softly goes well'. It's not often that you hear of men doing tapestry, but it had been made by my father. He told me that, many years ago, it was quite normal for sailors to take up tapestry weaving to kill the boredom of months at sea. This may have been true, but it was a strange thing for him to say… he, himself, never went to sea.

At the weekends, we would often go to watch the polo at Windsor Great Park. Prince Philip used to play, so on many occasions, the Queen was there too. This resulted in the occasional appearance of photographs of my parents in the Tatler. While they watched the chukkas, I would be climbing trees, eating ice cream, and waiting for a rare sighting of the couple that caught my attention far more than the horses. It was the Maharajah and Maharani of Jaipur in full Indian clothing, looking splendid and exotic but also strangely familiar. This only made sense to me years later. The fascination and allure of India is still very strong for me, but this first taste of the family of Jaipur fired my imagination and gave me the desire to go there myself one day.

*

The arrival of a television in the house was a momentous occasion. It was housed in a large cabinet of dark wood, and one had to wait for the valves to warm up before they projected the images from behind. When you switched the thing off, you could watch the little dot in the middle getting smaller. I suppose the television was mostly used to keep me quiet during Children's Hour, with the likes of 'Andy Pandy' and 'Muffin the Mule'. My main memories of the television, however, were when a great music show called 'The Six-Five Special' came on, straight after the six o'clock news. The show started with images of a steam train, accompanied by the theme song, "The Six-Five Special's comin' down the line, The Six-Five Special's right on time …"

It was introduced by Pete Murray, whose catchphrase was "Time to jive on the old six five", and was broadcast 'live'. Don Lang and His Frantic Five were the resident band, and I remember Cherry

Wainer playing her padded organ. Television was in black and white then, and so I never knew what colour her organ was – but I like to think it was pink.

Lonnie Donegan often performed with his skiffle group, but my first crush was over a young boy of 13, called Laurie London who sang, 'He's got the whole world in his hands'. The next crush came soon after, when I was taken to the local cinema in Woking to see Elvis Presley in 'Love Me Tender'. Up until then, I'd only seen movies like 'Fantasia' and 'Lady and the Tramp', but just one look at Elvis and – like many other impressionable young girls – I felt something different. Years later, I got to see him 'live' at the Nassau Coliseum in New York, when he was wearing his famous white rhinestone outfit. By that time, I was signed to RCA Records in America, and they gave me a piece of his shirt as well as every single and LP he'd ever made. Sadly, someone stole this small, but no doubt valuable, material from me years later.

*

When I was quite small, I sometimes went to school on the back of my mother's bicycle. Occasionally, Nixi and I would be on ponies, with my mother riding by our side on her old bike, known as 'the Bone Shaker'. The first time I ever made it into a newspaper was when I won a rosette at the local gymkhana in the leading rein class, aged three. My legs did sideways splits on the saddle, and I looked like a child in a Thelwell cartoon. My sister was always getting red and blue rosettes as prizes, which meant first and second place, whereas I had to be content with the yellows and pinks of the consolation class.

We kept ferrets as pets, which I love even now for their pungent smell, and while my sister kept budgies, I had a goldfish called Mrs Perkins. Through the years, as my fish would die, each one would be replaced by another, always with the same name. Sometime later, when the family moved to London, my father bought a child's grave made of white marble, and installed it on the floor of the dining room as a fishpond for Mrs Perkins, with a fountain spouting out of the mouth of a Roman head. When guests arrived for dinner, my father would turn on the fountain, then watch in amusement as the guests' bladders would give in to the sound of the trickle, and they'd be forced to use the loo with glass windows next door. It was meant to be frosted glass, but – in reality – the glass only seemed to offer any privacy from the inside. Anybody outside could see everything that was going on in the loo from the waist up, and most guests were nervous about using it once they'd seen how little privacy it offered.

My father always kept the lavatory door open when he used it himself, and sometimes he wandered around the house in the nude. One time, he answered the front door of the house in London absolutely starkers; the startled but understanding woman standing there said, "Henry, must you be so naked? You could at least wear a hat!"

As an 11-year-old, I thought this was rather a cool thing to say.

This nudist side of him carried on right into his eighties (by then, he was living in a warmer climate, which must have helped). He kept a toy train set at his house, and sometimes he'd get the whole lot out on the balcony, in the nude, of course, and then sit back and watch the toy trains go round and round.

*

While my father's reputation as a radiologist (with an excellent bedside manner) was growing, he decided to do his bit for society by employing home help from the nearby mental hospital called Botleys Park Hospital. Extraordinarily, its official name was 'Botleys Park Colony for Mental Defectives', with patients classified as "idiots, imbeciles, and feeble-minded or moral defectives." The hospital was intended to offer some sort of rehabilitation, but it didn't always work out too well.

One time, we took in a recovering patient to act as butler and general man about the house. He had formerly been an acrobat in a circus, but he was more memorable by the fact that he always left his flies undone, regardless of the number of times my mother told him to zip up. This was tolerated for a while, but he overstepped the mark when it was discovered that he was regularly peeing in the coal shed, causing a nasty smell to waft into the kitchen. At this point, he was sent back to the hospital.

After his departure, we next had a woman called Kathy, who tried to strangle my sister.

She also had to go.

*

Music played an important role in our house, not just for Mama and her hymns. My father played marvellous piano, by ear and never bothering to sight-read, all with a strong Viennese slant to his improvised pieces (and with snatches of the famous Austrian singer Richard Tauber thrown in). He always played classical music on the gramophone at a deafeningly loud volume. Before I was born, he had lived on Culross Street in London, with Tauber on one side and the infamous Tilly Losch on the other side; it was a real Austrian area for those who had come to London to escape the War.

I sometimes wonder if one ever mentally gets over the horrors of a major war. My father had been interned on the Isle of Man – one of the last to be let out of the prisoner of war camp – but he *never* spoke about the war years. It was all dusted over, as if it hadn't happened, although he did tell me that he had once had breakfast with Hitler.

My father remained friendly with the various Mitford 'Girls', but had the most contact with Diana Mosley. Once in London, when I was about 12-years-old, I opened the front door to find Sir Oswald Mosley standing there; I had to entertain him for half an hour as my father was late getting back from his doctors' practice in Wimpole Street. I remember asking him how he felt about the deaths of so many Jews, but sadly I can't recall his answer. He must have thought I was an odious and precocious child.

I once asked my father why he had been such a hit all his life with the ladies, and he laughed and said it was because of 'this', and at that moment, he stuck out his tongue which was very wide and long. Let's face it, a man who knows what to do with his tongue is always going to be successful with the women. He and I were both able to touch the end of our noses with our tongues.

Some of my father's early years were spent in Switzerland, in the Mittelschule in Davos. He was sent there as it was thought he had the early stages of TB, and the mountains were considered good for a cure. Apparently, the bracing mountain air made one feel very horny, resulting in patients leaping from balcony to balcony for a last shag before death. The sanatorium where this took place is now a well-known hotel, and I've seen the balconies and know it is possible to leap over them, having done it myself years later.

My father also spent part of his childhood in the Italian part of Switzerland – the Ticino – which was one of his favourite places. Hermann Hesse, the famous author, lived down the road at Montagnola, near Lugano, and my father said Hesse was like an unofficial godfather to him. He was often bounced upon HH's knees as a child.

Life in Ticino, in those days, must have been exhilarating, as this was the location of Monte Verita – in a way, the first hippie commune in Europe. There are photographs taken there, in the 1920s, of men with headbands and long hair and women dancing or posing provocatively in fountains, wearing nothing but diaphanous bits of chiffon. According to some reports, experimental drugs were there too, and it attracted all sorts of original thinkers, including Jung, and philosophers from all over the world.

There were many artists and performers there as well, such as Paul Klee and Isadora Duncan, and – as a young man – my father must have fitted in perfectly. He was always lucky in life, and was known as a great raconteur at the dining table, a connoisseur of good food, and, of course, a rascal with the women. He must have picked up these talents by being around stimulating people.

He was married before he took the plunge with my mother, to Anne-Marie Slatin, daughter of Baron Sir Rudolph Slatin. The Baron was always known as Slatin Pasha, as he had been the Inspector General of the Sudan in 1900-1914. I doubt if the marriage ended very well, as Anne-Marie went on to marry Prince Galitzine and one of her two sons, Georgie, told me that my father's name was mud in their house. No doubt he'd dallied where he shouldn't have with another woman, as this was his *modus operandi*.

*

From an early age, I was lucky enough to enjoy foreign travel, and most of the school holidays were spent going somewhere on the continent in the car. Dadster always had a large black car ("Any colour as long as it's black!") with a dramatic light on the roof. It looked like a police car, and other drivers would swiftly get out of the way as we approached. A few years later, it was forbidden to put such a searchlight on a car, so ours had to go.

Off we'd trek, with Nixi and me in the back, and a suitcase put between us to stop us scrapping. The destinations varied. A few times, it was Germany, Switzerland, or Austria, but one year we drove to Spain, where we stayed at the Marbella Club. It had a swimming pool, and I have a clear memory of a small child falling in one day, and being rescued by my mother.

All this time in cars meant that I was often whining to stop the car so I could go for a pee. This occurred so often that I got the nickname "Dan, Dan, the Lavatory Man."

I was also passionate about all things to do with cowboys, especially Davy Crockett, and loved to dress in a cowboy outfit whenever I could. I had a splendid pair of cowboy boots, unheard of in those days, and I swaggered around in them with a Davy Crockett hat on my head. One day, the milkman, who was delivering to our house, said, "Here's Dangerous Dana from Alabama."

These two uses of the name Dan explain how I got to change my name. When I was ten, I announced to my mother that everyone must now call me Dana. I would be famous when I grew up, I declared, and didn't want anyone who was not in the family to use my real name, Richenda.

According to folklore, the name Richenda should only be used in the families of Buxtons, Gurneys, and Frys. The story goes that many, many years ago, a gipsy carrying a baby had come to sell clothes pegs at the front door of one of my ancestors' houses. In those old times, a house known for its generosity would have a sign laid out by the gipsies, by the front gates, in the form of some stones or a knotted clump of grass. As all the ancestors were known for their charitable good works, the clothes pegs were duly bought by the lady of the house, who was also carrying a babe in arms. In the course of exchanging baby greetings, my ancestor asked the name of the gipsy child as she was looking for inspiration to name her newborn daughter, and the gipsy mother replied, "It's Richenda, which is the name for a Romany gipsy princess, and it can only be used in the direct line of us gipsies, but as you have always been kind to us and bought our clothes pegs, then you may also use the name, providing it only stays in this one line of your family."

The other Richendas I know, or have heard about, have all been relations, mostly from Norfolk. The elder daughter of Nixi is also called Richenda, while the younger one is called Dalila.

By the time we moved to London, I had managed to persuade everybody, including school teachers, that my name was now Dana. I even thought I had invented the name, but years later, I found out that it's not such a rare moniker and can even be a man's name. As I was a tomboy for all of my childhood, it seemed to fit well.

*

From the age of five, our winter holidays were taken up with skiing, with us all going away as a family. After a few days, my father would typically leave us, using work as an excuse to return to England; in retrospect, I think it was so he could juggle his love life. My poor mother must have known what was going on, but in those days, the stigma of divorce was pretty terrible. We tried out various ski resorts before settling on the place that was to become like a second home to me, Klosters.

In the early days, the ski equipment was basic, with terrible heavy boots that took an age to do up, and which often resulted in blistered hands and frozen feet. It is no wonder that my early memories of the sport weren't particularly pleasant, and I spent a lot of time howling. I remember saying to my mother, the first time I watched anyone skiing, "That looks easy. I know I can do it!"

How wrong I was. It took me five years to be able to ski well, and in those early days, everyone else – including my sister – was much better than me.

I also said the same thing to my mother when I first saw someone water-skiing. I was nine years old, and my father had rented a house called Villa Azalea on the shores of Lake Maggiore. It was here that I learnt to swim, and I spent the holiday almost living in the water while my mother and friends would sit on the terrace talking and drinking wine. One of the friends had been one of my father's ex-girlfriends, and my mother gave me some good advice years later. "If you want to keep your husband, then make friends with his mistresses and then you'll land up being better friends with them, and the man will eventually get squeezed out."

This is how it was with my mother. So many of her best friends had been Dadster's 'flings', and when the affair had fizzled out, and the woman in question was an ex, she often remained a staunch supporter of my mother – while hardly speaking to my father!

Back on the lake, something had caught my eye at the house next door. It was a speedboat containing three teenage brothers, and they all seemed like champion water-skiers to me. As usual, I said how easy it looked and that I could do it, and when they offered to teach me I immediately said yes, especially as Nixi had got up first time. Unfortunately, I wasn't even able to stand, and badly bruised my arms and my ego in my failed effort. I was to make up for it, however, a few years later.

So, summer holidays started taking on a regular pattern of days spent by the lake, whilst winter – and sometimes even Easter – holidays would find us on the ski slopes of Klosters. We would have Christmas and loads of presents by the tree around December 19th, and then take off to the Alps for the skiing.

Klosters has now become known as the place where Prince Charles liked to ski, sometimes with Princess Diana when she was alive, but life was very different there back in the fifties. For a start, it was full of writers and film people, and it was quite normal to see the likes of Greta Garbo, Gene Kelly, Irwin Shaw (more of him later), Deborah Kerr and Sam Spiegel wandering around the village, or sitting in the famous Chesa Grischuna, drinking and having lunch.

It is said that the English invented skiing in Switzerland. Davos, a few kilometres away, had the first toboggan run, but it was also used – at night-time – to transport dead bodies down the hill from the sanatorium after inmates had died from tuberculosis. The corpses were dispatched at night so that the other patients wouldn't get despondent over their deceased friends. The story of the sanatorium is well-chronicled in Thomas Mann's book 'The Magic Mountain', published in 1924.

There were always many English people in Klosters, often staying in the quaint Hotel Wynegg, and it was to this hotel that we started going every year. It almost seemed like a club; we'd always see the same friends at Christmas time.

Two events occurred during my early childhood which would have a major impact on my life, albeit in very different ways.

The first happened when I was only five and on holiday in Germany. Nixi and I had been left to stay with Dr and Mrs Best, friends of my father, while he and my mother went off to attend a radiological congress in Frankfurt. The house was in a small town called Eltville, and we had stayed there several times before, so I knew the Bests' three sons and their Alsatian dog.

Nixi and I were playing in the gardens next door with some local children, who were climbing and hanging from the crossbar of a football goalpost. I was the smallest in the group, and begged to be lifted up to swing with the rest of the kids. One of them helped me up, and I hung upside down like a monkey, though not as agile as one. The other children all moved off to play somewhere else, and nobody thought to help me down, so I was stuck clinging on to the crossbar. Eventually, I couldn't hang on any longer, fell, and hit my head on the paving stones below, fracturing my skull.

To this day, the impact of my head on stone was so strong that the memory of it is like it happened yesterday. With a tremendous flash of light inside my head, I felt as if I had seen my entire life and beyond, and I was stunned by the enormity of this feeling. It's a hard thing to describe, but maybe it's like when you see your whole life pass before you in a car crash, or get close to death in an accident. The feeling can only have lasted a second, and then the pain kicked in.

I was carted off to the nearest hospital by Dr Best and was given some kind of gas to calm me down before they did an X-ray. The doctors were all naturally talking in German, and as they put the mask on me, I thought they were trying to kill me. Nobody knew how to contact my parents or where they were, and I was really scared.

There's not much you can do after this kind of accident other than rest and wait for the fracture to heal. It was decided that I should be kept in the top room of Dr Best's house, with the bedroom door locked so I couldn't wander anywhere.

For a few days, I lay in agony while my parents were being tracked down. The pain was excruciating, and I don't recall being given any painkillers. The left side of my face had swollen up so much that I looked like the Elephant Man, with my mouth vertical so I couldn't even speak, only moan. It got to the point when I simply couldn't take it anymore and just wanted to kill myself, to put my damaged head out of its misery.

One day, I tried to open my bedroom door and – to my surprise – found it unlocked and the house deserted. I made my way downstairs and out into the garden, which sloped down to the edge of the River Rhine, a wide and fast-flowing stretch of water. At the end of the garden was a small gate that led to a riverside path where I had walked many times. I hadn't learnt to swim, and decided that the best way I could kill myself – and end my suffering – was by jumping into the swirling brown water. There were five steps leading down into the water, and as I walked down them I was sucked into the river and pulled under.

What happened next is not hard to write, though may be hard for some to accept. All I can do is to tell it exactly as I remember it.

As I sank deeper into the water, a strange Being, dressed all in white, lifted me up and out of the water, carried me back over the path and fence, and then laid me on the grass lawn of the garden.

Some may call this a hallucination, but I know that it really happened. I have no explanation for who, or what, this white figure was, nor even if it was male or female, but once I was laid out on the grass, in my muddy wet pyjamas, the figure was gone.

There is no way I could have got myself back out of the river, and when – at last – I was discovered, barely conscious on the lawn, I was carried back to my room and the door was firmly locked. I overheard someone saying that the dog, which had been sitting near me, must have pulled me from the water, but I knew that what I had seen was not a dog. I had no way of telling anyone what I had seen, as my mouth was too swollen to speak, and I couldn't talk properly for many weeks. I think I also realised that no one would believe my story, so I kept quiet and pushed it to the back of my mind.

After a few months, the swelling went down, and twice a week I would go to the hospital where my father worked to have ultrasound on my cheek to try to heal the last remaining injury from my accident. It was as if a hard lump of blood – the size of a golf ball – had got stuck in my cheekbone; there was talk that eventually I would need an operation. As luck would have it, some time later, I got hit on the cheek by a friend while playing, and though it was agony and I howled as usual, the ball of blood slowly drained away. To this day, I have what looks like a dimple in my left cheek, but you wouldn't notice it unless I pointed it out. It wasn't until I was 16 that the after-effects of this accident came back to haunt me, and it changed my life in a way I wasn't expecting. More of that later.

The second major event was that, on my tenth birthday, we left my beloved Fishers Hill. I felt as though my life was being destroyed when I was told we were going to move permanently to London. No more running free in the gardens, and no more swinging in the trees on my rope ladder. For the previous two years, my father had been commuting between London – where he would spend the week practising in Wimpole Street – and Woking where he would spend the weekends. Nixi was doing the same journey with him, as she had started going to a smart private day school in Sloane Square called Francis Holland School.

Back then, Fishers Hill had been in the countryside. Surrounded by woods with a long drive to the house, the tranquillity was lost when modern bijoux residences were built along the drive, all of which seemed to have huge glass windows so that you could see right into their living rooms. It sort of spelt the beginning of the end for us, as the drive where I had learnt to ride a bike, and trotted with my pony, had been changed forever. My sunny childhood was coming to an end, and I felt quite miserable about the prospect of moving to the capital.

Little did I realise then, how much this move was to change my life.

2: THE MOVE TO LONDON, AND MEETING BOWIE

The final day of the move from the countryside to the capital city was memorable for me as it occurred on my tenth birthday, and depressing though it was, I was soon busy with a new school and new friends.

My father had bought a large house in South Kensington, consisting of five floors and a basement. As the house was so big, I was put on the top floor, under the slanting roof, with wonderful wallpaper of bamboo and ivy design. My sister was on the floor below. She tended to keep to herself, with books for company, as she was always considered the brains of the two of us; I was thought of as the musical one.

The rest of the house was taken up by my parents. There was a huge four-poster bed on the next floor down, where my father also had a dressing room. The drawing-room was on the first floor, alongside my mother's sitting room, and on the ground floor was my father's study and library, with the dining room and see-through lavatory at the back. The basement was a cold dismal place where various au pairs would come and go, but it was damp with stone floors and – in the early years – it was not an area I went to much.

The house was on Thurloe Square, which surrounds a large private garden for the use of the residents (provided they have a key), and was one minute on foot from the tube station, and five minutes from Harrods. It was right in the heart of big museum territory, and we would often visit the Natural History, Victoria and Albert, or Science Museum and then walk up Exhibition Road to Hyde Park to feed the ducks on the Round Pond. Grown men, acting like boys, would often be sailing their toy yachts and remote control boats.

My mother would always take my sister and me past the bronze statue of Peter Pan, where I would count the carved animals, wishing we had real ones of our own as the cat and two dachshunds we'd had at Fishers Hill had died of old age before the move. Eventually, we got a Norwich Terrier called Snuffy, and when she died, I was given another named Sneezi, who remained my best friend until she died at the age of 15. Later on, many a boyfriend had to put up with her. Sneezi and I were inseparable, so it was a case of 'love me, love my dog', even though she would often embarrass me by running into a room full of people with my knickers in her mouth.

Francis Holland School was round the back of Sloane Square, conveniently close to home. I could walk there or ride my bike, but I would usually take the tube as it was only one stop away. The uniform was a nightmare of grey and blue, with pudding bowl hats in winter and straw hats for summer. The school motto was 'May your daughters be as the polished corners of the temple', and we were very well polished by excellent teachers. Never top of the class, like my sister, I managed to float somewhere in the middle for most of my time at school, with mathematics being the only disaster area.

The moment I got home from school, I would speed through my homework as fast as possible, then grab the key to the garden square and rush out to climb trees and hang out with some of the local kids. This came to an abrupt end one day when the gardener, who lived in the next-door basement flat, asked me to follow him into his gardening shed, whereupon he took out his cock and asked me to hold it. I yelled and ran out of the garden, and (even though I still live just around the corner) have never stepped inside since. I didn't dare tell my mother at the time, as I somehow thought it was my fault. I'd seen my father naked many times but never in the state the gardener was. Worse still, I would often have to pass him on the street, but I would ignore him and look away. When I did eventually tell my mother, she was totally shocked, but by then two years had passed, and it was too late to do anything about it. Besides, we all felt rather sorry for his long-suffering wife and two sons, so we decided to keep quiet.

Now I had every evening to fill with no outdoor playing, so I turned to music as consolation. I had been given a battery-run yellow Dansette record player for my 13th birthday, and I would play the few records I had over and over again.

It's amazing how one small action can change the course of your life. In my case, it was my sister Nixi throwing away an EP record of Bessie Smith singing 'I Need A Little Sugar in My Bowl'. I retrieved it from the bin and played it until the grooves were worn out, while totally falling in love with the music. Very soon, my favourites included Bessie singing 'Empty Bed Blues' and Louis Armstrong playing 'Muggles'. At the time, I didn't fully understand the words of Bessie Smith's song, nor realise that muggles meant marijuana.

Up at the top of the house, I would disappear into my fantasy world, dancing and singing to music. From the moment my mother gave me an old wireless, I would tune in every evening to Radio Luxemburg to listen to the latest hits. Radio played such a large part of British life in the fifties; television was still new, with only a couple of channels which were – of course – broadcast in black and white. It seemed as if the world stopped once a week as everyone tuned into their radios to listen to Tony Hancock's Half Hour. He's still my favourite comedian from the old school.

I had been given a baby grand piano for my tenth birthday that stood in the drawing-room, and I'd spend hours playing anything other than the things I was meant to be practising. I was quite sad when, many years later, the piano was sold as there was no space to store it.

With great pride, aged 11, I showed my mother my first composition, a simple piano piece called 'The Cuckoo Clock', but soon after that, I stopped trying to write down my compositions; it was too difficult to put what was in my head onto paper.

At one time, my mother used to think that I would become a concert pianist, but I always had trouble with sight-reading. I struggled through lessons of the usual 'Moonlight Sonata' and 'Fur Elise'; the dots seemed to make no sense to me. In fact, my sister was far better at piano and singing than I was, but – looking back – I don't think she had the passion for it as I did.

My piano teacher at school was called Miss Muriel Ashby, and she remains a wonderful memory to this day. She was a large-busted spinster with a bun at the back for her grey hair. I listened to her and, more importantly, she bothered to listen to me. She knew how hopeless I was at sight-reading, but must have seen I was passionate about music and had some talent. The school rule was that we were only allowed to play classical music, but after a lot of begging on my part, Miss Ashby agreed to teach me 'Take Five', 'Unsquare Dance', and 'Blue Rondo a la Turk', all of which were hits by the Dave Brubeck Quartet. Through this one act, she became my favourite teacher and helped to steer the course of my life in the direction that I knew I wanted to take. I didn't know exactly what road lay ahead, but I knew it had to be something to do with music.

I was never allowed to join the school choir, as I was considered too much of a giggler to be let loose in such a disciplined group. One day, I was due to perform a duet called 'Oranges and Lemons' at the school concert with my best friend, Carrots. We walked confidently onto the stage and sat on the double piano stool, but I was shaking so much with laughter that we didn't manage to play one note. We had to leave the stage in fits of giggles, to the horror of the headteacher and the embarrassment of my mother, who was in the audience.

My poor mother had to put up with quite a lot from her unconventional daughter. A good example of this was on one abnormally foggy day when it was impossible to see your own hand in front of your face. As we passed Harrods, she asked, "Why have you let go of my hand? What are you doing?"

"I've got my skirt over my head," I replied, "as one day I want to be able to say that I walked down Knightsbridge, in front of Harrods, showing my knickers!"

Years later, I did much better than that, by giving someone a blowjob in his white Rolls Royce while we were stuck in a traffic jam outside Harrods. This was the sixties, a time when my life was as swinging as the rest of London.

My world was now in South Kensington. One day, I noticed a sign in the local newsagents that said "Wanted, newspaper delivery boy." I went in and presented myself and got the job, and every morning at 5.30, I would turn up on my bike and do the paper round. I was paid twelve shillings and sixpence a week (about 12 pounds in today's money), increasing later to seventeen and six a week. To this day, I have always been an early riser, even if I've been up late the night before.

Between five and seven in the morning was when most of the world was sleeping, and I loved the silence when my brain was clear and the streets were mine to ride around on. Sundays were the worst as the papers had so many supplements and were very heavy, but I loved my job and never missed a round unless sick or on holiday. I was so proud to be making my own money. Christmas was a time when I got extra money as tips, and the most generous tippers were at two houses where the men would stand at the front door in their striped pyjamas with their cocks in hand, waiting for me to arrive with their newspapers. I often got flashed coming home from school too, maybe because I was already a big-busted girl, though possibly it was the school uniform I wore that was doing it. Why wasn't I quick-witted enough to hit them with some witty retort telling them to 'put it away'? Unfortunately, the smart replies only came to my mind when it was too late.

Around this time, I'd heard a record by Sandy Nelson called 'Let There Be Drums', and from that moment on I became hooked on drums and drumming. Once I'd saved up enough money, I went down to Shaftesbury Avenue, in the heart of London's theatre and film district, and made straight for a shop called Drum City. This was heaven on earth for me, and many a time I drooled by the window looking at the drum kits on sale. A lot of them were in bright sparkly colours, but I could only afford a plain white one made by a company called Ajax.

In the shop, I saw an advertisement for drum lessons, so off I went to an address in Archer Street in the red light district, just along the road from the well-known Windmill Theatre strip joint. Inside there were drums of all types and colours, together with the man who was to become my drum teacher for three years, Frank King.

At the time, I don't think I realised how lucky I was to chance upon such a great teacher, but years later I've met many an English drummer who has sung his praises. Frank played left-handed so that the kit he was playing on was a mirror image of mine – which helped in following what he was trying to teach me. Sometimes, as I was trying to do my triplets, paradiddles, and flams, he would hold pornographic photos under my nose to see if I would drop a beat. This was perhaps a slightly unconventional way of teaching a 13-year-old, but I didn't mind as he was so good at his job. Being his only girl student, he'd often overrun his time with me and not charge extra. Sometimes he'd get a bit over-familiar with me at the end of a lesson, but nothing too serious and I didn't mind. I'd got a great drum teacher and – to me – this was a small price to pay in order to learn to play.

Frank used to write a drum page for Downbeat magazine and was friendly with Buddy Rich, the hero for all drummers at the time. When Buddy was playing at The Talk of the Town, I would go with Frank and see as many shows as I could, amazed at what could be done with rhythms.

Frank also used to play drums on the children's television show, 'Crackerjack', and I would go along to watch. It was my first chance to go to a television studio and see how programmes got made, which would prove to be useful in the future.

Somehow, I also found time to be a Brownie, then a Girl Guide, and my ambition was to get as many badges up my arm as I could. This meant that sometimes my mother would help me cheat by saying I'd baked a jam tart myself – when, in fact, she had – thereby securing my cooking badge. She did the same for my knitting badge. I thought it was good of her not to be bothered about such trivialities as the truth. This was curious, though, as one of my mother's sayings was, "Oh, what a tangled web we weave, when at first we do deceive."

Being good at swimming and all things in the water, I joined two swimming clubs, the Dolphins and the Mermaids, which stood me in good stead when I moved on to water-skiing a few years later. How my mother had the time to get me to these places to train, I'll never know, as she also had a part-time job. She had trained as a physiotherapist at St. Thomas's Hospital, years earlier, and had given up her work to look after her children. But once we were settled in our London school, she started working at the Royal Hospital, Chelsea, which meant looking after the famous Chelsea pensioners. I'd often meet her there after school, and she'd usually be putting hot wax on the arthritic hands of some of the old boys, all of whom seemed ancient to me. One of the perks of this was that we could go into the Chelsea Flower Show for free with one of her patients. To this day, I remain a loyal fan of the Flower Show.

*

In 1962, South Kensington had two shops that fascinated me. The first was called Indiacraft and sold things like carved wooden snakes and incense. It may seem odd to mention that now – as you can buy Indian things everywhere – but in those days it was a rarity. I was already developing the habit of lighting incense every day, and I still do it when I'm at home.

The other shop was Mascalls Record Store, just opposite the tube station on Harrington Road. I'd go there so often to listen to music that eventually the owner, Harry Morgan, asked if I'd like to work in the store part-time after school. This was an offer from heaven for me, as it meant I could listen to music and get some pocket money too. I loved my time in there, standing behind the counter, chatting to the customers and, best of all, listening to the latest record releases.

Harry Morgan was a popular man with an easy-going manner, and it was not unusual to find ladies like Jackie Bissett and Vivienne Ventura hanging around him. Occasionally, I splashed out and bought myself a record, and for some odd reason, the first single I ever purchased was 'Wimoweh' by the Karl Denver Trio. However, pretty soon I'd moved on to Miles Davis's 'Sketches of Spain' and Jimmy Smith on his organ playing 'The Cat'. After that, my life seemed to be charted by what I was listening to at the time.

As I look around me now, I have a wonderful and rare collection of great Blues and jazz LPs, and with each record, I have memories of the things I was doing at the time; which lovers were around, which country I was in, what work I was doing, and how my heart was feeling, emotion-wise.

One day I saw Chris Blackwell, the founder of Island Records, unloading a box of copies of 'My Boy Lollipop' (which became a massive hit for Little Millie Small) from the boot of his car and taking them into Mascalls. The pop charts were made up of 'sale returns' of records sold at specific record stores around the country, and Mascalls was one of them. It was well known in the music business that you could buy your way into the singles charts purely by going into the listed stores and purchasing lots of copies of a particular record – though I'm pretty sure that's not what Chris was doing; he was just making sure that the shop had lots of copies for sale.

*

Not being a particularly good skier in my early years, it wasn't until I was 13 that I was good enough to join the junior team of Klosters racers. This was a club called 'Mardens', and its symbol was a bat, maybe to inspire the young British skiers to go like bats out of hell. We had slalom and downhill training sessions twice a day, and I would hit the slopes and try to get down as best I could without breaking anything. However, the music bug had planted its first seed in me, and I spent many an evening in my bedroom singing along to any record I could get my hands on, rather than partying.

When visiting Klosters, I used to take my Spanish acoustic guitar with me and would keep the other hotel occupants awake at night while I strummed my three chords. The walls were like paper, and on I would play until someone complained. This persistence paid off, as it was in Klosters that I made my first public singing appearance.

In those days, of the late fifties and early sixties, one of the pastimes after a day out on the slopes was to go to a 'thé dansant' (literally a tea dance). Still in our ski clothes and heavy boots, we would stop off in the Schwemmi Bar in the Grand Hotel Vereina, and dance to a quartet called 'The Four Camillos'. We would stay there until it was time to go back to our hotel, where we would have a bath to ease away the bruises of the day before heading out for dinner.

One day, it was announced that there was to be a singing talent contest. I really wanted to enter, so I practised a rather folky song called 'J'entends siffler le train', which had been a hit by a French star called Richard Anthony. I was 12-years-old and sang the song wearing skin-tight black trousers and a black top, whilst backed by the wonderful Four Camillos. The judges were Lex Barker, who had acted as Tarzan on the big screen (and also married Lana Turner), a very young Jane Fonda, and Roger Vadim. Roger had been married to Brigitte Bardot, whom he had made famous by directing her first big film 'And God Created Woman', and he was now trying to do the same for Jane (with whom he was having an affair).

I can't remember what I won in the contest, but I was presented with something for my performance, and as I held out my hand to receive my prize from Roger Vadim, he said to me, "Quelles poitrines!" which translated means "What breasts!"

You would probably get arrested if you said that to a 12-year-old girl these days, but things were different back in the sixties.

*

We usually had hot-looking instructors for the ski team. With tight ski pants, smart tops, and the great advantage of never falling over and getting covered in snow – like the rest of us – our two instructors always looked sexy, and very quickly became the pivotal thing in my life, both on and off the slopes.

By now I was getting quite good at ski racing, and had won something called the Vlasov scholarship which was awarded every year to two girls under the age of 15, and involved being given special ski training in Davos over Easter. We used to work hard and play hard, spending all day on the slopes, then passing the evenings in the local bars. It wasn't a drinking thing for me as I've never enjoyed the taste of alcohol, but it enabled me to listen to the local bands playing jazz and popular music. The fact that my two ski instructors played the drums, in two different local bands, meant that I would watch them play, rather than going to bed early to be in good shape for the following day.

In the ski resorts, they always say that the foreign girls lose their virginity to the skilehrers (ski instructors), and I was no exception. I had been part of one of the junior teams that went to Arosa for the British Junior Ski Championships, and as we were housed in a hotel away from parental guidance it was – I suppose – inevitable what would happen. On the first evening there, after dinner, I had a ski waxing session with one of the instructors. This was important, as having the wrong sort of wax on the bottom of your skis can significantly slow you down. Anyway, after this was done, he invited me to his room, and not really knowing what would happen (but knowing something probably would) I went with him.

It's not necessary to give him a name as he might want to forget the whole event, and in those days you could get six months in prison for sleeping with a minor. Although I was only 13, I looked much older, as I was tall, already large-busted, and had taken to putting blonde peroxide streaks in my waist-length hair. He knew my age, and in a way we were good friends – as much as pupil and trainer ever can be – and I absolutely don't regret it at all.

The actual sexual act wasn't so memorable, but the fact that it happened was. I had to lose it somewhere, so why not in the mountains, away from home and parents?

Of course, it wasn't long before I had a fling with the other ski instructor/drummer!

*

One evening when I was working at Mascalls, an elderly man with a walking stick came in and struck up a conversation with me. His name was Cecil Landeau, and he was an acquaintance of Harry Morgan, the record shop boss. After Cecil had left the shop, Harry told me that Cecil was a well-known impresario who had discovered Audrey Hepburn and also Shani Wallis, the girl who went on to play Nancy in the film 'Oliver'.

Cecil lived up Exhibition Road, near Hyde Park, and he took to dropping into the shop quite often to order records. One day, he asked me what I wanted to do when I left school, and I replied that I wanted to go on the stage, though I'm sure I didn't know in what capacity. I'd seen films and quite a few stage musicals, and by now television was a part of everyday life, but I also nurtured a childish dream to be in a television advert for Smarties (no doubt to get my hands on the chocolates).

When Cecil offered to give me private acting lessons, once and sometimes twice weekly, I readily agreed. Many people may have thought that he was a dirty old man, and indeed he did seem old to me, but he never did anything that was not polite and proper. Soon, he was introduced to my parents, who also approved of him.

My training consisted of learning and reciting great chunks of Shakespeare, and he even got me to learn the whole of the Rubaiyat of Omar Khayyam, which is no mean feat. Sometimes he would take over the Shaftesbury Theatre on a Sunday, when it was officially closed, and I remember doing the speech from 'Romeo and Juliet' where Juliet wants to be deflowered. If Cecil got a kick out of this, I never knew; he would sit high up at the back, in the 'gods', to make sure that my projection was good and my words audible.

*

At the age of 13, I took up another sport that was to occupy a lot of my spare time. My mother had met an Austrian lady called Lotti Warburg, who asked if I'd like to go water-skiing. Initially, I wasn't too keen as I'd tried it a few years earlier on Lake Maggiore and had been pretty hopeless. I agreed as I thought it would maybe help my snow ski training, so I went along with her to a lake in an abandoned quarry near London Heathrow airport called The Princes Club. It may sound very smart, but it certainly wasn't then.

Amazingly, I did rather well on my first attempt, and very soon I was going there every weekend. By the end of my first season, I had won a medal in the Junior Championships, though I have to be honest – there wasn't much competition (the sport was very much in its infancy then).

To enter the Championships, you had to be able to compete in three categories: slalom, jumping, and tricks (which entailed doing 360 degree turns and jumping backwards over the wash while holding the rope by your feet). Although I don't think I was the best skier, I was usually good at showing off in front of a crowd, and the discipline of being able to perform when required gave me a lot of self-confidence. It's thanks to water-skiing that I never suffer from stage fright or get unduly anxious.

I wasn't too brilliant at slalom, and was usually frightened while going over the jump as I sometimes went more than 25 metres before landing. However, I was the best at doing tricks. Falling is a necessary evil if you want to try something new and daring when water-skiing, and I did really well at this. I also had enough puppy fat on me to help survive the arctic British temperatures.

In those days, the rubber suits stored water in them, which was supposed to keep you warm, but the reality was that they just made you look huge. I would get pulled out of the water feeling like the Michelin Man, and looking like one too.

It was not long before I began to excel at the sport, and I was the British Junior Waterski Champion for four consecutive seasons. One year, when the championships were being televised, I even managed to make it onto the cover of TV Times, wearing a blue frilly swimming costume and matching hat. Soon, however, my interest fell by the wayside as I could see there was no future career in it. In any case, by then I had discovered the joys of the Marquee

Club, down Wardour Street in Soho, and that meant late nights, great music, and boys.

Soho was something else. A lot of it has been pulled down now, and it's certainly not the place it used to be, but in the early sixties it seemed to be the most exciting, vibrant place on earth. You always knew when you were in Soho, as there was something magical about the place. The red light district had a vibe to it, and I would enjoy wandering around looking at the women hanging out of the doors, and all the punters checking them out.

One day, when I was 13, a friend of mine who had a motorbike offered to take me to the Marquee Club. As soon as I walked in, I was hooked. A band was playing Blues so loud that I could feel it, and there was a real buzz about the place. The walls dripped with sweat on the red-and-white striped backdrop, and it was such an exciting place to be. The music was fabulous; I just adored being there.

The Marquee Club was one of the hotspots in town for 'live' music, and seemed to play Blues predominantly. Down the road were the Whisky-a-GoGo and the All Nighter, which had a blacker audience and lots of pill-popping. But my heart belonged to, and was loyal to, the Marquee Club. I had heard my first Blues at the age of 11, and by the age of 13 – going to the Marquee pretty regularly – I instinctively *knew* that Blues was the music for me.

Wardour Street was such a happening place in those days. Running off it was a little alleyway with a coffee bar, where I'd sit for as long as I could with my girlfriend Sara, watching people go past. We'd wait until there was a queue forming outside the Marquee, and would then rush out to get a place at the front.

Pretty soon, I was a regular at the Marquee. As I looked far older than my age, no one questioned me, and the great thing about Wardour Street was that I could walk home at the end of the evening. In those days, you could be out late at night without fear of any scumbag hassling you.

Thank God I had parents who didn't ask me where I was going all the time, and who were quite open-minded in letting me stay out late. I would have probably told them, had they asked, but it wouldn't have meant a thing to them because they wouldn't have known what a Blues club was. I just wanted to watch young men on stage looking hot and playing hot.

The bands playing there included The Who, The Action, Gary Farr and the T-Bones and Blossom Toes. The biggest draw, however, was The Yardbirds, and whenever they were on the bill, I tried not to miss them. Eric Clapton was my favourite on stage. He had a crewcut then, which was unusual as most musicians wore their hair long. He'd often be dressed in white, and when he played solos, he would close his eyes and throw his head back as if in a sort of Blues ecstasy. He played with real passion, straight from the heart, and somehow everyone felt it and could see it.

Julie Driscoll, who went on to have massive success with 'This Wheel's on Fire', was also often there, and I remember once being very envious of her when she was invited to get up and sing. How I longed to do this as well, but I didn't really have the experience and certainly not a big enough repertoire at the time. Luckily, I didn't have to wait too long for my turn.

I got to know The Yardbirds' manager, Giorgio Gomelsky, and his assistant Hamish, and soon became a regular at the other Blues venue they ran called the Crawdaddy Club in Croydon, which was a spin-off from the Richmond Crawdaddy (where the Rolling Stones first made their name). Croydon became a regular haunt for the Yardbirds, so I would sometimes go there with Hamish or Giorgio to see them. They would often play on alternate weeks, one night at the Marquee club, then one night the next week in Croydon. If I could get there, I would be there, and the good news was that I could always get a lift back home.

Giorgio was a very famous man in the Blues world and discovered many artists who went on to great fame and fortune. At one point, he looked after the Rolling Stones but foolishly didn't have them under contract. Just when he was about to sign them, Andrew Loog Oldham came in and stole them from under his nose.

Sometimes, I would go to the Marquee with my Spanish six-string guitar, which is what beginners always learnt on. Because I knew Giorgio and Hamish, the doorman used to let me into the club before the show started, while the musicians were still doing their soundcheck. So I'd get up front where I could really see the band, and watch Eric do his thing. One day, Giorgio came up to me and asked what I did. It must have been obvious I was still at school, but I said that I wrote songs and he said, "Get up on stage and sing."

As I was on my own, and had no band to play with me, I strummed my Spanish guitar and sang some of my own unpolished compositions. I doubt if I was very good, and Giorgio said that I needed guitar lessons – so he offered me Eric Clapton as a teacher!

A date was fixed for my first lesson, and not surprisingly, I was very excited about having guitar tutoring from my hero. Unfortunately, a few days before the appointed day arrived, I got a letter in the post from Eric saying that he couldn't make it as The Yardbirds' single 'For Your Love' had broken into the charts, and he and the band were going off on tour. Sadly, I don't have his letter any more, but one thing I do remember is that he had the most perfect italic handwriting, without a splodge of ink or mistake. He postponed my lesson for a later date, which never happened as the band just got more and more famous, and he was always on the road.

I can only imagine what it would have been like to have had guitar lessons from Eric. I can still remember the thrill of watching him play back in the sixties, and think that his show at The Royal Albert Hall with Delaney & Bonnie, in 1969, was one of best shows I ever saw.

The early sixties were the years that the 'American Folk Blues Festival' came to perform at Richmond, on the edge of London, and all the Marquee and Crawdaddy crowd were there. For Blues fans, this was a great way to see a package show with lots of top black American acts. The list was a joy: Sunnyland Slim, Sugar Pie DeSanto, Lightnin' Hopkins, Sleepy John Estes, the great songwriter Willie Dixon, Hubert Sumlin, Sonny Boy Williamson and – best of all – Howlin' Wolf. What a lineup. Sadly, there seem to be few touring shows as good as that now.

My all-time hero was Howlin' Wolf, but unfortunately, I didn't actually see him perform live as I had to get home by public transport and be up for school the next day. He must have been top of the bill and last on stage. Although I was lucky enough to see nearly all the Blues acts that played in London then, I'm still sad that I never got to see Howlin' Wolf, with his wonderful gravelly voice. The singers that were seen on British television never performed like him; their clothes were always tidy and they never seemed to sweat. In contrast, the real Blues stars dripped, howled, swore, laughed, drank, and strutted their stuff in such a natural way. It was this honesty in the music that appealed to me, with love, or loss of love, always being the main theme.

By now, I was a regular at the Marquee Club, and whenever I could go, I would be down there, getting my fix of the Blues. One evening, Friday the 6th of November 1964 to be precise, the headliners were Gary Farr and the T-Bones, but I was more taken by the lead singer in the support act, who were called Davie Jones and the Manish Boys. The singer was dressed in knee-length, fringed suede boots, a white baggy shirt, and a waistcoat, and the overall effect was something of a Robin Hood look. But most striking was his hair; it was shoulder length and lemon yellow, with a sort of Veronica Lake cut. This was around the time when the press was complaining about the hair length of The Beatles, but this guy's hair was far longer. It sounds so silly to even talk nowadays about the length of someone's hair, but back then it was so unusual that it was eye-catching.

I watched the band do their set, though I must admit that I can't remember anything about their music. Later, once the show was over and I was standing at the back of the club brushing my waist-length peroxide blonde hair, the singer came up to me from behind and – taking the brush from my hand – carried on brushing my hair while asking me if he could come home with me that night. Of course, I said yes. Little did I know, then, that this young chap would go on to become one of the best-known artists in the world, the iconic David Bowie.

We left the club together and walked the half-hour it took to get to my home in Thurloe Square, where I smuggled him past my parents' bedroom and up to the top floor. I did briefly wonder how I was going to explain his presence to my parents in the morning, though I didn't worry about that for long. We landed up in my single bed and, to be honest, I can't remember what we did. It was really late, it was a small bed, and I wasn't sufficiently experienced to fully know what I was doing. I'd had my moments with the ski instructors but was still pretty innocent, and David was also very young (though probably knew a bit more than me). I know we messed around a bit sexually, so let's just say that we spent the night together, horizontally.

In the morning, I had to go to school, so I needed to get him down past my parents' bedroom and out of the house. My mother and father must have heard us coming down the stairs because they both appeared on the landing. Straightaway I introduced him by saying, "This is David", upon which David shook hands with my father and then trotted off. My father told me afterwards that he thought I'd had a girlfriend with me, because of the long hair.

It only occurred to me later that David had needed somewhere to stay, as it had been too late for him to get home when we left the Marquee. I didn't know where Bromley was, back then, and it never crossed my mind that trains didn't run that late at night. As far as I was concerned, he just wanted to be with me. There was definitely a twinkle in his eye, and I guess there was a twinkle in mine too, but just as importantly, we spoke the same language… music.

How wonderful my parents were not to make a scene, or object to me bringing a boy home when I was only 14. They more or less let me do anything I liked; I was treated like an adult and trusted to do the right thing.

From that night on, David often used to come round and spend the night. Sometimes he'd call me and invite me to go to whatever gigs he was doing in London. He'd pick me up from school, which would cause a bit of a stir with my friends, and on some occasions, he would carry my ballet shoes as we walked back to my home. He even used to wait for me outside Cecil's flat until my drama lesson was over, after which we'd stroll back and go to the top of the house to be alone.

I knew it would never be a normal boy/girl relationship. We were far too young to get tied to one another, and in any case, I knew that there were other girls when he was on the road because that's what musicians do. Expecting anything like fidelity would have been ridiculous at our age, and I never wanted to be Mrs Jones or even his number one girlfriend.

What I did get, though, was time alone with him; time to explore what little I knew sexually, as well as time to talk about music. I was expanding my horizons and – best of all – David was giving me guitar lessons. The first song he showed me how to play was 'Love is Strange', an old Mickey and Sylvia hit, but he also listened to my compositions and told me to keep on at my songwriting. He used to encourage me to continue with my musical dream, as he too was chasing the same dream.

It didn't bother me that there were other girls around. He once told me that his previous band, The Lower Third, drove to gigs in an ambulance, and that, "…one day we all got hold of girls, and gave them one in Piccadilly Circus."

When I asked how they managed to do that in such a public place, he told me that the ambulance had frosted glass windows.

Having never expected or wanted a faithful relationship, I was just happy that we were good friends, who occasionally spent the night together. If he was going off on tour, he'd tell me what he was up to, and I'd be happy to see him when he got back. He'd ask if I'd written any new songs and I'd sing them to him, or vice versa. It sounds rather coy, now, but I was glad that somebody actually wanted to listen to my early musical offerings.

Often we'd meet in the Gioconda Cafe in Denmark Street, known in the business as Tin Pan Alley, which was where all the publishing companies resided. This was the place to be if someone needed a musician or singer to perform, and it was in the basement studios of many of the buildings on Denmark Street where the hits (or at least the demos of future hits) were recorded. As a result, the café was always full of musicians waiting to be called. David and I would spend many hours chatting in there, making a cup of tea last for as long as possible.

Our aim was always to get a publishing contract, with a record deal being a bonus. Having spent so much time sitting with David in the Gioconda, I knew that all along the street, on either side, were masses of publishers. At that time, neither David nor I really saw ourselves as performers; what we both wanted was to have our songs published, and I was lucky enough to soon sign with a publisher.

One afternoon, David came to the cafe and told me to follow him to the music store around the corner called Francis, Day and Hunter. We went into a little booth, and he gave me the earpiece and told me to listen to his latest single with the Manish Boys, which was called 'I Pity the Fool', with 'Take My Tip' as the flipside. He seemed so proud to play his new single for me, and I experienced the same thrill when I played him my first single.

David was always fun to be with. It was obvious, even then, that he was ambitious, and basically just wanted to work. We were very similar in that we both needed experience… anything that would take us to the next level. I recognised that in him, and he definitely recognised that in me.

Occasionally, we'd head off down to Carnaby Street, where David would have outfits tailor-made for him. You never saw him in an old pair of jeans and a T-shirt. Even in those early days, he dressed to draw attention, and heads always turned when he walked down the street.

His first TV interview was on the BBC's 'Tonight' programme with Cliff Michelmore, promoting 'The Society for the Protection of Long-haired Men'. If you watch the clip, you can see David has a twinkle in his eye, and you just know he's having a laugh, sending the whole thing up. It was a hoot, and very typical of the kind of thing he was trying to do at the time to get attention.

If there was ever anything interesting or unusual on the television when we were together, such as a programme about mime artist Marcel Marceau, he'd say, "We *must* watch this."

We used to watch 'The Strange World of Gurney Slade', starring Anthony Newley, whose voice David would sometimes mimic, as well as early black-and-white Ken Russell documentaries. He had a bright brain – something I have always appreciated in a man – and you wouldn't find him in front of the television watching brainless rubbish.

All things American seemed to interest him at this time, and he used to listen to US Armed Forces radio broadcasts. As a schoolboy, he had written to the American Embassy in London about his interest in American football, and they presented him with a full kit including a helmet. He told me that he had got his mismatched eyes from an injury he'd suffered playing American football, and it wasn't until years later that I found out this wasn't true! That permanently dilated pupil was, in fact, caused when his friend George Underwood punched him during a fight over a girl.

To this day, I have no idea why he made up the story about it being a football injury.

In 1965, one of the most popular groups around was the Monkees, whose lead singer was Davy Jones. David must have decided that there wasn't room for two David Joneses, and one day told me that he was now going to call himself David Bowie. He loved the movie 'The Alamo', and folklore suggests that it was Richard Widmark's portrayal of Jim Bowie in that film that gave him the idea for a new name. It didn't seem to make much difference at the time – it was just a stage name – and, of course, he never actually changed his name legally. He was David Jones all his life.

David once asked me to come to his home in Bromley, where he lived with his parents. It was a small terraced house out in the southern suburbs of London, and I had never been anywhere like it before. At my home we didn't watch television shows like 'Coronation Street', which depicted little houses in a row with backyards and washing hanging out to dry, so I had very little knowledge of the kind of working-class house where he grew up. I had grown up in a house with large rooms and was amazed at how small their living room was. It had three armchairs in it, all facing the television, with little bits of material on the back called antimacassars to soak up the Brylcreem that his father would put on his hair.

David's parents offered me tuna fish sandwiches, and then we just sat there in silence. They didn't really talk, and that flawed me a bit because I had grown up in a house where social intercourse was the norm. Even from a young age, I was used to dinner parties where you chatted, but they said nothing; they just sat there looking rather miserable.

After a while, they said they had to go out, leaving David and me alone. Once they had gone, David told me that – whatever he did – he would get out of this existence, come what may. This didn't surprise me; my main impression of the whole place was that it was emotionally cold. Nowadays, I recognise how an unloving childhood can affect someone in later years; if you don't get love when young, it makes it so much harder to know *how to give love* later on in life.

One time, we went to visit David's half-brother Terry, who was a few years older than him and was sadly living in a mental hospital nearby, called Cane Hill. That must have been tough on the parents, and when I saw the conditions there, it made a bit more sense to me as to why there was such a grim atmosphere in the family home. David was undoubtedly affected by Terry's condition, as he'd always looked up to him when he was growing up. The cover of the 1970 American release of 'The Man Who Sold The World' featured a drawing of Cane Hill Hospital, and the album included a number of songs about insanity including 'All the Madmen', which was supposedly inspired by Terry.

David also told me that he had a half-sister, but that she had been given away as a baby. He joked that he was worried that one day he'd land up in bed, making love to his own sister without knowing they were related. I think the idea even tickled him a bit!

It's very hard to talk about somebody that you've known as a mate, but who then becomes so iconic that everyone else sees them in a different light. We moved in and out of each other's lives for about ten years, and I just thought of him as a really good pal. Obviously, things changed when he became more famous, but nevertheless, the essence of David, and how he was when I met him, is what always stayed with me. He was my mate David Jones, and I never thought of him as 'David Bowie, the star'. Inevitably, most other people did.

*

When I was 15, Giorgio Gomelski offered me a managing and recording contract, but I didn't really understand it, and in any case, was too young for it to be signed without an adult. It was duly studied by my father, but somehow I never got round to signing it. Sometimes, I wonder how my career would have developed if I had signed with The Yardbirds' manager. Although I never did, Giorgio gave me the confidence to follow my dream, for which I shall forever be grateful to him. However, just at the time when Giorgio was waiting for me to sign, my life took a rather sudden and dramatic turn.

I had gone to Klosters for an Easter skiing break, and also to take part in the Ladies' Ski Championships in Davos. It had been a bad year all-round for skiers, as a couple of high-profile Swiss competitors had been killed in avalanches. Even though April was near the end of the skiing season, the mountains had one more trick to play.

It was a clear, sunny day for the British Ladies slalom competition, which was held on a very steep slope on a mountain range called the Jacobshorn. As I was still technically a junior, I had a high racing number which meant I had to go down the course later, when the better skiers had already left ruts in the snow. Most of the competitors had their skis off for waxing, and the judges had taken their positions from where they could check that both legs of each competitor went through the slalom gates.

My mother had volunteered to be one of these adjudicators, and she was sitting in the sun, ready to enjoy the day. I still hadn't got round to getting my skis off and was looking down at the course wondering how I was ever going to memorise it, when I felt someone (or so I thought) pushing me from behind. As I turned round to see who it was, I saw not a person, but what seemed like the whole mountain crashing down on top of me. At the same time, I heard screams and rumbling noises, and I tumbled down with my skis pulling me deeper under the snow.

There are two types of avalanches. There are the ones with powder snow that can suffocate you, as you feel like you are drowning in talcum powder, and there are the ones where the snow is packed hard and has cracked away in large chunks. This was the end of the season and so was the second kind, and was probably caused by many people using a steep area that was not usually skied on.

Down I went, with large blocks of snow swirling around and pulling me in all directions, a bit like crashing about in huge sugar cubes. The screams and rumbles lessened as I went deeper down, and then everything stopped, and there was silence. I was in total darkness, and I remember wondering if I was dead, but then I reasoned that I couldn't possibly be dead if I could ask myself such a question.

The problem was that I couldn't pinch myself to see if I could feel anything, as my arms were pinned down by the weight of the snow. It made no difference whether I had my eyes open or closed, as all was black and silent. Luckily, air was getting in through the gaps in the blocks of ice. I was probably upside down, and I knew my leg was badly injured as the pain had started; but there I stayed, trapped while pandemonium was going on above.

The whole slalom course and its timing equipment had been swept away, as had most of the judges and some of the competitors. As most had taken their skis off, they were able to ride this monster and somehow keep their heads above the blocks of snow.

In total, 30 people were swept down, but I was one of only two who had gone completely under. I had always used very distinctive metallic blue ski sticks, and by chance, one had been ripped from my hands, breaking the strap, and it was sticking up straight above me. My mother, who'd also been swept down, but was able to ride the avalanche, then started clawing her way up the slope, shouting for me.

A strange but comical thing happened, which she told me about later. As she was struggling up and was calling for me, a man came up to her. He was typically English, dressed in old-style skiing clothes with an anorak with lots of draw-strings hanging from it. He put his hand in a large pocket and produced a white printed card and said, "Ah, Mrs Gillespie, I've been looking for you. I've got your invitation to the Ski Club of Great Britain drinks party."

He then handed her the card while she carried on searching for her potentially dead daughter. This gave us all a laugh when we were finally able to sit down and look at the funny side of things.

Helpers had started to search under where my ski stick was sticking up, and I was duly found, pulled out, and put on an ambulance sledge, known to skiers as a 'blood wagon'. Irwin Shaw comforted my shocked mother with a flask of whiskey that he always carried with him when he went skiing. He had become famous for writing 'The Young Lions', which was later turned into a film with Marlon Brando, but a lot of people later knew him because of his book 'Rich Man, Poor Man' which became a television series. He remained a close friend of my mother and me until the day he died, and Klosters – which was his main residence – has been emptier for me ever since his demise.

For me, Irwin was a star on the day of the avalanche, because as I lay strapped on the sledge that was going to take me down the hill, he asked me if I wanted anything. "Chocolate", I replied weakly, and soon I had a pile of Mars Bars balanced on my chest. I couldn't actually eat them as my hands were strapped in, but the thought was there, and he remains a hero to me to this day.

I was whisked off to the Klosters doctor where my leg was bandaged up. The ligaments and cartilage had been ripped to pieces, and my left leg seemed to go in every direction, which made me feel queasy just to look at it. However, I was young and strong, and after two months of hobbling in plaster, and being back at school – but obviously not dancing – my life returned to normal.

3: IN THE BASEMENT

In 1963, Cecil Landeau persuaded my parents to let me leave the safety and good breeding of Francis Holland School to go to a stage school called The Arts Educational.

I had to audition and was accepted as a drama student rather than a ballet student, though one had to learn both. Let's face it, I was hardly the type to be gracefully lifted up by a male partner, in a pas de deux, with me wearing pointe ballet shoes.

'The Arts Ed' was situated in a marvellous old building on Hyde Park Corner which was sadly demolished shortly after I left, and replaced by what is now the Intercontinental Hotel. On my first day there, the headmistress, Mrs Cone, a very stern woman who seemed about 90 years old, called me out in front of the whole class and said, "Your bust bodice is too high!"

I was rather embarrassed as I had no idea what she was talking about, but soon realised that she was referring to my bra. Even then, I was considered a big girl, and the lunches I was served were what the school called the 'diet lunch' of crispbread and cheese with an apple. As a result, I was constantly hungry, so would head straight for the chocolate when I got home.

At Francis Holland School, I had been average in all academic subjects other than mathematics, but at the Arts Ed I was suddenly elevated to being nearer the top of the class. Most of the children were only interested in the dance side of the school, and other subjects took a back seat. Every morning we had normal classes, but the routine was often broken by someone going off to do an audition.

Between lessons, I used to take my old Spanish six-string guitar and disappear down near the boilers in the basement to compose naive love songs. It didn't take long for me to form a band with three of the boys. I was on drums, and we used to practise after school in my bedroom at the top of my parents' house. We had our first gig at an event called Big Beat '64 (although it was actually in 1963!) at The Vaudeville Theatre on The Strand. Millie 'My Boy Lollipop' Small also performed in it.

Cecil was convinced that I should go to the Royal Academy of Dramatic Art, RADA, and managed to get me an audition. A black velvet dress with a white lace collar was bought specially for the occasion, and was never worn again. I had to do two pieces, one Shakespeare and one more modern, so I did my usual deflowering speech from 'Romeo and Juliet' and also a soliloquy from 'Gigi'.

As one had to be 18 to be accepted, and I was only 15, we lied about my age on the entry form. They told me that they were going to offer me a place and all would have been well had not the then-head of RADA, John Fernald, called up the Arts Ed to congratulate them on one of their students getting in. The fact that I was underage became clear during the call, which was rather embarrassing for all concerned. A compromise was found, and RADA said they would keep a place for me in two years' time, while I stayed on at the Arts Ed.

That was never to be, as two years is a very long time when you are young, and I was to leave the Arts Ed at 15, just before the law was changed to require all children to stay until they were 16. The whole world was waiting for me out there, and I was eager to get started.

*

It had been obvious for a while that my father was spending more and more time out of the house. He used to say things like, "I'm just going out for a walk", and then he'd not come back for hours. Eventually, it became common knowledge that he had a 21-year-old mistress called Lorna Lambton. She had bought a house on the other side of Thurloe Square, so my father didn't have to walk far to reach her, and this soon became their love nest. Subsequently, my father decided that honesty was the best policy, and suggested to my mother that Lorna move into the big house with us. His idea was that my mother would have the top half of the building, where Nixi and I had been, and he and Lorna would be in the bottom half. It may sound an odd arrangement to many people, but for a while, it really did work. Thus, Lorna became part of the family, and remained so for 27 years.

Lorna was the granddaughter of the Earl of Buccleuch, and had a brother called Michael who gained a moment of notoriety during the famous Profumo trial that almost bought down the government of the time. Christine Keeler, when asked by the judge if she was a prostitute, replied that she wasn't, as she was engaged to Michael Lambton of Hambros Bank. A few years later, Lorna's cousin, Lord Lambton, was exposed in another sex scandal. The family name became quite well known to the press.

My mother didn't stay lonely for too long, either. She had met a man in Klosters that she'd known years earlier as he was a distant cousin of hers. He was called The Honourable Thomas Hazlerigg (always known to me as Tom), and they fell in love, got married, and he moved in with her at the top of Thurloe Square. If one was casting a film and wanted someone to look like the perfect upper-class English gentleman, then Tom would have got the part. He was the model of correctness too, which suited my mother as she'd had enough of my father's philandering ways.

The result of these moves was that I now had two sets of parents under one roof.

I moved into the basement, and this was wonderful for me as I got to decorate it in orange and black, with all sorts of splashes of colour and Oriental hangings. The combination of red lights and permanently burning incense made it feel like a harem. Very soon, the dark hallway was lined with tapestries, and the living room was filled with objets d'art collected from travels all over the place. The walls were covered in cases of stuffed birds and animals, and knowing how big an animal lover I am, my friends were surprised by my interest in taxidermy. I explained that as I didn't have live animals (other than my dog) in the house, I had to make do with stuffed ones, though – within a year – I had added two real cats.

The living room had a sofa bed where people would crash if they weren't staying with me in my bedroom, and it was here that I kept my musical instruments. There was an upright piano, as my baby grand couldn't get down the stairs, a selection of guitars and – of course – my drum kit. I'd also acquired an ancient two-channel recording machine called a Vortexion, which allowed me to overdub backing vocals on my demos. Musicians used to come over, and sometimes we'd get together, around the machine, to record songs.

There was also a large carpeted bathroom with a big sofa where my friends would sit chatting while I would bathe. Very Bohemian! The bedroom was big too, and finally I'd got a double bed, above which I hung an old Temperance Society certificate which I'd bought in a junk shop several years earlier. The moral side of drinking didn't bother me, it was the taste I loathed, and that hasn't changed to this day. Still, it makes me a cheap date. Only the kitchen was small, but that was never a problem as all I cooked was brown rice and vegetables, which I would feed to any visiting hungry musician, including Bowie. Last but not least, I had a little back garden where Sneezi could go out and pee.

Often, my father would come downstairs to see what I was doing, and if I had friends with me, he'd sometimes sit and talk, or flirt if there were girls there. He didn't seem to mind if someone was smoking a joint. He always said to me that if I had to choose between drinking or smoking a joint, go with the hash as it was far less dangerous. Indeed, he told me that he had prescribed a tincture of cannabis to some of his patients in his early years as a doctor, before he specialised in radiography, though I can't remember what ailment needed such a remedy.

*

One of the best things about Thurloe Square is its location, right in the heart of London; bursting with cafes and restaurants. In the sixties, it had the added advantage of being near two really good 'music and hang out' clubs, both within three minutes' walk from home.

The Cromwellian Club on Cromwell Road regularly had 'live' music. The crowd would often be musicians on a night off, music journalists getting drunk, and general liggers and lovers of good music. The Cromwellian became a real happening place in the mid-60s; it was where Jimi Hendrix made one of his first appearances in London in October 1966.

Among the regulars who played at The Cromwellian were Brian Auger's band The Steampacket, featuring Rod Stewart and Long John Baldry on vocals. Long John left in 1966 to form Bluesology, which included a young piano player called Reg Dwight, now rather better known as Elton John. Another of the bands was The Artwoods, featuring Art and his brother Ronnie Wood. Ronnie went on to find fame in The Small Faces, The Faces (with Rod) and, since 1975, as 'the new boy' in the Rolling Stones. Ronnie and his then-girlfriend – the stunningly beautiful Chrissie – became regular visitors to my basement, and his 1965 diary published by Genesis Publications contains several entries describing our get-togethers. We'd sit together in the local Wimpy Bar if there was nothing else to do, or head back to my place to hang out.

The Cromwellian Club was my favourite hangout, but sometimes I would stroll over to Blaises on Queensgate to check what was happening there. According to Melody Maker journalist Chris Welch, this was a venue, "where musicians, agents, managers and writers allowed themselves to be deafened whilst imbibing quantities of alcohol."

Sometimes I would go to The Troubadour, which at the time was the 'in' folk club in town. Bert Jansch and Davy Graham used to appear there, as did Paul Simon. Paul was over from America, playing solo, and lived just around the corner from me at St George's Court. One day, he asked me over to his place, and when I got there, I found him packing his bags. I asked him why he was leaving, and he said he'd just had a call from America about a recording that he'd done a year earlier with Art Garfunkel, called 'The 'Sound of Silence', which had suddenly become a big hit in the States. Apparently, the producer had added drums and other instruments to the original recording – without Paul's knowledge – and it was this that took a traditional folk song from obscurity to number one. He was now 'Homeward Bound'.

*

Over the next few years, my flat became a popular meeting place for musicians and other interesting characters, who used to land up there at the end of the night if they couldn't get home. After all, a taxi was a bit of a luxury if you were an impoverished musician.

One evening, my friend Sara Troup and I were with Mick Avory and Pete Quaife, a couple of the members of The Kinks, at The Cromwellian. We came out of the club, walked up to Hyde Park and jumped over the fence to go for a swim in the Serpentine. Obviously, we didn't have swimming costumes with us, so we all went in starkers. Sara and I leapt out of the water first, and it seemed like a good idea at the time for us to hide the boys' clothes before they realised what was happening. After a lot of giggling and running around, we took pity on them and let them have their clothes back, and we all ended up at my place.

On another occasion, the same guys and I were celebrating my 17th birthday (which was the next day) in the Cromwellian. Once again, we found ourselves back in my basement at the end of the evening, and all crashed in bed. I should say that I kept my knickers on, as did the others, and nothing happened as it was all rather innocent. In the morning, I woke up to the sound of my father coming down the stairs singing "Happy Birthday To You". The guys were still fast asleep, and there was no time to hide them. He opened the door still singing happy birthday until he saw his daughter in bed with two men, at which point he stopped rather abruptly. Mick and Pete both sat up in bed, so I felt I ought to introduce them. Dadster smiled, and said it was the first formal introduction he'd had to friends of mine for a long time.

What a liberal father I had. He didn't seem to mind what went on, and his study was right in front of the steps leading down to the basement, so he would see all my friends who would come to visit.

"That's OK, she's young and enjoying herself", he would explain.

On one occasion he even bought me a vibrator from Harrods. He didn't tell me what to do with it, and the picture on the side of the box didn't help much, as it was of a woman holding the vibrator against her neck. This was well before the time when every magazine and newspaper was writing about female orgasms; it took me some time to work out what to do with it!

*

Back in the early sixties, everyone wanted to be close to the King's Road in Chelsea. It's rather lost its sparkle now, but in those days, it was a joyous, magical place, especially in the summertime. It was a time of peace and love, with people out on the street having fun. Sitting in the 'Chelsea Kitchen', I would eat egg and chips for a few pennies, or hang out in the 'Picasso', from where I'd watch the whole world go past. Great looking girls and guys, musicians, models and actors, everyone would be walking along the King's Road.

Most musicians, especially working-class ones, couldn't afford to live in Chelsea, and a lot of them never had a place where they lived all the time. More often than not, they would rent some cheap place for the whole band in somewhere like Bayswater, a part of London that is not so affordable now. There would often be three or four of them living in one place, and it would be fair to say that their standards of personal hygiene and tidiness left a lot to be desired.

Rolling Stone Brian Jones used to live in a little converted house on Elm Park Gardens, just off Gloucester Road. I can't remember where I first met him, but it must have been sometime in the early sixties. There was nothing sexual between us as I was just a bird among the few girls who turned up there. Anyway, I remember walking in and seeing total chaos, just mess everywhere. Some of the other Stones, I think Keith and Mick, were also dossing there, and were living in complete squalor.

When the Rolling Stones exhibition came to London a few years ago, there were full-size recreations of the place the Stones lived in the early sixties, and my friend Gered Mankowitz asked if I wanted to go and see it. I thanked him but said *no*; I had seen the real thing, and had no need to see it again!

The kind of people that the Stones and many of the other bands were hanging out with – typically dope smokers and acid takers – used to come from families with money who lived in areas like Kensington or Chelsea. These were people who went to great schools, had wealthy backgrounds (and so were 'trust fund babies'), and had parents who were often away a lot or, like me, had a separate flat in their parents' house. This made Chelsea a very alluring place in the sixties.

One day in 1965, I was invited to join the Stones on a boat trip up the Thames. Some footage of this strange event can be seen on YouTube, and it was reported in the London Evening Standard.

The boys were being taken up the river to be presented with a record award by Anita Harris. Charlie Watts looked unutterably bored, Keith Richards was quiet and Brian Jones less than cheerful. On the other hand, I rushed around the boat somewhat over-excitedly before (according to the press report) shooting a reporter with a gun loaded with blanks, smashing his glass of whiskey and cutting his hand. Whilst I don't remember shooting anybody, I did indeed carry a starting pistol with me, which was used when I was doing water-skiing tricks. Maybe that explains it.

Another band I knew in those days was The Animals who rented a flat quite close to me on Old Brompton Road, and for a while I hung out with the guitarist Hilton Valentine. Their piano player at the time, Dave Rowberry, had taken over from Alan Price in 1965, and according to singer Eric Burden had been chosen partly because he looked a bit like Alan.

It was common knowledge that Alan was not that popular with the other band members, because he had been the only one who had turned up at some management meeting and, as a result, was the only one who signed for the rights to the Animals' huge breakthrough hit 'House of the Rising Sun'. This was a song he didn't actually write, as it was an old traditional folk song but, as a result, he got all the songwriters' royalties. Poor Eric Burden had to sing it every night for the next 20 years, knowing that all the royalties were going to Alan Price.

Dave Rowberry was famously quoted as saying of the band: "They were a bunch of cunts when I joined them and were a bunch of cunts when I left!"

Dave was a great piano player, and subsequently played in my band for many years. He was on several of my albums, including the aptly named 'Blue Job'. Sadly, I had to sack him when his drinking got out of control; it really upset me at the time because he was such a great musician. When he used to get drunk, he'd sometimes say, "Oh Dana, I love you", although nothing ever really happened. I adored the man, but it's best never to fuck the musicians you work with, because it always goes wrong. We had a great relationship, but in my opinion, drink ultimately killed him.

Dave was invited to join the reformed Animals in 2003 for a tour of Europe. The band turned up one day outside his front door to pick him up in the group bus, and when there was no reply, they broke the door down to find him dead, flat on his face in front of a whole wall of pictures of me. It was almost as if he'd built a shrine.

Years later, Elton John was interviewed at the European launch of MTV in Amsterdam, which I also attended. He said that the first band pianist he was inspired by was Dave Rowberry when he was in the Mike Cotton Sound. A few years later, I was at a birthday party thrown by Elton at Home House, for my pal Mike

Hewitson, who worked as Elton's personal assistant for over 30 years. I was pleased to be able to thank Elton for praising Dave on such a high profile occasion, and to tell him that Dave had spent many years in my band.

*

'Ready Steady Go' was the top weekly pop television programme at the time. This was the first TV show that promoted black artists, like Muddy Waters, as well as other great American acts like Jerry Lee Lewis. The show was recorded at Studio 9 in the Rediffusion Building in Kingsway, London. David Bowie and I would head straight to the Green Room to network with others in the music business and also meet guys from the music press. If you chatted to the important press people and photographers in the Green Room, sometimes you would get a mention in the music papers. The thing to do was to turn up at the studios in the afternoon, when the soundchecks had been done, then start networking with the music biz folks who were there.

The show had a 'live' dancing audience, chosen from the hippest and most fashionably dressed people from the local clubs. I would gyrate with all the other kids, enjoying the latest hits and trying to get noticed every time the cameras came near. You couldn't miss the approaching cameras as they were huge, and they often appeared on the screen. Dave Clark (of the Dave Clark Five, who had lots of hits in the sixties) now owns the old tapes, and I keep hoping he'll find some footage with me on. Sadly, he hasn't found any yet; however, there was a documentary shown on television in early 2020 when I think I spotted myself.

In the early days, the programme was presented by Dusty Springfield, who was very friendly with one of the producers, Vicki Wickham. Vicki co-wrote (with Simon Napier-Bell) the English lyrics to Dusty's hit, 'You Don't Have to Say You Love Me'. The main producer was a guy called Elkan Allan, who had a rather disconcerting habit of only talking to my chest. When the show became more popular, the presenters were Keith Fordyce, Cathy McGowan and Michael Aldred.

If David wasn't around, I would sometimes go to the studios with my best friend Sara, who was a very good looking blonde. Girls of that age always have a 'best friend,' and we spent a lot of time together. Through Donovan, whom I had met in the Green Room, I got to meet his managers, Peter Eden and Geoff Stephens, and soon afterwards they became my managers for a short time. Geoff wrote the novelty hit 'Winchester Cathedral' which The New Vaudeville Band took to number 1 in the charts.

Peter Eden and Geoff Stephens were very supportive of me, and introduced me to a guy called Barry Kingston at Southern Music Publishing House in Tin Pan Alley. He became my next manager. I was happy to sign with Southern Music because it was a publishing house right next to the Giaconda Café, where I used to spend so much time with Bowie. It had a little studio in the basement.

The date was fixed for my first recording session, but when I turned up, it had been cancelled as the engineer had blown his brains out, there, that very morning.

A new date was arranged, and it was decided that I should sing a folk song called 'Donna Donna'. It is actually a traditional folksong about a poor cow being taken to market to be slaughtered, but I guess I wasn't really thinking about the merits of vegetarianism at that time. Donovan came in and played guitar for me, and for some strange reason, an ocarina player was also brought in. This was the folk era, so ethnic instruments were considered cool. The B-side was one of my songs called 'It's no use saying if'. It was always a good idea to have a self-penned song on the B-side of singles, because the songwriter of the B-side got the same amount of money as the writer of the A-side when it came to royalty payments.

In 1965, the producers decided that 'Ready Steady Go' should be broadcast 'live', so its new name would be 'Ready Steady Goes Live'. Donovan was on the first 'live' show, and he was so popular that they extended his run to three weeks in a row; unheard of at the time. By the end of this stint, 'Catch the Wind' was a hit, and Donovan was a star.

Donovan had made it by breaking the mould of wearing a suit on stage, as he would dress in denims, including a blue denim hat. So when 'Ready Steady Goes Live' booked me to go on straight after his appearances, I chose to wear a similar look, albeit without the hat. This was unusual, as girl singers would inevitably wear a dress in those days.

I was booked to appear on 'Ready Steady Goes Live' on the 29th of April 1965, a month after my 16th birthday. Also on the bill were Georgie Fame and the Blue Flames, Chubby Checker doing 'Lets Twist Again', and The Searchers. 'Donna Donna' had been chosen as Melody Maker's Record of the week, and I sang it 'live'. I had no clue what I was doing, I didn't know what a monitor was, and I had no idea about microphones.

Like Donovan, I was booked to return the following week, so I must have done alright on the first show. This time, the Spencer Davis Group were on, promoting 'Keep on Running', which became a huge hit. Others on the show were the Walker Brothers ('The Sun Ain't Gonna Shine Anymore') and the Nashville Teens, who had a big hit with 'Tobacco Road'. John Hawken, the pianist with the Nashville Teens, later joined my band.

On this show, I sang a song that Bowie had taught me, called 'Love is Strange', with the Les Reed orchestra backing me. Unfortunately, the monitor wasn't working properly, and I couldn't hear the music. I wasn't experienced enough to deal with this situation and – with Les and his musicians way over the other side of the studio – I had trouble finding the note to come in on. It must have sounded horrible, going out 'live', but that is how one learns, by making mistakes.

The more gigs I did, the better I got, and I was learning fast. One particular show which was rather unusual was a BBC television programme called 'Gadzooks'. I was quite excited about it because also on the bill were The Who, Gene Pitney and Marianne Faithfull. Unfortunately, I didn't get to meet any of them in the studio, as the producer of the show, Barry Langford, decided that I should sing on water skis.

When I say sing, I – of course – mean mime.

My song was filmed back at the Princes Club near London Heathrow Airport, and all I can remember was that it was fucking freezing. Normally, I would wear a wetsuit when water-skiing, but I assume the producer was rather fond of seeing girls in bikinis because this is how I was told to appear. Looking wet and bedraggled, as well as being blue with cold, was hardly the best way to present a song, but I was game for anything, and it produced quite a bit of coverage in the press because (in those days) some newspapers would use any excuse to publish a photo of bikini-clad girls. They did, at least, let me come to the studio fully-dressed the next time I was on Gadzooks. The other performing acts were The Hollies, The Who, Anita Harris and The Four Pennies, together with compere Alan David.

The Hollies were riding high in the charts when I supported them on some of their Sunday concerts on the Britannia Pier, Great Yarmouth. In fact, my next single was a Hollies song, 'Pay You Back With Interest', recorded for Pye Records at their studios in Marble Arch. If you haven't heard it, then you are in good company, because – let's just say – it didn't trouble the charts. The same fate befell another Pye single, 'Thank You Boy', released around the same time. At least they both had Gillespie compositions on the B-sides: 'You're A Heartbreak Man' and 'Adam Can You Beat That'. Despite the records not selling, I did, manage to find time to have a bit of a fling with Hollies guitarist Tony Hicks (and an even shorter one with Graham Nash).

Most of the girl singers then were not singing their own compositions, but I was determined to be different and to become known as a singer/songwriter. Folk music was very 'in' at the time, and my voice hadn't yet developed enough to do more than folk songs. I could sing in tune, but I didn't have the chops to belt out a song.

That was to come later.

4: MAKING MY NAME IN THE MUSIC BUSINESS

Whilst I had a good social life for one so young, I really needed to know how to take my career forward, and was happy to accept any gig that came my way. It wasn't just experience that I wanted, I was also determined to be financially independent from my parents, so I needed to start earning my own money.

When the first paid gig came in – playing folk guitar at the opening of a new garage in Taunton – I was happy to do it though I doubt it was an earth-shattering experience for the smattering of people who bothered to turn up. Folk music in a petrol station doesn't really work too well, and the agent who booked me must have been off his rocker. At least when I did my second gig, in a Norfolk folk club, some of my relations turned up to support me. Although I didn't plan it that way, it seemed like the folk music scene was where I was headed; it was an obvious music style when armed with a guitar and a clear young voice.

Around that time, I received a telephone call from Victor Lowndes, who was head of the Playboy Club in London – the British version of Hugh Hefner, I suppose. Victor had seen a photograph of me water skiing in a swimming costume, and wanted to know if I'd be interested in posing for Playboy. I took the short walk to Victor's luxurious house near Harrods in Montpelier Square, Knightsbridge, alone.

Victor ran his operations from there, so the place was full of people running around, with telephones ringing all the time. He made it clear from the start that he fancied me, but also quickly realised I'd be too young to do a photoshoot for Playboy as I was still under 16. We nevertheless became friends, and I would often be invited to his legendary star-studded parties, and as a result, became a party girl for a while. The reality is that I have never really enjoyed parties, and even now, I go with big reservations, usually wondering why I bothered in the first place.

On party nights, his house would be full of bunny girls and models, and a fair number of celebrities. Actors such as Bennie Carruthers, Jim Brown (both of whom appeared in 'The Deadly Dozen'), Harry Baird ('The Italian Job'), and Ian Quarrier were regular attendees. Everyone was beautiful, and everything was available, and to an impressionable 15-year-old it was like a fantasy world. There was a lot of flirting going on, and people would disappear upstairs and reappear an hour or so later, obviously after some sort of rough and tumble. Sometimes, Victor would withdraw into a bedroom with two girls at a time. It all made my experiences with ski instructors, and even David Bowie, seem pretty innocent in comparison.

Film directors Roman Polanski and Jerzy Skolimowski also joined the hedonistic crowd, and when I first met Roman I did end up spending the night with him in a nearby mews house that he was renting. Whilst I certainly didn't look my age, I was old enough to know what I was doing, and in any case, I was curious and adventurous. I learnt early on not to say something was another person's fault, knowing that it takes two to tango.

I saw Roman a few times after that but knew he just wanted one night stands, which I wasn't interested in. In any case, when his wife Sharon Tate was in town, there was definitely no hanky-panky. A year later I met him again, this time with Sharon (who was then pregnant), and I can honestly say I had never seen such a beautiful-looking girl. How he coped with the Charles Manson murder of his wife and unborn child, I can't imagine.

*

One night, when I was at the Cromwellian, some Italians came in looking for 'extras' for a film they were making. They needed people who looked 'groovy', who could represent the youth of the swinging sixties, and said that anyone who wanted to be in a film should turn up at a particular address the following day.

So the next day, a bunch of us were taken out to the edge of London to start filming. I wore a mini skirt and white boots, and took my guitar as they had asked me to bring it along.

The film was called 'Fumo di Londra', meaning 'Smoke over London', and featured Alberto Sordi, the prominent Italian film star. Even to this day, if I tell people in Italy that I was in that film, they go into meltdown because Alberto was the biggest name in Italian film at the time.

On another occasion, The Who drummer Keith Moon and I were invited to be in a film, and we both agreed to be involved. I had got to know Keith quite well, and he was a lot of fun. I can't now remember what we were filming, and don't know if anything was ever made of the footage or indeed whether it still exists. However, what I do remember is that at the end of the day, we ended up together in a hotel room, where we had something of a horizontal marathon over the next couple of days. Typically Keith managed to consume A LOT of speed, which certainly kept him up all night…

Keith truly was a great character, never bland or boring. He was the nicest sort of lunatic, a genuinely wild eccentric. Sometimes, when he was a bit the worse for drink, he would bang on my front door, demanding to be let in. On occasions, he would just pass out; other times, we landed up in bed.

He was a wild musician, with a great sense of humour, and his wildness was no act; it was for real. In those days, he had no TVs to throw through windows, or Rolls-Royces to drive into swimming pools. Everything written about him is true; he really lived life to the full and had an enormous appetite for drink, pills, and sex. He was a big consumer of purple hearts, and all those pep pills meant he could go on for hours and hours. He didn't really care when or where we were, his kick was shocking people, and we had wild sex in some pretty strange places. Once, when The Who had done a concert on the Britannia pier in Great Yarmouth and their fans wouldn't let them off, Keith dragged me onto a pleasure boat where we 'passed the time' until the fans had dispersed. On another occasion, we ended up in the Tunnel of Love in Battersea Funfair.

*

At the time, I was very weight-conscious because whenever I went to an audition, they would say, "You can have this part if you lose a bit of weight".

So my father suggested that I go to see a man called Doctor Robert (the doctor rumoured to be an inspiration for The Beatles' song of the same name on their 'Revolver' album). He had a practice in Harley Street, and his waiting-room would always be full of models and actresses waiting to go in and see him. You'd pay a fiver, be in his room literally for ten seconds, he'd give you an injection through your tights, and you'd go away with a load of pills and come back the next week and give him another fiver.

I did this for a couple of months until, one day, over breakfast, my father said I was looking a bit grey. I'd lost some weight following my visits to Doctor Robert, and my father insisted on seeing the pills that had been prescribed for me. He took them away and had them tested, and found that they were pure speed.

*

My next chance to be in front of a camera was in a little-known film called 'The Secrets of the Windmill Girls', starring Pauline Collins, Harry Fowler (from 'The Army Game'), April Wilding, Martin Jarvis, and various other well-established English actors. It was made in 1965 and, again, I was booked to sing and play guitar in a short skirt and a top with a plunging neckline. I'd written a song especially for the film, which I foolishly agreed to sell outright for £25. Nowadays, I think this would have been against the law, but I was happy to have the work, and all I had to do was strum my guitar at a party scene and sing my song with gusto.

The Windmill Theatre ('We Never Close' was their motto) had been an established strip club in Soho that had survived the war. Many well-known British actors, including Peter Sellers and Harry Secombe, had started their careers there by 'entertaining' the punters – no doubt getting heckled in-between the strippers' performances. The film was a low budget affair that told a rather weak story of two of these girls. You didn't see bare breasts in those days, just nifty camera work involving fans and other objects, so that the censors were satisfied – even if the audience weren't.

The film sometimes turns up late at night on rather obscure television channels. It's very dated, and (not deliberately) hilarious. It was initially released in Britain as part of a double bill with a film called 'Naked as Nature Intended', part of which was filmed at a nudist camp, so clearly the package was very much aimed at the dirty raincoat brigade.

After the film came out in 1966, without any big fanfare or premiere, I got a call from one of the two producers who asked me to come to his office in Old Compton Street (now perhaps the gayest street in London, and known as Old Campton Street for obvious reasons).

My appointment was at six o'clock in the evening. Rather naively, I didn't think there was anything odd about having a meeting when nobody else would be in the office. During the filming, I had never actually met the producer, so I suppose he had only seen me when he had watched the film. Anyway, it soon became apparent that he didn't particularly want to talk about my career. He offered me a drink, and I took a bitter lemon. As I was about to sit down, he hit a switch that instantly turned the sofa into a bed, so that I fell backwards, spilling my drink all over him. There then ensued a farcical situation of him, with his trousers round his ankles, chasing me around the desk with me shouting "No!" before managing to make it to the door. It was a bit like a scene from a Brian Rix farce, and needless to say, I was never asked to work for his company again, which was fine by me.

The only other time that I had to fight someone off in a similar scenario was a few years later.

A friend of mine called David McEwen had secured me an appointment with the famous American record company boss/producer Ahmet Ertegun by telling him that I was looking for a record deal. I really wanted to see if I could get signed by an American company, to try to break out of the British pop scene. The only time that we were both free to meet was at eight in the morning, as he was flying back to America later that day. As it was a Friday, I had gone to the Bermondsey antique market, at dawn, to check out if there were any bargains, so I was definitely not dressed in anything unduly provocative, just jeans and a top.

Our meeting was at the Dorchester Hotel on Park Lane, and I arrived clutching the two L.P.s I'd made. I was surprised to find that he didn't have a record player in his suite, as the purpose of the meeting was supposedly for him to listen to my recordings.

He asked what I'd like for breakfast, and I said porridge. While we were waiting for the food to arrive, I chatted away but couldn't help noticing that his hand was moving up and down inside the trouser pocket of his wide Oxford bags. I was in a quandary as I didn't know whether I should react or ignore it, so I pretended I didn't know what he was doing. There was always the chance that he was just scratching himself, so ignorance seemed the best option. The breakfast arrived, but the moment the waiter had left the trolley behind, Ahmet got his cock out and made a lunge at me. Once again, a sort of slapstick situation took place, with him chasing me around the trolley and me saying "No!" The final insult was when he came all over my porridge. I left in disgust, and didn't even get to eat my breakfast!

This episode has never diminished my admiration for the work of Ahmet Ertegun and his brother Nesui, as Atlantic Records signed some of the top Blues musicians in the world. It did illustrate, however, that great men can still mess up when thinking with their cocks!

It wasn't until a few years later that I met Ahmet again, on Mustique with Mick Jagger, when he turned up for Colin Tennant's 50th birthday party. He leered at me from his half-closed eyes, but I chose to play it cool and just gave him a frosty look. I was hurt that he hadn't taken me seriously when I had come to him in good faith to talk about music, and he'd had his mind on other things.

Having accepted that I was in a business that relied on looks, it definitely did not mean that I was prepared to sleep with someone to advance my career. I'd already discovered that I was more likely to be in the newspapers if I had my top button undone and breathed in at the right moment, as that was what all the press photographers were after. Nothing more than cleavage was ever shown in the sixties press, but I knew that it was the game one had to play to get noticed, which then hopefully turned into work.

My first real taste of standing alone with my guitar on a big stage was in 1965 when I was booked to do a summer season of Sunday concerts at the Britannia Pier in Great Yarmouth. This was in an era when most people still had their holidays in Britain, so pop package tours were arranged at the seaside resorts to entertain the holidaymakers. I was the bit of fluff that came on and sang four or five songs, strumming away on my guitar as a warm-up act before the big names. I was paid £25 for a concert, but as this didn't include travel or accommodation expenses, I used to hitchhike to the gigs in order to save money.

Sometimes, after a show, I would crawl under the tarpaulin of a pleasure boat left on the beach, and sleep there. My mother would have had a fit had she known where I was spending the night.

The best thing about these concerts was the opportunity to get to know the other acts on the bill. There was always a lot of hanging around backstage, and – as the only female performer – I'd get most of the offstage attention. There was a different star name each week, and during my run, The Hollies and The Who both headlined, as did Donovan, whilst the artists lower down the bill stayed on for a number of weeks.

P.J. Proby was the star one week. He sported a ponytail with a big black bow in his hair, often wore a velvet suit with a Beau Brummell look, and when he stepped on stage, the girls went crazy and screamed at him. He managed to get through the show without splitting his trousers, something for which he was to become infamous. Our paths were to cross again a few years later.

One of the local newspapers reported on my performance, "Dana has achieved success in a short space of time and is rated highly to become one of the future top recording stars in the country."

What a load of twaddle some people write!

On another occasion, Tom Jones and his backing band The Squires were the star attraction. The audience was again full of screaming women, and when Tom gyrated his hips in a way that was reminiscent of early Elvis, the crowd screamed even more. 'It's Not Unusual' was just starting to storm the charts, and Tom was becoming one of the big names in the music business.

During his performance, Tom wore an open-fronted red frilled shirt, with a medallion in full view, and a little bolero jacket. As I was watching from the wings, he walked to the side of the stage mid-song and handed me the jacket. When his act was over, he walked off stage and, without saying a word, he took his jacket from me and planted a passionate kiss on my lips. Heady stuff for a 16-year-old who was still learning the ropes. He then disappeared into a waiting boat that would take him to dry land before the fans could mob him.

Going back to my then budding music career, I was once described in the press as "the female Donovan", and one journalist wrote, "Dana (it rhymes with spanner) is actually a friend of Donovan." As a result, many people thought I was going out with him, but it wasn't true – my friend Sara did go out with Donovan for a short time, but I had my eyes on another 'folkie'…

5: BOB DYLAN

In April/May 1965, Bob Dylan undertook his first concert tour of England. He was still performing folk songs at the time and, ridiculous as it may now seem, some of the English newspapers were even suggesting that Dylan was a poor man's Donovan.

At a press conference at the Savoy Hotel in London, on April the 26th, Dylan was asked whether he had heard of Donovan. He replied, "Donovan what?" After he gave a similar answer to several more questions, arrangements were made for the two of them to meet at the hotel later on. As my friend Sara was hanging out with Donovan at the time, she heard about this, and we decided to go along.

We duly turned up at the Savoy, and somehow found our way into the area where Dylan was holding court to a relatively small press reception of mainly journalists and photographers. Many of them weren't there for long, as they would take some pictures, get a few quotes, and make sure they had a few free drinks, before rushing back to the office to write their copy.

These days it would be impossible to walk unchecked into an event like that. It helped that I already knew some of the journalists from the New Musical Express and Melody Maker who were there, as I'd often bump into them at the Speakeasy. I guess I was a familiar face to them as it wasn't the first time I'd been to one of these press events; sometimes, a journalist would tip me off about a record reception somewhere, for whoever the star might be, and I'd just turn up.

Dylan was 23 then, and already a big name in the music business. The first time I saw him, he was dressed in an open-necked shirt, jeans, and boots. He chain-smoked all the time and later admitted to a journalist that he was smoking 80 cigarettes a day. Joan Baez was present, but she was due to leave a few hours later to fly back to America.

Once the journalists had finished asking their questions, Dylan came over to me, and we chatted for about 20 minutes. There was definitely some sort of spark between us, which was unusual for me as I tended not to be drawn to Americans. I must admit that I found him attractive. I usually go for all the things that you can't see in a man, like a good heart and an interesting brain, and this he had plenty of. Whilst I can't say that I was there just because of his music, the moment we started talking I did find his persona magnetic. I really hoped to see him again.

After a while, Dylan had to leave to go to another event. Somebody said that he would be at a huge reception that night, at the Dorchester Hotel, hosted by his label CBS Records, and I said to Sara, "We have to go, I've got to meet him again."

Determined to get into the reception, I ran home to change, and oddly enough can still remember exactly what I chose to wear: a little mini-dress and some hideous shoes.

We had no invitation but thought we might be able to talk our way past the door. However, I hadn't realised that security would be so tight. We got to the entrance to the ballroom where the reception was taking place, and I could see in through the main door and past the crowd to where Tony Bennett was on stage singing. Several other CBS stars like The Byrds were also there to perform.

Unfortunately, when Sara and I tried to go in, we were confronted by bouncers who – despite our best efforts – would *not* be won over. Refusing to allow the minor disadvantage of not having an invitation to deter me, I persuaded Sara to follow me in through the front lobby of the hotel, where we tried to make it look as though we were guests. Then, seeing a waiter carrying a silver tray of canapes, I decided we should follow him, and this led us to the staff area and down a long labyrinth of corridors. The waiter disappeared through one door, and I opened the next one, only to find that it was actually a false mirror that led straight into the main ballroom where the reception was being held.

I found myself standing at the top of a small flight of stairs. Sadly, the same two unfriendly bouncers who had stopped us getting in earlier also saw me above the heads of the crowd. They started making their way towards me, pushing the guests to one side, and their expressions suggested they were planning to throw us out. Just before they could say anything, Dylan spotted me and said, "Let her through, she's with me."

He then stepped forward to kiss me and say hello. One of the photographers there snapped a few shots of us together, which appeared in the press the next day.

The two bouncers retreated, leaving me on the protective arm of my knight in shining armour. He asked me for my telephone number, which I happily gave him, and this became the start of a curious friendship that continued for many years.

The next day, when I came home from school, my mother said somebody called Bob Dylan was on the telephone. I dropped everything and was straight off to his hotel. I'm not quite sure what I thought was going to happen, though I must be honest and admit that I half expected to spend the night there. In fact, I stayed for the next few days, for as long as Dylan remained in England.

Like most rock stars on the road, Dylan's hotel suite was full of people; friends, publicists, management, together with D.A. Pennebaker and his film crew, who were making a documentary about Dylan's 1965 tour. This was subsequently released as a black and white feature film called 'Don't Look Back'. The opening sequence was filmed in a side street at the back of the Savoy Hotel on the 8th of May, and Dylan mimed to his song 'Subterranean Homesick Blues' whilst holding up a set of cards, on which selected words and phrases from the lyrics of the song had been written. It has since become an iconic clip.

I was around for quite a lot of the filming, though stayed pretty much in the background. The only time I appear in the film is when Dylan comes into an empty Royal Albert Hall, and I'm sitting there – peroxide blonde in jeans and black suede Chelsea boots – awaiting his arrival. One of the extras on the DVD release of the film is a set of commentaries, in which you can hear Pennebaker swapping anecdotes with Bob Neuwirth, Dylan's good friend and touring buddy. When they get to the bit where I'm in shot, Neuwirth says, "That's Dana Gillespie. Al Grossman says she sings while surfing and she gave me her new LP which is really good."

Al Grossman, who was Dylan's then-manager, must have confused surfing with water skiing, but I didn't care; it was the bit about the LP being good that I liked best.

*

Back in the hotel suite, there was plenty of the usual 'hanging out', with Dylan's friends often dropping by. On one occasion, Dylan said he liked the pair of flowery bellbottomed trousers I was wearing, and asked if he could try them on. He looked pretty good in them, and I didn't mind when he said that he had to pop out for a couple of hours for some filming, and left wearing my trousers. The 'couple of hours' turned into almost 24, and while he could fit into my trousers, I couldn't fit into any of his. So I was stuck in his suite, wearing just a shirt and a pair of knickers.

I can't now remember what excuse I gave my parents when I finally got home. I doubt I told them I'd been keeping Bob Dylan's bed warm. On other nights, when we were together, I would slip out of his bed in the early hours and sneak back to my parents' house before they woke up.

After each concert, Dylan would tear out of the hall into a waiting limousine, dragging me with him. We'd have to run like mad to get into the car before all the stampeding screaming fans got hold of him. Being on stage for 2½ hours used to take a lot out of him, and when he came back to the hotel at night, he'd drink red wine to unwind before bed. What was I there for? Well, I think he just wanted someone warm to keep him company.

Soon it was time for Dylan to return home to America. I may have been young, but I knew that this was not what you would call a proper love affair. We were just having fun, as musicians do on the road, and while I hoped I would see him again, I understood that it might never happen.

*

Being in Dylan's company was always great, and so I was really excited when I heard that he was coming back to London for another tour in 1966.

In the early part of the year, I had been touring Europe – playing in Belgium, Holland, Germany, and Finland. This included performing at the Folk and Blues Festival in Antwerp alongside Donovan, and appearing on a television programme in Belgium singing 'Donna Donna'.

In those days, journalists could go to the airport and stand on the tarmac to welcome somebody famous. When Dylan got off the plane in London, and some reporter asked him, "What are you most looking forward to seeing in England?", he replied, "Dana Gillespie's jugs", which I suppose I should take as a compliment!

Dylan certainly seemed to have had a fixation with my bust around that time. New Musical Express reported on a press conference in London, on the 3rd of May 1966, at which Dylan was in one of his less than talkative moods, offering fairly bland responses to the questions until, according to the NME report, '…someone mentioned folksinger Dana Gillespie. Dylan brightened visibly – he practically tore his face in half in his effort to smile.

"Is Dana here?" he asked. "Bring her out. I got some baskets for her."

'Regretfully Dana was not there and the conversation reverted to monotone inanities again.'

Having sat through a number of Dylan's press conferences around that time, I can understand why he used to get rather tetchy. He is a deep thinker and, when interested in the subject matter, a good conversationalist, but being asked stupid questions would always get him annoyed. There's a famous clip where someone was interviewing him and asking really ignorant questions like, 'Where were you born?' or 'What's your favourite colour?', and you can just see him thinking 'What the fuck?! Talk to me about something of interest'. He was quite monosyllabic a lot of the time when talking to people he didn't know, so rather than let a conversation drop, journalists would just carry on waffling and thereby piss him off.

Dylan rang me shortly after arriving in town, and I went straight over to see him at his hotel. We ended up spending a lot of time together while he was in London. Strangely enough, the bedroom in the suite had two single beds rather than a double bed.

Dylan had a reputation for being cold and aloof, and he certainly could be like that, but we would often spend hours just chatting. On one occasion, he told me that he'd like me to record one of his songs, backed by Manfred Mann. They had already enjoyed considerable success with covers of Dylan songs, most noteably at that time with 'If You Gotta Go, Go Now' which reached number 2 in the UK singles charts in September 1965. Sadly, nothing ever came of this suggestion, though Manfred Mann's cover of 'Just Like A Woman', recorded in July 1966, went to number 10. I have no idea if that was the song that Dylan had in mind for me to sing – it would have required some changes to the lyrics – but it was probably a better choice for me than Dylan's 'The Mighty Quinn', a number 1 single for Manfred Mann in 1968.

He could certainly be pretty outgoing when friends came to visit. One guy who was usually around was Bob Neuwirth. The two Bobs would chat and laugh for hours, and loved teasing people. One day, Dylan asked me, "Can you get your hands round your back, like this?" as he reached behind to clasp his hands together. I was wearing a tight top and hadn't realised what they were looking at until they both fell about laughing.

I had walked into a tit trap.

There were nights when the Beatles or the Stones would drop into the hotel, sometimes bringing their wives or girlfriends with them, but mostly just to hang out and play the newest tracks they'd recorded. Not showing off, just saying 'this is what we've been doing' in the studios.

The Beatles had learnt by this time how to escape all the screaming fans, as they would arrive in a black-windowed limo, and be dropped off at the back security door of the hotel. Once inside Dylan's suite, they were just a bunch of mates hanging out together and having a good time, though it always seemed to me that Dylan had a closer affinity with George Harrison than the rest of the Beatles.

It was the start of the period when the Beatles' music was getting quite psychedelic, and acid was creeping into everyone's lifestyle. One night, John Lennon turned on the record player and played a test pressing of 'Tomorrow Never Knows', which they had just recorded. It would become the last track on their next LP, 'Revolver', which was released in August 1966. The recording tape had been played backwards in the studio by their producer George Martin, to create what was then a new and very unusual sound. Dylan responded by playing 'Rainy Day Women 12 & 35', which repeats the line 'Everybody Must Get Stoned' and seemed entirely appropriate as they then sat around, listening to music, drinking, and smoking joints until the early hours.

Another time when the Beatles turned up, they all brought their ladies with them. Cynthia was with John, Jane Asher was with

Paul, Maureen was with Ringo, and Patti Boyd was with George. All the naughty boys went into Dylan's bedroom, where they had quite a party, drinking more wine and smoking more dope. I spent the evening going back and forth between the two rooms, checking that people got 'cups of tea and things'. It was the very early days of smoking dope, and I remember the girls sitting quietly outside, obviously thinking, 'what the fuck are my men doing?'. They certainly weren't invited in to have a joint.

John must have been really quite difficult for Cynthia to deal with in those days. In fact, he drank so much that night that he passed out on the bed I was sleeping in. I hasten to add that I was in the bed and he was on it, and so there was a blanket between us. Anyway, it was the closest I got to being able to say that I'd slept with John Lennon.

Paul had left quite early because he had to get Jane home. He was always really well behaved, as was Ringo. It was basically John and George who were the experimenters.

It seems funny to think now that I was alone in a room with Dylan, probably the best-known songwriter in the world, and the Beatles, unquestionably the most famous group in the world. However, when you are hanging out with musicians a lot, it didn't seem anything special at the time.

Somehow, the press had caught on to the fact that I was seeing Dylan romantically, though horizontally might be a more accurate description. Then again, I was seen out on the town with Dylan on several occasions, so can't complain about them writing about the two of us together. I remember once going with him to a famous restaurant called 'The Tratt', or 'La Trattoria Terrazza' to give the place its full name, in Romilly Street, Soho. It was very trendy in the sixties, and you'd see actors and celebrities like Michael Caine in there. Allen Ginsberg was with us, and although I knew he was a poet, I didn't really know much about him at the time. He was famous for having taken lots of acid and for having lived in India. Marianne Faithfull was there too, and she certainly had the hots for Dylan and was quite keen to pull him. However, she was with John Dunbar – the man she married the following week – so couldn't really do anything about it. She does suggest in her autobiography that I may have got in her way, "Meanwhile, elsewhere in the hotel unbeknownst to me, he's fucking someone else. Dana Gillespie, if memory serves."

Another evening we went to Blaises nightclub to see John Lee Hooker, and, according to a contemporaneous news report, "With Dylan was Dana Gillespie, she was smiling nervously at people and Dylan was talking a language all his own; English words but in a sequence of phrases that could be understood only by his close friends."

Dylan's 1966 tour was famous for being the first time an electric band had backed him. He would play an acoustic set in the first half of his shows then The Band (who were known as The Hawks at the time), joined him for the second half. He was often heckled by 'fans' who would shout 'Traitor' and 'Phoney' because they didn't like the new direction he was going in; during some shows, there would be walkouts. This was particularly the case with his two concerts at The Royal Albert Hall in London. The Beatles were in the audience for one of these shows, and afterwards George Harrison described the angry fans as "idiots".

It wasn't just some of the fans who were unhappy. The Times newspaper review of the second concert at The Royal Albert Hall stated, "In the first, and infinitely better, half of the evening, Mr Dylan gave an agreeable solo rendering of some of the songs for which he is best known: in the second half he was accompanied by the thunderous quintet who made it virtually impossible to distinguish a single line of the lyrics." *The Times, 27 May 1966*

After that show, Dylan and I talked about how he felt. Although I never heard him say anything derogatory about British fans, I know he was very surprised by the response, because he had felt that England was far ahead of any other country in pop music. At one concert on that tour, I read that he said, "Oh come on. These are all protest songs. It's the same stuff as always, can't you hear?"

By the time the tour reached London, when the audience booed and jeered, he just rocked louder as if to annoy them.

On the final night of Dylan's London visit in 1966, an impromptu departure party somehow landed up at my basement flat in Thurloe Square. It was packed with rockers and rollers, amongst whom was Rolling Stone Brian Jones and his girlfriend Anita Pallenberg. At some point in the evening, after Bob had left for the airport, Brian said we should leave my place and head off to a party at a flat on Cheyne Walk by Chelsea Embankment, which was owned by a well-known interior designer called Christopher Gibbs.

Having just passed my driving test a few weeks earlier, after only six days of lessons, I hoped Brian and Anita wouldn't notice what an inexperienced driver I was, as we climbed into my little grey Austin A35 car and headed off to Chelsea. Also with us was quite a character in London called Prince Stash de Rola, the son of the famous Polish/French artist Balthus.

For some reason, Anita and I were both dressed in rugby shirts, which we wore as mini-dresses. It was only when we got to the flat that we discovered that the 'party' consisted of just the four of us, as the owner of the flat was in his bedroom with one of his boyfriends and never appeared. Brian was egging Anita and me to get it on together – perhaps for him and Stash to watch – but more likely so they could both join in. Someone produced some glasses containing a mysterious liquid, and we all took a gulp of it. I didn't know what it was, so really didn't know what to expect, but subsequently found out that it was the hallucinogenic drug mescaline.

Instead of it turning me on, and making me hot to trot for a foursome, I'm afraid to say that I bottled out and went home, saying I wasn't feeling well. Driving at about two miles an hour, clinging to the wheel, and seeing the traffic lights going to every colour other than red, amber, and green, it's a miracle I got home in one piece. I recognise now that I was lucky not to have been stopped by the police. Looking back, I probably could have handled girl-on-girl action if I *hadn't* been on mescaline, but I think I was just too young then to deal with the drug or myself. I've had it since then, and always had an amazingly good time, finding it offers me most profound experiences.

Why did I leave my own party to go off with them? Well, when you have people like Brian and Anita saying 'let's go somewhere' then you go, as they were both fun company. As for Stash, he continued hanging out with the swinging crowd, and has the unusual distinction of having been busted for drugs with both Brian and Keith Richards, on separate occasions.

I think that was the last time I saw Brian alive. Sadly, like so many of my old friends from the sixties, he soon afterwards went to join that Great Rock and Blues Band in the sky.

*

Dylan didn't come back to England for a long time after his 1966 tour, and it wasn't until 1974 that we met again. By then, I was living in New York and performing at a club called Reno Sweeney's. I was booked to sing there for a week, but one of the nights was a special gala show. David Bowie, Bette Midler, Dudley Moore, Janet Leigh, and Raquel Welch were all in the audience.

The afternoon of the show, I went to the venue to do the soundcheck. As I went in, I saw the back of what looked like a tramp buying a ticket for that evening's performance, but when he turned around, I realised it was Dylan. Whilst I was delighted to see him, I was also rather worried as I had flu, my voice was shot to pieces, and I didn't know if I could get through the show that night.

We arranged to meet later, but by the evening I still felt dreadful. Before the show, I sat huddled in my little dressing room feeling like death, wishing I was a million miles away and knowing that I had a house full of celebrities to face with a failing voice. I instructed my minder/ bouncer, whose name was John Bindon (more of him later), that I wanted no visitors in the dressing room.

What happened next was reported to me by my then-boyfriend Leslie Spitz (more of him later, too) who had seen the whole episode. Apparently, Dylan turned up outside the dressing room and said to Bindon, "I'd like to see Dana. Can you tell her that Robert Zimmerman is here to see her."

Unfortunately, Bindon, not recognising the scruffy man who was talking to him, said, "I don't care if you're Bob Fucking Dylan, you can fuck off."

I was mortified when I heard this later, but at the time I knew nothing about it.

After just about managing to stagger through the show, I went home to bed to die, while everyone else went off to Bette Midler's party, so I missed seeing Dylan again later that night. Poor Bindon didn't feel too good either, when he was told what he had done.

*

It was in 1997 that I got a call from Dylan's U.K. agent, Barry Jenkins, telling me that Dylan had requested that I be the opening act on his British tour. What an honour and how pleased I felt.

Two days before the tour started, my doorbell rang, and there was Dylan himself standing on my doorstep. We spent the next four hours together, him lying on my sofa drinking fennel tea while we swapped stories about what we had each been up to, and reminisced about the old days. I asked him how many children he'd got and he said he wasn't sure, but he thought seven or eight. He might have been joking, though, as he was laughing as he said this. He also talked a lot about his home life, and how proud he was of his son, Jacob.

There is one story that he told me that sticks in my mind, which was about when he toured with the Grateful Dead in 1987. He had thought it would be a piece of cake to get up and sing his songs with the Dead, as he had been doing most recently with Tom Petty and his band, but the Dead were a totally different animal. They wanted to do songs that he'd long forgotten, and he surprised me by saying how he felt his confidence slipping away – knowing he would never be able to remember all the lyrics from his old songs.

It got to the point where he felt so uncomfortable about this, that he told the band that he'd left something at his hotel, then walked out of the rehearsal room with no intention of returning. Apparently, he felt so bad he was ready to quit the tour. Fate, however, led him into a little nearby bar where a jazz band was playing in the back of the room, and as he stopped to listen to the musicians – and especially the singer – a kind of revelation came over him; he said it was almost like he was being propelled into another dimension. Somehow, he suddenly knew that he had the power to go back to the Dead and sing those old songs that had previously scared him so much.

From the moment he returned to the rehearsal rooms, he said he never looked back. He had been on the edge of giving up singing completely, yet something in that little bar had triggered off a new start in him. Jokingly, he said that maybe one of the Grateful Dead, probably Jerry Garcia, had slipped a little something in his drink; acid maybe? Whether that's true or not, I don't know, but whatever it was – it worked! He never looked back, and nowadays the man never stops touring. What a legend!

It was sweet of him to share a story like this with me, as it showed that if someone like Dylan can have a crisis of confidence, then he is ultimately just as human as the rest of us. A few years later, he recounted parts of the story in the first volume of his autobiography, 'Chronicles Volume One', and reading his book reminded me of him lying sideways, feet up on my sofa, sipping his fennel tea.

One thing that made me feel good as we chatted was that he liked my songwriting, and one song in particular called 'Blue Temptation' which had been on one of my albums for Wolf Records. This was high praise indeed from His Bobness. The fact that he liked my Blues was all that mattered to me.

As we reminisced about the old days, I reminded him of the Bindon story, which he had mercifully forgotten. When I asked why he had contacted me after all these years, about the upcoming tour, he said it was because he had seen a good review of one of my Blues albums in Billboard magazine, and this had jogged his memory. He said this reminded him how nice I was, which I felt he said with sincerity. Normally, describing somebody as 'nice' can be a bit damning, but this was a compliment coming from him: a man who never wasted words.

He then did something that I admire in any man with brains; he looked along my bookshelves to see what sort of things I read. He wouldn't have found any novels in my library, as I love books on history and all things spiritual and philosophical. Instead, he pulled out an Indian paperback, full of quotations from world religions, and asked if he could have it. I said yes, of course.

Later that night, after he went back to his hotel, it got me thinking that if Dylan likes books of uplifting quotes then I had several exercise books full of such things; sayings that I had collected over the previous 20 years. Right then, I decided to put a book together, which was published two years later with the title 'Mirrors of Love'. It is full of quotations to do with love, gleaned from all religions and many philosophers, a lot of them from the Sufi tradition. My father had always said that one should write down any clever or pithy sayings, and I had followed his advice. I was lucky enough to have the Austrian, Jorg Huber – in my opinion, one of the best artists in the world – to do all the illustrations, so it is really also an art book. There will be more of Jorg later.

Many of the quotes were then set to music, which I recorded with a producer called Nick Hogarth at his studios, and this was subsequently released as a CD, also called 'Mirrors of Love'. So I have Dylan to thank for inspiring me to produce the book and the music, and I sent him a copy of both, the moment they were published.

On my wall at home, I had a number of pictures of the famous Indian spiritual guru, Sathya Sai Baba, who by then was playing an important part in my life. Dylan saw one of the photographs and laughingly said, "That's the guy who materialises jewellery."

I was surprised that Dylan knew who Sai Baba was, and about His miracles, but then he explained, "George (Harrison) told me all about Him, as he went to see Him in India with Ravi Shankar and He was materialising lots of jewellery!"

We both laughed at that, although maybe for different reasons, as I have seen Sai Baba produce a piece of jewellery, and many other things, seemingly out of nowhere. I never understood it, but it was an amazing thing to behold.

When Dylan was leaving, he said he was going to visit George Harrison the next day, so I gave him some of the Sanskrit albums I had made, and asked him to give them to George.

*

The last night of the tour was at London Wembley Arena, and though I wasn't originally booked to do this gig, Dylan insisted that I must play it too. I was lucky to have the London Blues Band backing me on the tour, so I had the best guys on stage with me, though the late addition of the Wembley show meant that I had a problem. Chris Hunt, my drummer at the time, also played with Lonnie Donegan, and months earlier had been contracted to play that same night with Lonnie. So I had the difficult task of trying to find a good drummer at short notice, and everyone I knew was busy that night. In desperation, I went through my telephone book one more time, searching for anyone who could drum for me, and the only man I hadn't called was Roger Taylor from Queen.

Although I didn't know him that well, we had bumped into each other a few times in London and Mustique, and so I decided to give it a try.

Taking a deep breath and hoping he wouldn't be pissed off, I rang him and said, "Roger, this is Dana. I have a huge favour to ask. I know you are used to playing big venues, but can you play with my band at Wembley Arena in three days' time, supporting Bob Dylan? I hope you don't mind me asking you."

He was an absolute angel and said it was no problem at all. Within two hours, his drum technician was on my doorstep to pick up a tape of the songs we were going to play, so he could learn them. If there's one thing I adore in a person, it is professionalism, and Roger certainly had that. My ratings definitely went up when the crowd saw who was on drums that night, and to this day I am grateful to him for his generosity of spirit. He even refused the paltry gig money I tried to give him afterwards, which was just as well as I couldn't have afforded his normal Queen fee; not on the money that support acts get.

During the course of the tour, I didn't really see much of Dylan backstage, because he would normally arrive at the venue shortly before he was due to perform. However, at Wembley, he turned up early and listened to my whole set from the side of the stage, which really pleased me as I suppose a part of me wanted to prove myself to him musically.

Many years later, I was asked by Howard Sounes, the author of 'Down the Highway – The Life of Bob Dylan', about my time with Dylan. I am quoted as saying, "He is amusing, he is spiritual. As for the promiscuity, at least he's honest. Women prefer to be seduced by a brain rather than a bollock. Brains go a helluva a long way."

Actually, the word used in the (American) publication was bullock, not bollock. That must have confused many readers – *Women prefer to be seduced by a brain rather than a bullock*!

6: RECORDING WITH JIMMY AND ELTON: THE DECCA YEARS

After I had made a series of singles on Pye records, I was taken to meet Dick Rowe, the boss of Decca Records. He was well known in the business for having been the man who turned down The Beatles, so it was only natural that he would offer me a contract to make two albums! According to the 'Ready steady girls!' website: "When Decca's Dick Rowe spotted her, he was quick to sign her up. He is reported to have been less interested in her singing ability than in, er, two of her more visible assets."

Whatever the reason, I was happy to sign the deal, as going from singles to albums seemed like a step in the right direction. Dick introduced me to the man he wanted to produce the album, Wayne Bickerton, who had just been working with former Beatle Pete Best, and we started collecting songs for my first album.

In those days, if you didn't have your own band, it was normal to use session musicians on albums, and mine was no exception. Two members of Manfred Mann – Mike Hugg and Mike Vickers – played for me, as did Big Jim Sullivan, who also played guitar on Bowie's first Deram album, and Blue Mink founder Herbie Flowers on bass. Two other musicians on the album were John Paul Jones and Jimmy Page, who only a few years later would become the bass player and guitarist, respectively, in Led Zeppelin.

From these sessions, I got to know Jimmy very well as we had a similar interest in Indian music, and we would sometimes go to see Ustad Vilayat Khan or Ravi Shankar in concert. Jimmy produced and played on the first single taken from the album, called 'You Just Gotta Know My Mind', which was a sort of surfing song written by Donovan.

Jimmy was devastatingly good looking, as well as being a fabulous guitarist. He cut a really striking figure with his black hair and dark eyes, almost like a gypsy, and seemed to always dress in black. At that time, he was also interested in black magic, and was to be found reading up on it and collecting anything to do with Aleister Crowley, the English occultist and ceremonial magician. My recollection of Jimmy was of a nice, polite, gentle, lovely fellow, and although I knew I was not a big love in his life, we did have a bit of a 'thing' going for a time, on a no-strings-attached basis. It was fun, and I'm happy to say that, more than 50 years later, we are still friends.

Jumping forward for a moment, towards the end of 2007, I got a call from one of Jimmy's assistants asking if I would like to go to the Led Zeppelin reunion concert at the O2 Arena in London. I was touched that Jimmy had thought of me and enthusiastically accepted, but then realised that I had a problem as I was due to play a gig in Portugal a couple of days before, so wouldn't have time to collect the tickets. Jimmy's people told me not to worry, and that the tickets would be couriered round to my home in good time. The day before the concert, there was a knock on my door at the agreed time, and there was Jimmy himself with my two tickets, which I thought was pretty cool.

The show brought back so many great memories from the days when the Zeps ruled the world. My guitarist from The London Blues Band, Jake Zaitz, came along with me, and he was over the moon to be asked as he had always been a fan of the band. These tickets were like gold dust, as over a million people had applied, and the venue only held 20,000. We sat in the VIP area with wives, ex-wives, and friends of the band like Jeff Beck and Lulu, and watched what was described by Mojo magazine as "the gig of the century".

Jimmy has been to see me playing on a few occasions with The London Blues Band at the 606 Club in Chelsea, and there is always a buzz of excitement in the group when we know he is in the audience.

Anyway, back to the sixties. The album was called 'Foolish Seasons', and after a rather frustrating delay, it was finally released through Decca on the London label in May 1968, strangely only in the US and not in the UK. The cover photographs of me standing with a palomino horse, wearing a headband and in a low cut kaftan, were taken by Gered Mankowitz, who was very well known then for having shot the Rolling Stones and, later on, Jimi Hendrix. As well as the numerous iconic shots he has taken of musicians throughout his career, he took some of my best photographs too (including the cover of this book).

I was very proud of 'Foolish Seasons' at the time, and was happy when it was re-issued recently by Rev-Ola Records in a double CD set called 'London Social Degree', along with my second album 'Box of Surprises'. The title track of the recent re-release was written by Billy Nicholls, who is probably best known for writing 'I Can't Stop Loving You', a hit for both Leo Sayer and Phil Collins. It's funny to think that both Billy and I were teenagers when the song was recorded, because the song was obviously about LSD, though I don't think the record company had a clue.

One song on 'Foolish Seasons' that I still really like, though sadly didn't write, is called 'Dead'. I suppose it was unusual for someone so young to sing about preparing to commit suicide, and it's certainly a weird song. Although my voice is still quite folky, it does show that – even at this early stage – I had Blues leanings.

Billboard's contemporaneous review of Foolish Seasons introduces me as, "A new singer from England who has a style sure to make the grade in the US market."

Sadly it didn't.

Producer Wayne Bickerton was disappointed by the lack of commercial success of 'Foolish Seasons', which he said was "due to Decca's lack of promotion". He gave this as an excuse for leaving Decca to join Polydor, where he had huge success in the early seventies with The Rubettes, for whom he wrote 'Sugar Baby Love' and their eight other Top 50 hits.

*

The Yardbirds were still my favourite band, and I was interested to see how it would work after Jimmy Page took over from Eric Clapton. Jeff Beck was also playing in the band then, and he and Jimmy would sometimes come round to see me together. Those were the good old days of tea and crumpet!

Musicians were always great fun to hang out with, and I have such good memories of those days. Although I occasionally got involved with some of them in the horizontal sense, we were always friends first and foremost. Whilst it was definitely a period when having a good time was high up on the agenda, this still came second (albeit a close second) to the actual work of making records.

Another 'interesting' character I met around that time was Allen Klein, the controversial American business manager for numerous singers and bands, including both The Beatles and the Rolling Stones. I was introduced to Klein at the Dorchester Hotel by Jeremy Clyde of the singing duo Chad and Jeremy, who were very successful in the States in the early sixties, though strangely enough not so much at home in the UK.

Klein obviously liked big-busted English birds, and whenever he was in town, he used to call me and I'd go over and spend afternoons with him in his hotel suite. There were times when I'd be in the bedroom and he'd be meeting members of the Stones or The Beatles in the next room; with Klein, I was always kept out of view, which was very different from when I had been with Dylan a couple of years earlier. I suppose Klein looked on me as a bit of entertainment for him, and although he was unpopular – by being so ruthless in his business dealings – I personally liked him, and learnt a lot from him about the music biz.

Nobody really knew about my thing with Klein as he was a married man, so it was not something either of us talked about. Most of my musician friends would have thought I was crazy to spend time with him, but I have always had a soft spot for short, Jewish, ruthless men who get what they want when they want it.

I suppose it's fair to say that I was quite outrageous in the sixties. For example, when I was 18, my father bought me a mink coat with a purple lining from Harrods, which I would wear to go out in with nothing on underneath. Although I still have the coat, I obviously can't wear it outside anymore because I would probably be pelted with eggs. Nowadays, I just use it as a dressing gown, at home, when the heating breaks down.

*

By the time work on my second album started, I was much more confident, especially as I had Mike Vernon as producer and a Blues band called Savoy Brown as my musicians. It was called 'Box of Surprises', and this time was released in the UK, but not in the US. Unlike the first album that took weeks to finish, this one was done in a few days and featured all my own compositions. It was thanks to Dick Rowe that Mike had enough faith in me as a songwriter to do this album, because – in those days – girl singers never recorded their own self-penned songs. As usual, Gered took the cover photograph, which featured me sitting on a coffin surrounded by stuffed animals (except for my Norwich Terrier, Sneezi, who was sitting on my lap), holding the hand of a corpse sticking out of said coffin.

'Box of Surprises' includes a song called 'For David, The Next Day', which generated some online excitement amongst Bowienuts in 2013 when David issued an album called… 'The Next Day'. Was my song about David? Yes, it was. Was he referencing my song all those years later? Well, it would be nice to say he was, and I guess it is not impossible. After all, his video for the lead-off single from his album 'Where Are We Now?' showed David wearing a 'Song of Norway' T-shirt, which many said was a message to Hermione Farthingale, his girlfriend in 1968-9, who had left him to appear in a film of the same name. So was David sending a message to me? Who knows? Probably not. More likely it's just a coincidence, and it goes without saying that we can't ask him now.

It's always been a joy to work with Mike Vernon, who was considered the king of Blues recordings. He'd started his own label called Blue Horizon, and whenever any great American Blues artist hit town, Mike would be there recording them, using the cream of the London Blues scene. Guitarists like John Mayall, Peter Green, and Eric Clapton were just a few of the guys who played with the visiting stars, but it was Mike Vernon's passion and dedication to the Blues that kept everyone going.

Over the next 40 years, I did four more albums with Mike. I sat next to him in the studio and learnt so many tricks of the trade that, even now, I often think of him when I'm producing an album myself and some of the useful tips he gave me.

Funnily enough, Bowie had recorded his first album with Mike Vernon when we were both on Decca, though Bowie's was released on a subsidiary of Decca called Deram. That album had some pretty unsophisticated stuff on it – 'Little Bombadier' is not exactly an early version of 'Moonage Daydream' – and the less said about one of his other productions for Bowie, 'The Laughing Gnome', the better!

In March 1968, Bowie invited me to come and see him perform with mime artist Lindsay Kemp at a tiny little place in Notting Hill called The Mercury Theatre, which only held about 30 people. The production was called 'Pierrot in Turquoise' and was described as "An entertainment of Mime, Music and Dance". Bowie sang a number of songs from his Vernon-produced debut album, including 'When I Live My Dream', but just as importantly had the opportunity to develop his mime skills by performing alongside Lindsay. They would famously work together again, in 1972, on the Ziggy Stardust shows at the Rainbow Theatre in London.

With the royalties from my albums barely paying my phone bills, I had to find other ways of earning money. One of these was to sing on cover versions of singles for a company called Avenue Records, which was run by a guy called Alan Caddy who had originally been a member of Johnny Kidd and the Pirates ('Shakin' all over') and The Tornados ('Telstar'). These records were called 'Top of the Pops', though had no connection with the TV programme of the same name, and featured current top 20 hits but sung by other artists. They usually had a dodgy-looking bird in a bikini on the front cover, and the singers never got a name-check on the album sleeve. We would get £25 each for a backing vocal session, but for a lead vocal we got £50.

The songs were intended to sound as close as possible to the originals, though – if you listen to them now – you would have to say that some were rather more successful than others! It is quite hard for me to remember which songs I was on, though I know I did 'The Night They Drove Old Dixie Down' by Joan Baez, 'That Same Old Feeling' by Pickettywitch and 'Chirpy Chirpy Cheep Cheep' by Middle of the Road, and was part of the group that did 'Sugar Sugar' by the Archies. I knew I'd really made it to the Big Time when, whilst hanging out with some friends before going on to the 100 Club, I heard my voice singing one of these cover versions over the sound system of the Wimpy Bar on Oxford Street!

Alan tended to use the same singers: Madeleine Bell (who went on to front Blue Mink) if it was a soul sort of song, myself if it was folky or pop, and David Byron, who had a terrific rock voice and who later on became the lead singer in Uriah Heap. Kiki Dee and

Lesley Duncan were also around then, together with a funny little chap called Reg Dwight.

A slightly chubby fellow with glasses, Reg's dress style at the time was to wear a kind of schoolboy blazer jacket with piping. He was quite shy, but had a fabulous voice and was able to cover many of the big hits. Unlike many of the other musicians I worked with then, he never tried it on with me.

I'd sometimes see Reg at the Cromwellian, and we'd say "See you at the studio", meaning the Pye studios by Marble Arch where the sessions were recorded. I never hung out with him socially, as he wasn't part of the South Kensington crowd. Let's be honest, I don't think he had any interest in coming round to my place, as it was probably all a bit too hetero for him. Not that I think he was out of the closet then; in fact, I'm not sure whether he knew that he was even in the closet. He was, however, hanging around a lot with Long John Baldry, who made no secret of his sexual preferences and was known to everyone as Ada.

One day, Reg came to Pye studios and said that he'd just signed to Dick James Music, and his single, 'Lady Samantha' was going to be released. He also told us that he had changed his name to Elton John, combining the first names of Bluesology's sax player Elton Dean and lead singer Long John Baldry. It was one of the best moves he ever made. Can you really imagine him becoming a global superstar if he had kept the name Reginald Dwight?

I liked his first album, although it didn't initially trouble the charts. Funnily enough, he continued doing the cover albums even after he had his first big hit in the UK with 'Your Song', and his hugely entertaining autobiography 'Me' contains amusing stories of him recording what he calls, "some terrible album sold in a supermarket for fourteen and sixpence." In one of them, he describes his attempt to cover a song by Robin Gibb of the BeeGees. "I stood there, wailing away, fingers clasped round my neck, desperately trying not to look across the studio, where the other session singers, David Byron and Dana Gillespie, were clinging on to each other and weeping with laughter."

We also had real trouble recording a cover version of 'Back Home', a chart-topper in 1970 for the England World Cup football team. David, Elton and I had to pretend to be the entire squad of 30 players, a task that was so ridiculous that we all got an uncontrollable bout of the giggles, preventing us from recording anything for what seemed like ages. Elton recorded more cover versions than any of the rest of us, turning his hand (or should I say voice) to a wide range of different types of songs, and although he was always very professional in the studio, he could be hilarious at the same time. It was rumoured that he had got engaged to a girl, though called it off after Long John Baldry talked him out of it, as described in his hit 'Someone Saved My Life Tonight'. In those days, you couldn't really come out of the closet and hope to have a career, even though a lot of the top performers were gay.

People have asked me about when I first met Elton, or when I first met Bowie... did I know they were destined for megastardom? The simple answer is no, I never thought of them like that. Nobody believed that you could be big in America in those days; America was so far away, and to take a flight to America was like going to the moon. Musicians just thought they'd like to get enough gigs to get them through the next few weeks, or secure a record deal. Obviously, they hoped they'd get on 'Top of the Pops' or 'Ready Steady Go', but never really thought about global fame. Bowie was a mate I hung out with, and Elton was a guy I'd sometimes see at the Cromwellian, or in the studios when we were doing covers. Even when they became huge, to me they were still my old pals.

Alan Caddy had a bit of a soft spot for me, and used to come round to my place to drop off the original singles of the songs we were going to record so I could learn them. I don't know if he did that for the other singers, though somehow doubt he was as regular a visitor to Elton's place. He once got me to record the whole of Cabaret in Pye Studios, with me playing Liza Minnelli's character – Sally Bowles – backed by a full orchestra. Everything was done at musicians' union rates, so if you fucked up, and the session went past the union approved finishing time, the whole orchestra (of maybe 40 people) were on double money. That certainly used to focus the mind. To this day, I've no idea what happened to the Cabaret recordings; they're probably lost in a studio vault somewhere.

*

Another way I was earning a crust was by singing every night at a lowlife place called the Crazy Horse Saloon. It was not one bit like its namesake in Paris; for a start, it was in Baker Street, and had topless barmaids instead of long-legged glamorous dancers. My mother would have been horrified if she had known.

From what I could see, a lot of the clientele were politicians or off-duty detectives from West End Central. The place was owned by a businessman called John Bloom, who had made a fortune selling discounted washing machines before his company went spectacularly bust.

Bloom was a larger than life character who would arrive in the back of his Rolls Royce to inspect his club, often dressed in a black snakeskin or leather suit. He 'auditioned' the girls that worked as hostesses in his office, and had a railing to which he would sometimes tie up one of the girls due to some misdemeanour that he thought they had committed. Every time he walked past, he would give the girl in question a slap on her arse, not so much to cause her pain, but because he just loved the sound of spanking. He liked his girls to be dressed in black PVC or leather, and was altogether a bit too fond of the bondage look.

As he was Jewish, he was quite strict about not working machinery between Friday night and Saturday night. Instead of switching on lights, like on a normal day, he had sonic light switches installed, so when he clapped his hands (or slapped one of the girls), the lights flashed on and off.

Bloom liked having me around at the club, as he was happy to have a well-spoken voice answer the telephone; occasionally, I would turn up in the daytime. He also had some other more unusual tasks for me. As he famously loved orgies, he would ask me to look through piles of magazines to see if there was anything that I thought might be suitable for his tastes. So I would spend my time looking for adverts like 'Girl into S&M would like to meet like-minded man'.

Another time, I told Bloom that I was going to Geneva to stay with my mother, who was living there at the time with my stepfather. Bloom responded excitedly saying that there was a guy in Geneva who organised orgies, and could I go and see him. I went to check him out, and reported back that he seemed extremely normal and that I couldn't imagine him in a room full of naked women with loads of whips.

On one occasion, I walked into Bloom's office when he was with Freddie Laker, founder of one of the earliest 'no frills' charter airlines. Bloom was conducting the meeting while a girl was giving him a blowjob under the desk; 'multi-tasking' I guess. After the meeting (and blowjob) was over, Bloom said to me, "Well, I think you had better check out Freddie Laker's charter flights for me."

Nobody knew what a charter flight was then.

He continued, "I'm going to send you to Los Angeles, and while you're there, I've got this address in the Hollywood Hills for you to have a look at…"

So off I went, aged 17, knowing nothing about America. Bloom gave me a hundred dollars to survive on, together with the address, and wanted me to report back on what the orgy scene was like, so that he could decide whether or not to go himself.

Nobody was at LA airport to pick me up, so I got into a taxi and asked the driver to take me to the address in the Hollywood Hills that Bloom had provided. We drove up through Beverley Hills, past all the movie star homes, and finally stopped outside a large house which looked down over Los Angeles. I rang the bell, was shown in, and couldn't quite believe what I was seeing. There was a full-on orgy underway, with about 40 people at it, in every position known to man – several of which were most certainly NOT known to me! I stood at the entrance holding my little suitcase, while everyone else there just got on with what/who they were doing.

Because I had to wait for the return charter flight, I ended up spending a week in the Hollywood Hills. Whilst I was there, I saw people being peed on and all sorts of other weird stuff, but I just thought, 'Well, if that's what they're into… They don't do this sort of thing in South Kensington – or if they do, I don't know about it'.

Bloom must have liked what I told him about Los Angeles because, a few years later, he went to live out there.

*

At the Crazy Horse, my job was to stand in the corner of the dance floor together with a backing trio, singing boring old songs like 'I Can't Give You Anything But Love'. No one really bothered to look at me as I was fully dressed, albeit in a little black dress with a bit of cleavage, so I was no competition for the topless barmaids. My fee was £25 a week, for which I had to sing five songs every evening. I'd do my set, then get into my little Austin A35 and drive off to do the same thing at two other clubs that Bloom owned.

One of them was called Rasputin's (in Bond Street), and the other was the 'A.D.1520' where all the staff were dressed in medieval clothes, (basically an excuse to get the girls to look like busty wenches). The barmaids made money from tips given by inebriated customers, and if a customer offered to buy me a drink, I'd ask for a vodka and orange. The girls at the bar would know not to put in the vodka, and would slip me the pound that it would have cost.

Another wheeze the girls had to make money was with the sale of champagne. They got paid by the number of corks they handed in at the end of the evening, so it was normal for a girl to sit with her punter, call her pals over and get the punter to give them all a glass of champagne, then order another bottle. What the punter didn't know is that, often, the girls would distract him by pointing at something, and the moment he looked away they'd slop their drink onto the floor. He then had to pour out another glass, and then buy another bottle. The carpet was made of something that must have been very absorbent as the girls were all at it, throwing drinks away; by day, the club was often quite squelchy underfoot. There were also a few potted plants around that would get 'watered' in champagne.

The floorshow every night was pretty seedy. Apart from my five songs, there was a magician and several strippers, one of whom did her act with a boa constrictor. The snake was kept in a basket in the girls' changing room and was given a few rats to eat each week; it only ever got out when it was time to do the act, which involved the stripper simulating all the usual sex things with this poor snake. One night when she was doing the dance of the seven veils, it bit her on the wrist, and she had to be rushed off to St. George's Hospital, clad only in her four remaining veils. An hour later, she returned to the club, with a bandage on her hand, to remove the rest of her veils.

For about six months, I stuck with this mad job as I needed any work I could get. Actually, I was quite happy because I'd never seen such a world before, and I've never regretted the experience. Bloom was a bit of a naughty guy, but I got on well with him, and with his extremely nice wife.

A strange postscript to this story is that, back in 1964, a young David Jones had cheekily written to Bloom asking for financial support for his then band, The King Bees. Bloom responded by introducing David to a contact in the music business called Leslie Conn, who hired the King Bees to play at Bloom's wedding anniversary party. Although their set apparently went down badly with the guests, Conn saw enough in the performance of the lead singer to decide to become David's manager shortly afterwards, and to produce his first single.

*

Making a living was still important, and I was always on the lookout for other opportunities to raise my profile, as well as money. On the 20th of January 1966, the Chelsea Post published an article about me saying, "Dana's ambition is to become a top international film star, and with two films behind her she may well fulfil it."

With a total screen time of about 5 minutes in those two films, I doubt that the likes of Sophia Loren or Ursula Andress were quaking in their stilettos. The good news was that more film parts were soon to come my way.

Hammer Films, then a British institution for horror, Frankenstein, and cave girl fantasy films (guess which I was in) invited me to appear in a film called 'The Vengeance of She'. It was intended as a sequel to the very successful movie 'She', which starred the aforementioned Ursula Andress, and which was based on the Rider Haggard story. However, Ursula had now made her name as a Bond Girl and was going to cost too much money, so the producers hired an actress called Olga Schoberová instead, who at the time called herself Olinka Berova. The producers thought she would be the next Ursula Andress. They were wrong.

The director cast me as a drunken girl who dances provocatively with some man on a dancefloor. It was a non-speaking role, and why they thought of me for the part, I can't imagine.

Even though it was such a small part, I must have done well enough, because I was invited back to audition for the next Hammer film. The boss of Hammer Films, a really lovely man called Michael Carreras, said he would give me a screen test for 'The Lost Continent' starring Hildegard Knef, but that I first needed to lose some weight. This was clearly going to be easier said than done, but I was determined to do what they wanted, so literally didn't eat a thing for three weeks, consuming nothing more than water and lemon juice. By the time of the screen test, I could hardly stand and felt quite dizzy, but the diet had done the trick and I got the part. The producers told me I had been chosen because I had been a waterski champion and would have to spend a lot of time walking on the 'sea'. What they didn't tell me then, was that the water was only about three inches deep.

After the screen test at Elstree studios, they took me to lunch in the studio restaurant, and I can still remember now that I had a huge plate of roast beef (I was eating meat then), roast potatoes, Yorkshire pudding, the full works. Everyone had said that because I hadn't eaten for three weeks, my stomach would have shrunk. Well, it hadn't, and I just went straight back to normal eating with no problem at all. Christopher Lee, the star of numerous Hammer horror films who was perhaps most famous for portraying Count Dracula, was having lunch at the same restaurant and managed to get my telephone number from me. Although he called and asked me over for a drink, I knew that wasn't all he wanted and decided to say no.

Soon, after putting off Dracula, I was fitted into my outfit, with a plunging cleavage of course, and shown onto the set. Once the filming started, it wasn't long before I discovered the joys of the food trolley. All day there were bacon sandwiches, sausage sandwiches, egg sandwiches, biscuits, endless cups of tea, and then it was lunchtime! After lunch, there was more of the same.

Unfortunately, I hadn't yet discovered that the more you eat, the fatter you get. Mercifully, my costume was made of chamois leather, which conveniently stretched, and if you watch the film you can see that I'm thinner in some shots and larger in other shots. It wasn't my fault; I blame the food trolley.

'The Lost Continent', or 'The Lost Cuntinent' as I inevitably called it, was an adventure film based very loosely on a book by Dennis Wheatley called 'Uncharted Seas'. It's about the passengers and crew of a ship sailing from Africa to South America who are attacked by pirates and descendants of the Spanish conquistadores, and featured an assortment of man-eating sea monsters, a giant crab, and some killer seaweed.

My role was that of the usual native girl but with one difference; I had two huge balloons attached to my shoulders – theoretically containing enough air to keep me afloat in the water – thus preventing me from falling into the man-eating Sargasso Sea. The water itself was filled with strange squirming snakes and other fierce-looking rubber serpents, which were controlled by a man, out of shot, letting air in and out to make them look alive. With my very low-cut top and push-up bra, my tits were up under my chin, and if you then add the two balloons, it looked like I had four huge inflatables attached to my shoulders.

After the film was released, I went to the Fulham ABC cinema to see it incognito. When my balloons and I appeared on the screen, the whole audience fell about laughing, as did I. Thank goodness no one recognised me on their way out.

One of the other cast members was a stunning looking girl called Sylvana Henriques, who was making a name for herself in the modelling world in those days. In one scene, we were on a raft trying to escape an exploding ship, and the film crew had pyrotechnics firing Phosphor B into the air. There were great blobs of this burning stuff flying around, which ate through whatever they landed on. Predictably, some landed on the raft that we were standing on, burnt through the wood, and went to the bottom of the water, still glowing. Unfortunately, a lump of Phosphor B also landed on Silvana's back, and the poor girl started screaming, but nobody did anything because they thought it was part of the scene. Eventually, she had to be carted off to hospital, and I often wonder whether she got a good compensation payment. She did come to see me sing, recently, at the 606 Club in Chelsea with her husband, but I forgot to ask her.

Around this time, Gered and I went to see Marianne Faithfull, who was appearing alongside Glenda Jackson in 'The Three Sisters' by Chekhov at the Royal Court Theatre, Sloane Square. Gered and I sat through the play, then met Marianne after she came off stage, and Mick Jagger joined us for dinner at a trendy Chinese restaurant called 'The China Garden' on Edgware Road.

Marianne was wearing a red see-through chiffon blouse, with no bra. You had to be pretty bold to wear something like that in those days, and the Chinese waiters didn't know where to look as they served the noodles.

I've always felt life with Mick must have been quite tough for Marianne. She'd had her hit single ('As Time Goes By', written by Mick and Keith), and was very dependent on other people to find new songs for her. She became known as the beautiful blonde who'd had a hit with a Stones song, and cycled around topless in a film called 'Girl on a Motorcycle'. She also acquired some extra fame after an alleged encounter with a Mars Bar, although she always said that this never happened. It is probably an apocryphal story, but it is the stuff that legends are made of, so she is stuck with it.

Another character I got to know around then was Ferruccio Lamborghini, creator of the eponymous sports car company.

We met when I was draped over a car at the Earl's Court motor show. In those days, it was usual to have tasty-looking birds at car shows, whose job seemed to be to enhance the bonnet of a car by lying on it. I remember exactly what I was wearing: suede Spanish boots, a miniskirt, and a fringed cowboy jacket with a hand-stitched label inside saying 'Stolen from Bud Flanagan'. My Uncle Carl had been friendly with Bud, who very popular at the time as a member of 'The Crazy Gang'. Bud always had these labels in his clothes and gave Carl some spare ones, which Carl then passed on to me.

Ferruccio paid me a lot of attention and said that he would like to spend some time with me in Modena, Italy. He was entirely honest about what he had in mind; he told me he was married, but that he had another house on the edge of the town and wanted to install me there. I responded by saying that he would have to talk to my father about this, but that in any case I was starting a film the next day ('The Lost Continent').

That afternoon, he turned up at our house in Thurloe Square and had a very civilised conversation with my father. Thankfully, Dadster said that he thought that I wasn't quite ready to go off and be Lamborghini's mistress, which I assumed would be the end of it. Ferruccio nevertheless continued to send me the odd telegram, saying how he was longing to see me.

About six months later, my mother and I were going to Florence on holiday, so I sent Ferruccio a message telling him I would be there. He replied, saying that he would send a car for me, as Modena wasn't far from Florence. So a Lamborghini duly turned up, driven by a very hunky driver, and off we went. The car was really low and went super-fast, so when the driver hit the accelerator, I felt like I was having a facelift and that my tits were in the back seat.

When we arrived in Modena, I was met by Ferruccio, who took me around the factory and then on to his 'second' house, where he tried to leap on me. He had wanted me to live in a little house in the middle of nowhere so he could come and hump me every so often, but I told him that this just wasn't going to work. I had no friends there, and it just didn't seem like a very good idea. Reluctantly, he accepted that – as I was only 17 – that was the end of it. The dishy driver took me back to Florence and I never saw Ferruccio again. I did, however, spend the next 24 hours with the driver at my hotel; he may have been in trouble when he finally made it back to Modena. It wasn't his fault; he was absolutely shagged out.

*

This wasn't the first time that fast cars and dishy drivers had caught my attention. One year, while we were holidaying in Italy, my mother was invited by stockbroker Jack Durlacher to watch the Grand Prix at Monza, and she took me along. We were right down by the track with the Lotus team, and I can still clearly remember how exciting it was to watch from the pits and hear the cars going past at what seemed like incredible speeds.

We also attended the post-race dinner at the beautiful five-star Villa d'Este on Lake Como. All the drivers and owners were there, including Jackie Stewart, Graham Hill, Jochen Rindt and Joe Sieffert, as well as the very sharply-dressed Enzo Ferrari. I thought it was funny to find a number of the drivers in a large room at the hotel, racing toy cars around the track of a huge Scalextric set.

I would never describe motor racing as my favourite sport, but a couple of years later, in 1966, I did get a part as an extra in John Frankenheimer's movie 'Grand Prix', which starred James Garner, Yves Montand and Eve Marie-Saint.

*

The good thing about working for a film company is that they usually have a press department, who are keen to promote their artists. As a result, I was constantly being photographed, and these images used to turn up on the cover of magazines like 'Titbits' and 'Parade' – weekly publications that kept the British man up to date with what was happening in the world of film and glamour, provided cleavage was on view. Very tame by today's standards, but quite bold back then.

Talking of cleavage, I didn't get a bra that properly fitted me until I was 17. A friend of my mother, Katie Boyle (most famous for her role as compere of the Eurovision Song Contest), said that she must take me bra shopping, so off we went to a shop in Knightsbridge which specialised in made-to-measure bras. When I told Jimmy Page about this, he used to laugh and would sometimes ask me to tell him what it was like going bra shopping with Katie Boyle. I guess this story used to titillate his fancy.

It was clear to me that the only way to find work was to get an agent. Although I'd had a couple of managers by 1968, it was the agent who got you gigs. I finally ended up with a company called Starlight Artists, fronted by a man called Peter Walsh. Their roster of artistes was pretty good: Fleetwood Mac, the Tremeloes, the Spencer Davis Group, the Troggs, Marmalade, The Easybeats, and The Nashville Teens.

Before long, I found myself being sent off to gigs in new places, clutching my guitar and hoping nobody would notice that I didn't play that well, just well enough to get the songs across. There was a man working at the agency called Clifford Davis, and he helped me a lot. His main act was Fleetwood Mac, and he became their personal manager. All was going well until the band broke up, at which point Clifford started up a new band, *also* called them Fleetwood Mac, and sent them out on the road. All hell broke loose, lawyers were brought in, and it took ages to clear the mess up. I can't really say whether what Clifford did was right or wrong as it didn't involve me, but it did bring me into contact with the original Fleetwood Mac frontman Peter Green ('Albatross', 'Man of the World', 'Black Magic Woman').

Clifford told me that Peter Green always felt extremely guilty about the amount of money he made in the sixties with Fleetwood Mac, and that Peter ordered Clifford to give it all away. Clifford didn't, but apparently put it in a bank account for him to return to Peter. Whether he ever did, I cannot say.

Peter Green was at his peak as a guitarist then, and the band could do no wrong. Not only would I often see Peter at Clifford's office, but we'd bump into each other at gigs and I always had a soft spot for him. He was petite in build, had long dark curly hair and just hearing that sound he made from his guitar was wonderful. His instrumental hit 'Albatross' was so unusual, and stayed at No.1 in the charts for ages.

Once he'd had his mental troubles, Peter disappeared from the music scene and I'd heard that he'd taken a job as a gravedigger, although I never actually saw him with a spade in his hands. Rumour also had it that this happened because he'd taken one tab of acid too many, but everyone I knew took the stuff back then and it didn't seem to send any of them over the edge.

He would often be seen at the bar of the Golden Lion in Fulham, which was round the corner from where he lived. As this was one of my regular places to play, I'd stand at the bar and talk to him, noticing that he'd grown his fingernails so long that playing would have been impossible. This quiet man never said anything bad to me about his ex-manager but then he never said bad things about anyone as he was a genuinely sweet person. He was also the guitar mentor to Danny Kirwan who joined Fleetwood Mac for a few years. After he left the band, I got to sing on Danny's solo album 'Hello There Big Boy!'.

Years later, when Peter had decided to play again, he and I met in Norway at the Hell Blues Festival. He was still charming, although one could see he was moving and talking a little slowly. In his heyday, he'd been everyone's favourite and could do no wrong. That's how I like to remember him.

*

Performing at folk clubs and other venues was not the only thing that kept me occupied. An opportunity arose for me to try my hand in a musical, when I was chosen to perform in a not very successful production called 'Liz'. It was loosely based on the Greek story of Lysistrata, who stopped the Peloponnesian War by getting the women to withhold sex from their menfolk until they stopped fighting. The show premiered at the Marlowe Theatre, Canterbury, in the summer of 1968 and starred Ron Moody, fresh from his Golden Globe-winning triumph as Fagin in Lionel Bart's 'Oliver'. He was supported by a large cast including Bill Maynard, Nicholas Smith and (according to the over-enthusiastic local newspaper) "10 gorgeous girls headed by the gorgeous Dana Gillespie".

It was written by a guy called Peter Myers, and based very loosely on a play by Aristophanes. In reality, it was a bit like the Benny Hill Show, with scantily clad girls running around and saying silly things. After a run in Oxford, it was supposed to transfer to the West End, but I'm afraid it never got there, basically because it wasn't very good. It did, however, give me a taste of what it's like to be part of a travelling show, and how to cope in strange bed and breakfast lodgings, often with minimal comfort. The camaraderie of the cast always made it bearable, and it helped me to learn the ropes about performing in the theatre.

I also made a short appearance in a very Sixties film called 'Hold on: It's the Dave Clark Five' starring – wait for it – The Dave Clark Five. This was a TV special, and was one of those films that became popular after the release of The Beatles' 'Hard Days Night', where the band rush around doing nothing much, and occasionally bursting into song. In my first scene, I appear dressed in a vest and mini skirt, standing on a vibrating machine which made my bust shake like jelly. In another sequence, Dave lies down and thinks he's getting a massage from me, but when he looks around he finds it is actually an old crone. It was all in good innocent taste, with maybe just a hint of light-hearted sleaze. It wasn't as good as the films the Beatles were making, but didn't do the band much harm as they were consistently in the charts. Dave subsequently sold it to Disney, who censored my wobbling bits.

The cast of the film makes interesting reading. As well as Dave Clark and the other four band members, there was Richard Chamberlain (Dr. Kildare, The Thorn Birds), and Lulu, together with French President Charles de Gaulle, Russian leader Nikita Khrushchev, US President Lyndon B. Johnson, and British Prime Minister Harold Wilson. Check it out if you don't believe me!

Perhaps my most surprising appearance on screen (in this case television) was when, at the grand old age of 20, I was invited to appear as a guest on BBC's 'Going for a Song' with Max Robertson and resident connoisseur Arthur Negus. It was nothing to do with songs, but instead was a popular quiz show about antiques, in which a panel of 'experts' were shown an object and had to say how old it was, and what it was worth. In a way, it was the forerunner to 'The Antiques Roadshow'.

Unfortunately, the week I appeared on the programme it was all about silver, and if you don't know your hallmarks, you are fucked.

I don't know my hallmarks.

I was fucked.

It's all a little hazy now, but back in 1969 I guess I just held the objects and hoped I said something intelligent. I can't have been that good because I lost out in the quiz to the BBC DJ Mike Raven.

It was time to bid farewell to the Sixties, a decade when I had grown up fast, and say hello to the Seventies. Time for me to settle down and act responsibly? Not a chance!

7: LIFE WITH THE BOWIES

The start of the seventies found me performing in a musical called 'Catch My Soul', known affectionately by the cast as 'Scratch My Hole'. The expression 'Rock Opera' was very new then, and this was ground-breaking stuff. It was the story of Othello, using the original words from the Shakespeare play but with the characters occasionally bursting into song.

It was an amazing production, with a set design that made the stage look like Shakespeare's Globe Theatre. One review referred to the costumes as being "a motley collection ranging from a bejewelled buxom harem of wenches through hippies to the Wild West. The outstanding confusion of the evening was Othello in green battledress, resembling a blackfaced General Eisenhower without the golf clubs."

Othello was played by the man who produced and put the show together. Jack Good was already famous for television pop shows like 'Oh Boy', 'Thank Your Lucky Stars', and (in America) 'Shindig', but he obviously wasn't content with just being the man behind the scenes; he wanted to shine on stage too. So, in order to look the part, he shaved his head and – because he was obviously the wrong colour to play Othello – blacked up every night.

Jack was also going through a bit of a religious conversion at the time, so before the show started, he would play recordings of hymns and sacred music over the tannoy system into the dressing rooms at the theatre. Later in life, he went off to live in Santa Fe, and I heard that he joined some kind of monastery.

A key moment in the show sees Othello stab Desdemona to death. On one particular evening, Jack pulled out his dagger (it was a fake knife, in which the blade retracts into the handle), and somehow the blade flew out of the handle and into the audience. This obviously made killing her somewhat difficult, so he 'stabbed' her with the handle, yelled "Aargh", and put his head in his hands. The show must go on! Unfortunately, when he took his hands away, his fingers had left ten white dots on his 'black' head, which made him look like an alien from outer space. The entire cast on stage started giggling, which inevitably reduced most of the audience to hysterics.

When it came to giggling on stage, I was definitely an offender, and as we were quite a young cast, discipline wasn't really top of our agenda. We just wanted to have fun every night.

Jerry Lee Lewis had played the part of Iago in the original U.S. production, so the producers chose another American for London, namely the bearded actor Lance LeGault. He was famous for hanging out with Elvis Presley, and had appeared in several of Elvis's movies, including 'Girls! Girls! Girls!', 'Kissin' Cousins', 'Viva Las Vegas' and 'Roustabout'. He went on to have a successful television career, appearing in shows like 'The A-Team', 'Magnum P.I.', 'Knight Rider' and 'Dallas'. In the show, he performed 'Canakin Clink', Iago's drinking song, and even appeared on Top of the Pops singing it with me as one of his backing singers. The tape was probably wiped by the BBC many years ago.

The original role of Cassio was played by Tony Joe White in the American production, but in Britain was portrayed by P.J. Proby. We had already shared a stage, several years earlier, when he was the star of the Sunday variety show in Great Yarmouth, and it was good to see him again. Proby had once been described (though not by him) as being better than Elvis, though having seen them both perform live, I can tell you that he definitely wasn't. He did have several successful singles in the sixties, including both 'Maria' and 'Somewhere' from the musical 'West Side Story', but his career had stalled somewhat after he split his trousers during concerts in both Luton and Croydon in January 1965. Believe it or not, this was front-page news at the time, and he was banned from performing in several theatres and on television. He was quoted as saying, "I did not split my trousers. My trousers split. I had nothing to do with it."

On most nights, he was on good form, although sometimes he could be slightly erratic. There was one time when he completely missed his entry cue, leaving me alone on stage with no idea what to do next. In the story, Iago drops a handkerchief, which my character – Emilia – finds and gives to Cassio. In typical Shakespearian fashion, this causes all sorts of problems and ultimately leads to Othello's downfall. One night, I picked up the handkerchief and waited for Cassio to take it off me, but unfortunately, Proby was pissed in his dressing room and missed his cue. So there I am, stuck by myself for about five minutes, looking like an idiot and waiting for somebody to push Proby on stage to collect the bloody handkerchief. To this day, I recall those few minutes as feeling like an eternity. You can't really ad-lib with Shakespeare. Now, with more experience, maybe I'd hum a melody to fill the time.

One evening when 'Catch My Soul' was not being performed, Proby was booked to sing in a club called Barbarella's in Birmingham, and he asked two other girls from the show, and me, to join him as his backing singers. We went to the soundcheck in the afternoon, and he was in great voice. Unfortunately, he was then left in a dressing room with loads of booze, and by the time the show was due to start, he was completely sloshed and could hardly stand up on stage.

The moral of the story is *never ever leave musicians with nothing to do, and a lot of alcohol.*

I recall something similar, many years ago, at a huge festival in Belgium. The band and I got there early, about eleven in the morning, and the organisers showed us to a caravan loaded with bottles of Remy Martin. Predictably, by the time we went on stage, the whole band, with the exception of me, was absolutely paralytic. Needless to say, the gig was awful but like most outdoor festivals, the audience were also pretty legless. I made a decision not to work with heavy drinkers any more and if I have to audition a new band member, the first thing I ask is how much they drink. Give me a mellow dope smoker any day!

In 'Catch My Soul', I was originally booked as one of the three girl backing singers who stood on a specially-lit balcony, looking down onto the stage. Every night, I wore the most outrageous costume in the whole production; thigh-length pink boots and a fringe thing with loads of cleavage on show. As a result, I got a lot of attention when it came to first night reviews. The Manchester Evening News reported on October 27th 1970, "The high spot of the evening was the lady in the chorus with the biggest boobs Manchester has ever seen. Catch my Soul is worth going to see for these alone, and if you can take your eyes off her for a second you will see a phenomenal production the like of which has never before been seen in the English theatre."

Bianca was initially played by Pat 'P. P.' Arnold, who had sung backing vocals on Ike and Tina Turner's huge hit 'River Deep Mountain High' and was also the first person to have a hit with the Cat Stevens song, 'The First Cut is the Deepest'. Marsha Hunt took over the part after Pat Arnold left and, when Marsha's contract expired and they couldn't find another suitable black girl singer, I got the role. It was a step up for me, and I loved it.

Once the show reached London, it was put on in the coolest venue in town – the Roundhouse in Camden Town – before transferring for six months to the Prince of Wales Theatre in the centre of London's Theatreland. It had come far since opening in Birmingham and Manchester, and I was having a ball. After the curtain came down, I would do what anyone in their twenties was doing at that time, which was to go clubbing. The scene was full of action, and sleep was the last thing on my mind.

Scratch My Hole got me loads of publicity. The 23rd of December 1970 edition of Melody Maker, by way of example, printed an eye-catching photograph of me beneath which it states, "We have printed a picture of a lady with large breasts for your further delectation. Her name is Dana Gillespie and her heart is in the right place."

Yet again, more journalistic twaddle!

The January 11th 1971 edition of the London Evening News contained an article by Penny Graham about "a girl who has a lot to get off her chest". I am quoted as saying, "Living with a Playboy pinup bust is not easy, unless perhaps you happen to be a playmate. Superstructure of this kind makes you a target for lusty wolf whistles and lewd remarks."

Interestingly, this article – like many of the period – mainly focuses on my boobs and, extraordinarily in these days of female equality, was written by a woman.

*

David Bowie and I were seeing a lot of each other at the time. When he was staying around the corner from me in South Kensington, he would often come by to tell me about his latest conquests or newest ideas for songs. One time he called me up and said, "I've just written this song half an hour ago. I'm coming over right now to play it to you, so you can tell me what you think."

He appeared at my front door a few minutes later with his guitar, and Gered Mankowitz and I were the first people to hear him sing 'Space Oddity'. We didn't realise at the time what an iconic song this would become.

It wasn't necessary for me to sing my latest compositions to him for approval anymore, as I had now signed as a songwriter to Immediate Records, the label owned by Andrew Loog Oldham, the flamboyant manager of the Rolling Stones. Once a month, I would go to a studio to record demos of my latest compositions, working with loads of really good musicians such as guitarists Chris Spedding and Ray Russell.

Jack Good asked if he could manage my career and I did initially sign to his agency, but shortly after that, my life took another turn. Like me, Bowie had been going through a few managerial changes, and he often used to say to me that we both needed a decent manager. One day, he rang up and said, "I think I've found the perfect man for us." He took me to an office in Regent Street and introduced me to Tony Defries.

From the moment I met Tony, I adored him. My first impression of Defries was that he was like a large, hairy bear; he was slow-moving, self-confident, and softly spoken. He usually had a big cigar in his mouth or his hand, and when he talked, he swayed from side to side like a moored ship. He gave off an air of dependability, and I felt I could trust him. I've always had a soft spot for guys who would put their hand on my shoulder and say to me, "Let me take care of this for you".

That sort of thing was heaven to my ears, especially when it came from someone who knew what he was talking about. Defries didn't talk nonsense – he was sober and didn't get stoned – and that is just what you need in a manager. Over the years, I've lost count of the number of managers I've met who wanted to party as hard as their artistes. That was the norm back in the seventies, resulting in many showbiz casualties, but Defries was too smart to get wasted. He just let his artistes get on with it while he struck deals, plotted careers, and talked legal jargon till people either glazed over or gave him what he wanted. For a start, he got David untangled from his past management deal, which basically meant breaking a contract and sorting out the mess afterwards. He did the same for me too, though that wasn't so difficult as Jack Good was happy for me, and gave me his blessing.

Defries had a legal background and worked in a music management company called Gem Music Group with a guy called Laurence Myers. Their offices were always buzzing with up-and-coming musicians and songwriters, all hoping to forge careers in the music business. One fellow who was often hanging around was Paul Gadd; he would find fame a couple of years later as Gary Glitter. When he was performing regularly on Top of the Pops, none of us could have predicted his shocking fall from grace in the 1990s.

Tony McCauley was another songwriter who was often in the office. He wrote 'Love Grows (Where My Rosemary Goes)', 'Baby Now That I've Found You', and 'Build Me Up Buttercup', amongst many other hits. At the time, he was going out with singer Sylvia McNeil, who was to be the original Mary Magdalene in Jesus Christ Superstar until… well, that's a story for later.

*

Bowie called me up one day and said, "I've just met a woman who I think you'll get on with."

He never invited me to meet any of his others, either because they were one night stands or – as was the case with Hermione – he was too busy just being with her. Little did I know, at the time, that David's new woman would become his first wife.

Angie writes in her wonderful book 'Backstage Passes', "One day David took me to Dana Gillespie's house. We banged on the door, and there she was, my new best friend."

She and I instantly hit it off, and have remained friends ever since. She was – and still is – an absolute joy to be around, and always supportive of everything I do. Sadly, she now lives in America and so I don't see her very often, though we keep in touch by email.

Born in Cyprus to an American father and Canadian mother, Angie was sassy and loud, feisty and funny. A tall, slim blonde and bursting with energy, she had been schooled in Switzerland, could speak French fluently, and was very bright. She soon became a positive force in Bowie's life, and shortly after we met, they both came to see me in 'Catch my Soul'. She promptly renamed my flat as 'The Bunker', a name that stuck for as long as I lived there.

Angie had always been open about her bisexuality, and I think Bowie liked her craziness and joie de vivre. They both said that they had slept with the same man – Calvin Mark Lee – though not at the same time. This was a novel story to give to the press, and it made good copy.

Angie continues, "There was no physical resemblance between us, since I was built like a boy and she (Dana) was very voluptuous, but we both knew we were in this world to celebrate it: to eat, to play, to make art, music, love, whatever was creative and productive. She and I and David and Ken, her boyfriend, all made love together that night."

The fact that we all jumped into bed together may sound pretty outrageous, but that's how it was then. There was nothing serious or meaningful about it; it just felt like a good way to break the ice.

Angie mentions my 'boyfriend' Ken, and there is a strange and rather sad story about our short relationship.

Ken Petty was a rebel, a writer, and an anarchist who came from Sunderland, and he opened my eyes to a very different world to the one I had grown up in. There was an instant connection between the two of us, but it wasn't destined to last, as he announced after a year together that he wanted to go off – alone – and explore Morocco. He promised to send me postcards from his journey which duly arrived for a couple of months, after which I heard nothing.

Very early one morning I received a call from the British Embassy in Tangiers saying that Ken's body had been found by the roadside on the edge of town, and that my telephone number and photograph had been found on him. They told me that he had died of heart failure, which seemed very odd as he was only 26, and that he had been found with strange markings on his body.

His body was flown back to Sunderland and the markings were never mentioned again, but it left a question in my mind. Ken had told me that he was investigating a story that humans were being sacrificed near Tangiers, either for some kind of strange sport – a bit like cockfighting – or maybe connected with a black magic ritual. He was going to tell me about it when he had found out more, but I never heard from him again. Could he have landed up a victim himself, by getting too close to the facts? I'll never know.

Anyway, back to Angie. Some people have said (and it's in a few of the books that have been written about Bowie) that she and I were lesbian lovers. OK, we did sometimes end up in bed together, but it was always when David was there, as he was the kingpin. When he wasn't there, we were just the best of friends. We would go shopping, hang out with people, and be outrageous in public.

From 1969-1972, Bowie and Angie lived in a place called Haddon Hall in Beckenham, a suburb to the south of London. The house was huge, and kind of weirdly Gothic, but sadly is not there anymore as it was demolished in the eighties and replaced by a block of flats. Bowie had rented a flat on the ground floor for which he paid about seven pounds a month.

Although the house was enormous, the flat itself only had a few rooms. When you walked in, there was this great big open space with a minstrels' gallery, and a marvellous stained glass window at one end. Bowie and Angie were in a bedroom off the hall, where they had a television and a load of dramatic furnishings, including the chaise-longue where the cover photo for 'The Man Who Sold the World' was taken. There was a small kitchen where Angie would rustle up some food, and a large garden where the famous photographs of Bowie in his Mr. Fish man-dress were taken. The band used to sleep on mattresses up on the minstrels' gallery.

In all the time I knew him, Bowie was never interested in normal, boring, blokey things. If something on television caught his attention, such as Japanese kabuki theatre, he would call out, "Quick, it's on!" and we'd all climb onto his bed to watch the programme with him. Many people in the music industry are curious for philosophical things, and Bowie was no exception; he liked to immerse himself in esoteric subjects.

One evening, when Bowie was on one of his first trips to America, Angie and I were together in Haddon Hall, and he telephoned in a state of great excitement. He'd just been to Roswell, "…a place where aliens landed and which the Americans now keep quiet about. I've seen an alien and the FBI are keeping it quiet."

It was about midnight, and he went on and on about it, saying, "You know it's happened, it's true, the aliens exist."

David was very, very enthusiastic, though it wasn't clear whether he had literally seen something, or if he had met people who had. The latter is actually more likely now I think about it. Anyway, he said that two aliens had landed in a spacecraft and that their bodies were being preserved in ice so that they didn't fall to pieces. His enthusiasm was so contagious that we both believed him!

Angie used to enjoy dressing David and me up, as she was great at finding clothes and was always really inventive with style. When I look back through my old photographs, I can easily see the outfits that had Angie's touch to them; lots of glamour, sparkle, high heels, and originality. Left to my own devices, I would have stayed in a shirt and jeans, but I was happy to have her take such an interest in the image side of things as it was never my main priority. David just let her get on with it too, as we both recognised that she had style and she knew how to use it. She used to buy Bowie's trousers for him, and he was so slim that both of them would be able to wear them. She bought most of the clothes he wore, even his high heels were bought by her, and when he stepped out, heads would spin, which was how he liked it.

Angie was highly instrumental in helping David to create the image and persona of Ziggy Stardust, though I don't think she ever got the credit she deserved for her role in making him a star. She was the one who had the drive and ambition, whilst — strangely enough — he could be rather shy and retiring. It was Angie who brought in the hairdresser Suzy Fussey to cut David's long hair and create the famous Ziggy mullet. Angie also persuaded me to get my long hair cut around that time, which was a great decision because I got rid of my hippy look.

Various musicians would turn up at Haddon Hall, and from this group, the Ziggy Stardust band 'The Spiders From Mars' was born. Drummer Mick 'Woody' Woodmansey and bass player Trevor Bolder both came from East Yorkshire, as did guitarist Mick Ronson. 'Ronno', as I always called him, was fresh off the train from Hull when Bowie first introduced us. He was a beautiful-looking man with the longest eyelashes you've ever seen, and a lovely Yorkshire accent.

Musicians tend to seek comfort wherever they can get it, and Ronno, who was pretty broke and homesick when we first met, did share my bed occasionally. It was never going to be a boyfriend and girlfriend thing between us, and it certainly wasn't a love affair; it was more a way of passing the evening. All this was long before he and Suzy, who in due course married Ronno, became an item. I never encroached on his love affairs, and vice versa. It was more a case of 'mates with benefits'.

*

Bowie and I were both busy getting songs together for our respective new albums, and Defries arranged for us to record a demo album at Trident studios, with seven of David's songs on one side and five of mine on the other. He had 500 copies pressed to try to secure a record deal for Bowie and me, and it has become known as BOWPROMO. If you have a copy, then put in in the safe, because it has become one of the most valuable Bowie collectables. Poor Laurence Myers, in his excellent book 'Hunky Dory, Who Knew?' writes that he had a pile of these promos, "…cluttering up my office, so once they got a record deal I threw them away."

I'm sure he regrets that now.

Funnily enough, speaking to Laurence recently reminded me that – around this time – I suggested that Dudley Moore be brought in to play piano on some of the sessions. I knew Dudley musically, but obviously Rick Wakeman must have got in there first. Amusingly, Laurence writes about my idea, "This was a very commercial thought, but Dudley didn't respond to Gem's letter of invitation."

If he had, maybe we would remember Dudley for his piano playing on 'Life on Mars', rather than as the star of '10' and 'Arthur'.

In any case, if you are interested in this period, I would strongly recommend that you read Laurence's book. Not just for his statement that, "Dana didn't reach her potential at the time, but later developed into a fine Blues singer." Thank you, Laurence!

One of the tracks on my side of the demo album was a song Bowie had written for me called 'Andy Warhol'. The original version, with Ronno on bass and Bowie on 12-string acoustic guitar and backing vocals, together with my five songs from BOWPROMO, were recently reissued on my double album 'What Memories We Make'.

I also sang 'Andy Warhol' when Bowie performed on the prestigious John Peel Radio Show in June 1971. Bowie didn't really like the song that much at the time, which might be why he gave it to me. Then again, it wasn't much later that he gave one of his best songs, 'All The Young Dudes', to Mott the Hoople, so maybe he was just happy to help me out by giving me a good song. When he heard how it sounded with Ronno playing electric guitar, he decided to record it himself for his 'Hunky Dory' album.

The John Peel show, recorded on the 3rd of June 1971, and broadcast on the 20th of June, was the first time Bowie and the guys who became the Spiders from Mars played together live. Trevor only arrived from Hull the day before the recording, and had to learn the songs overnight. Bowie wanted to get his mates involved, so George Underwood, Geoff MacCormack, and I were all included. John Peel introduced us as "David Bowie and an astonishing number of friends."

The set list mainly featured songs from what John Peel said, "….could very well be called Hunky Dory, that's if we can find out how Hunky Dory is spelt."

It included 'Kooks' (which Bowie introduced by saying, "They phoned through and said my wife had had a baby on Sunday morning, so I wrote this song about the baby"), 'Queen Bitch', and 'Song for Bob Dylan', together with two songs that didn't make it onto the final album, 'Bombers' and 'Looking for a Friend'. I sang backing vocals on a number of the songs, including 'It Ain't Easy', which was to end up on the Ziggy Stardust album, again with me on backing vocals.

Bowie introduced me by saying, "This is another friend of mine, who lives in London. And she's a very, very, very, very, very, very, very excellent songwriter, and she hasn't been recorded yet with her own compositions and needless to say tonight is no exception. She's doing one of my things that I wrote for her. It's called 'Andy Warhol', and this is Miss Dana Gillespie."

I guess Bowie forgot that I had made two albums for Decca in the sixties, featuring many of my own compositions, but I wasn't about to contradict him on-air, particularly after he had been so kind about my songwriting.

It's a mystery why Bowie wrote 'Andy Warhol' for me. Bowie was clearly fascinated by him, though apparently they didn't really get on that well when they first met. I myself did meet Warhol at the Factory in New York a few years later, but not with Bowie. The Warhol Factory made a screen print of me, based on a photograph by Terry O'Neill, and it was used as the cover image on my RCA album 'Ain't Gonna Play No Second Fiddle'.

Bowie did get one up on me, though, by finishing 'Hunky Dory' and getting it released before I'd finished my album, 'Weren't Born a Man', so it was Bowie's version of 'Andy Warhol' rather than mine that was heard first. In the end, because of my commitments in 'Jesus Christ Superstar' (about which later), which would have prevented me from being able to do any promotional activity, my album didn't get released until late 1973. My version of 'Andy Warhol' was released as a single, and there was a rather cool video made of it, which you can see on YouTube.

A few days after the John Peel show was recorded, Bowie, Defries and I travelled to Glastonbury in Somerset on Saturday, the 19th of June 1971, where Bowie was booked to perform at the second Glastonbury festival. He hadn't performed live for nearly a year, and he was keen to get back up on stage.

It was a very warm summer day, and we decided to walk to the festival site from the railway station. Bowie wore a floppy-brimmed hat, a pair of yellow, high-waisted twenties-style Oxford bags, and a 'magician's coat' that Angie had bought for him at a shop on the Fulham Road.

By the evening, the weather was dreadful, with heavy rain and traditional Glasto mud. Bowie was scheduled to play at 7.30 pm, but technical problems with the sound badly messed up the running order, and he finally took to the stage at 5.00 am the next morning, greeting the dawn with a short set. He played a selection of old and new songs: 'Bombers', 'Oh You Pretty Things', 'Quicksand', 'Kooks', 'Changes', 'Amsterdam', 'Song for Bob Dylan', 'The Supermen', and finally 'Memory of a Free Festival'. As he sang the line about the sun machine coming down, the sun itself appeared, its rays shining off the side of the silver pyramid stage. People were waking up in their sleeping bags, having been frozen all night in the mud, and came out to listen and watch. It was a quite extraordinary moment, which I was reminded of when David returned to headline Glastonbury so triumphantly 29 years later.

*

Angie and I had many adventures together, some of which are somewhat graphically described in 'Backstage Passes'. Her recollection of some of them isn't quite the same as mine, but I guess the passage of time, together with Angie's extraordinary imagination, resulted in the differences between what she wrote and what I remember.

One of these incidents occurred during a trip we made together to Italy, a few weeks after David and Angie's son (then called Zowie) was born on the 30th of May 1971. David felt that Angie needed to get over the birth by going away with me for a few days, so off we went to stay with my mother on Lake Maggiore, while David was left behind holding the baby.

In her book, Angie describes a violent storm which caused a power cut in the house. She remembers that we were naked in bed together "tangled up like a couple of Kama Sutra yogis", and that my mother walked in and caught us. My memory of this night is somewhat different. Yes, we were naked on the bed as it was mid-summer and very hot that night. Yes, my mother did come in, but only to bring us some candles because there was no electricity. We both fell about laughing because we realised what it might have looked like to my mother, and the fact that she brought in candles somehow only made it funnier. Angie's rather sexually explicit description just goes to show how two people can have totally different memories of the same event.

There is another story from the same trip which again demonstrates our different memories. The background to this is that Angie and I had gone off to see an Italian band called I Giganti. They had done an Italian-language version of Space Oddity, so Angie wanted to check them out. Somehow the whole band ended up back where we were staying, and we carried on partying until dawn.

Angie describes me and one of the musicians saying goodbye to each other in the middle of the road, in what can politely be best described as a very passionate clinch. Once again, I have to differ from her story. She makes it sound as though she saved my life by running into the road at three o'clock in the morning to stop oncoming traffic whilst my friend and I were otherwise 'distracted'. That is definitely not what happened, and I will tell you how I can be so sure about that.

There was no traffic because the road was closed.

And even if that was not the case, Angie's description of my (imagined) sexual contortions are arguably physically impossible. Never mind, I love her dearly, and will always forgive her occasional flights of fantasy.

After Angie and I had spent a few days together in Italy, David started calling increasingly often, saying how much he was missing Angie and pleading for her to come home. Maybe he just wanted her to come back to relieve him from nappy-changing duties? Whatever the reason, she cut short her holiday and flew back to Britain to keep him happy.

For several years, most Sundays were spent with David and Angie at Haddon Hall, and we had some pretty wild times. As David became better known, more and more people would turn up, and in his book 'My life with Bowie', Woody Woodmansey tells of coming downstairs at Haddon Hall one morning to find several naked women dancing around. I'm pretty sure I wasn't one of them!

*

Bowie originally intended to produce my 'Weren't Born a Man' album, and there were a couple of songs on it I wrote about him, namely 'Dizzy Heights' and 'Eternal Showman'. By the time the studios were booked, and all the songs put together, his career had taken a massive upward turn and he went off for a short trip to America, leaving Mick Ronson to take over the producer's role.

The recordings were all done in Trident Studios, just off Wardour Street in London, which was the same studio Bowie recorded 'Hunky Dory' and 'Ziggy Stardust' in. The studio musicians included Rick Wakeman (fresh from playing on Bowie's 'Hunky Dory' album) on piano, Bobby Keyes on sax (perhaps best known for touring with the Rolling Stones and playing the saxophone solo on 'Brown Sugar'), Terry Cox (who played on Bowie's 'Space Oddity'), and Barry DeSouza on drums with Ray Cooper, who has played with Elton John for nearly 50 years, on percussion. The strings were arranged by Ronno and Del Newman, and Del also played synthesiser. I originally wanted Paul Buckmaster as the arranger, but by then he was so busy doing Elton's stuff that he wasn't available. That's why I took Del, and he did a great job.

Lou Reed sometimes turned up with Bowie at the Trident sessions; Lou was the first man I ever saw wearing black nail varnish. Ronno was very serious during the recording sessions, as he didn't like too many disturbances, and co-producer Robin Cable was also quite earnest. It wasn't party time, unlike when I did my next album, which was crazy from start to finish. It was perhaps fortunate that Iggy Pop was in America at the time.

The title song, 'Weren't Born a Man', had been co-written by me and my boyfriend at the time, Mick Liber. We'd met when he was playing in one of my favourite bands, 'Ashton, Gardner and Dyke', who had a huge hit with 'Resurrection Shuffle'. I'd known Tony Ashton, Kim Gardener and Roy Dyke since the early sixties when Ashton had been in a band called the Remo Four. Mick, who had moved into the Bunker with me, had played on 'In a Broken Dream' by Python Lee Jackson with Rod Stewart on lead vocals, and on the strength of this record, Mick got a solo deal. As he didn't sing himself, he chose 'Weren't Born a Man' with me singing, as his first single, and it was released under the name 'Libido'. Sadly, it disappeared without a trace, but I'd always believed in the song and chose it as the title track of my album.

Initially, I wrote it for my friend Sandra Wood, who was my assistant at the time. She had been in 'Catch My Soul' with me, and when Defries told us we must all travel first class and have personal assistants, I asked Sandra if she wanted the gig ('Catch My Soul' had just finished), and she said yes. So we went off to America together and had an absolute hoot. She later married the guy who managed The Tourists (Annie Lennox and Dave Stewart), which later morphed into the Eurythmics.

Sandra and I were really good friends, and would often say to each other, "It's such a shame you weren't born a man", because we had the perfect relationship, only – obviously – there was a dick missing between us. We were just great mates, and the song was written for her.

It's not a song about being a lesbian. We never did that kind of thing, unless there was a man there, which did happen once or maybe even twice… I'm still not entirely sure why people thought it was a lesbian song, and if anyone thought it was, they got it completely wrong. So guess what? The BBC decided it was a lesbian thing, and banned it. "We haven't exactly banned it," said a rather huffy BBC spokesman, "we're just not playing the record."

At least the Daily Mirror let me put my point across, after the usual tit references. In their March 12th 1974 edition, under the heading "Dana's Big Front", Deborah Thomas wrote, "Dana Gillespie's new record 'Weren't Born A Man' must be the year's biggest understatement, for there is no getting away from it, Dana is all woman, every 44-26-37 inch of her. She wrote the song when she and a girlfriend were sitting in a flat one evening commiserating over absent boyfriends. Now the 24-year-old singer has found the song about bisexuality frowned on by the BBC. "I don't think it should be banned", Dana says, "I wrote it in all innocence and it has been totally misconstrued.""

Another song on the album, 'Mother Don't Be Frightened', was written after I had taken some LSD. I woke up the next morning and wrote the song as a kind of open letter to my mother. The song featured the soon-to-be Spiders from Mars: Ronno, Trevor Bolder and Woody Woodmansey, and the orchestral score was done by Ronno, who had recently done a similar job for Bowie on his 'Hunky Dory' album, including on the classic 'Life on Mars'.

Most people remember my 'Weren't Born A Man' album – if they do at all – because of the cover shot by my friend Gered Mankowitz. The intention was to make it obvious that I hadn't been born a man, as I wore a black corset, black stockings and suspenders, very high heels and a feather boa. It seems rather tame by today's standards, but it was quite risqué then.

Defries seemed genuinely interested in my songs and was happy for me to just carry on creating, which is really all any songwriter wants to do. Bowie was, of course, his number one act and I had come on board at his suggestion, but soon we all became like a family: Bowie, Angie, myself and Mick Ronson, with Tony Defries in the role of father figure.

It was around this time that Defries gave me a Polaroid camera, and encouraged me to take as many pictures as I wanted. These days everyone clicks away on their mobile phones, but in the early 70s the ability to take 'instant' photographs was new and exciting.

Over the next few years, I took hundreds of these pictures, often capturing visiting friends like the Bowies, Mick Jagger, Jeff Beck, Iggy Pop, Marianne Faithfull, Jenny Agutter, Kiki Dee, Lionel Bart and many, many others. Sometimes, I handed the camera to a friend to take pictures of me, a number of which are probably not suitable for publication. It's not surprising that we used to call them 'Pornaroids'! I have, however, selected some pictures of friends relaxing out of the limelight for inclusion in this book, many of which have not been seen before.

In the Marbella Club,
aged five.

Aged three, with Oma.

My mother, Dadster, sister Nixi and I,
attending a wedding when I was six.

Dadster - my fascinating, gregarious,
often womanising father.

My mother with her second husband,
The Hon. Tom Hazlerigg.

Clockwise: Eric Clapton, playing at the Marquee Club, around
the time that he (nearly) became my guitar teacher;
with The Hollies at the Ready Steady Go studios; singing to
Alberto Sordi in the film "Fumo di Londra".

Early days as a folk singer, aged 15.

British Junior Waterski Champion.

Me and Sara Troup on the steps of Thurloe Square.

Clockwise: An article about Dylan and me from Disc and
Record Echo in 1966; another article, from New Musical
Express - I learnt at a very young age that journalists often
misquote you; with Dylan, at a record company
reception at the Savoy Hotel in London.

From one of my early sessions with Gered Mankowitz.

From Gered Mankowitz's photoshoot for my
"Foolish Seasons" album in 1968.

David Bowie and I always favoured the 12-string
guitar because it made a fuller sound.

With Tony Beckley on the set of "The Lost Continent".

Me and my balloons from the same film.

With David Bowie in May 1971, shortly before he
recorded his "Hunky Dory" album.

In the basement. Those walls could tell some stories.

Me, Tony Defries, and Bowie at The Roundhouse
in London to see Warhol's "Pork".

Gered Mankowitz's original artwork for
"Weren't Born A Man". It attracted quite a lot of attention!

With Long-Legged Liz at the same session.

No wonder Defries was smiling!

My dear friend Angie Bowie; having dinner with Mick Ronson.

Trevor Bolder

Defries, Dana e Ronno

Trevor Bolder, bass player in Bowie's Spiders from Mars; with
two of my favourite men in the seventies - Tony Defries and
Mick Ronson.

Defries e Ronno

Tony Defries and the incredibly talented Mick Ronson; Ronno
and Suzy - his guitar playing and her hairdressing
played a major part in the huge success of Bowie's
Ziggy Stardust.

Bindon e Angie

John Bindon and Angie in the Bunker; performing
"Andy Warhol", the song that Bowie wrote for me.

Freddie

Suzy and Mick Ronson; Freddie Burretti, who designed a
number of Bowie's iconic outfits in the early Seventies.

With Ahmet Ertegun and Princess Margaret in Mustique.

The infamous picture I took of John Bindon
and Princess Margaret in Mustique.

Watching on as Lady Glenconner greets
Princess Margaret at Colin Tennant's 50th birthday party.

Colin Tennant with Princess Margaret and
Lady Leonora Litchfield at the 50th birthday bash.

Colin Tennant greets
Bianca Jagger.

Lionel Bart with my
mother and Colin Tennant.

Singing for
Princess Margaret in
Mustique.

Performing in "Jesus Chris Superstar" – I am on the right of
the picture, behind Paul Nicholas who played Jesus.

me in 'The Tempest'

Jenny Agutter

Playing Juno in "The Tempest" at
The National Theatre, where I shared a
dressing room with Jenny Agutter.

me, Zowie, Marion e Angie

the Bowies!

Nanny Marion looks after Zowie while Paul Jabara,
Angie and I recover after a night out;
at home with the Bowies.

Angie Bowie

Zowie Bowie

Angie looking beautiful; now a successful film director
called Duncan Jones, I knew him as Zowie Bowie.

Clockwise: Lou Reed (back to camera), Mick Jagger, Bowie, Jeff Beck, Ronno, and me at the Cafe Royal party following Ziggy's retirement in 1973; Bowie and me at the same event; dressed for a quiet evening at home, in the Bunker 1973.

Out on the
town with
Angie.

Glammed up for
Mainman in 1973.

Next two pages: Bowie on the Diamond Dogs tour in the
United States and Canada, 1974; David's backing singers Geoff
MacCormack and Gui Andrisano, with guitarist Earl Slick;
me and Bowie's piano at the Sherry Netherland hotel.

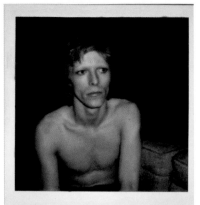

Bowie

David Bowie

Bowie

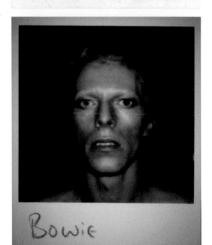

Bowie

Bowie

Bowie

Bowie

David e Jack

Bowie - Diamond Dogs

Bowie e Band in Montreal

Jeff, Earl Slick e Guy

Propping up Bowie's piano

Mick Jagger at the Bowies' suite in the Sherry
Netherland Hotel, New York; David and Angie, chilling out.

The adorable Cherry Vanilla; me with whizz-kid
drummer Simon Phillips and Sandra Wood - taking it easy.

Mainman montage,
put together by
Tony Defries's
wife Marlene;
one of my Mainman
promotional stickers.

Mainman promotional
photos.

Mainman promotional photos, taken in London and New
York; Raquel Welch and me, after a gig at Reno Sweeney's,
with Tony Defries's then-girlfriend Melanie.

My "Andy Warhol" screenprint.

Phill e me

Recording "Ain't Gonna Play No Second Fiddle"
with Phill Brown at Island Studios, and the Mainman
advertising poster for the album.

Gered Mankowitz promo photos taken at home.

Posing in the Bunker, and showing off my Janet Reger knickers
bought by Angie Bowie.

Me with Richie Hayward, the drummer in one of my
favourite bands, Little Feat; two great friends -
Marc Bolan and Angie Bowie.

Wearing an outfit designed by Natasha Korniloff.

Peter O'Farrell looking up in "Playthings".

On the film sets for "Byron's Mine" and "Sink or Swim"
(the island was Lanzarote).

8: MUSTIQUE

While the record company was waiting for the best time slot to release 'Weren't Born a Man', I really needed 'live' work to make some money and keep me occupied until the album was launched.

I used to read the weekly music papers to see if there were any auditions going for work; indeed, this was the way that Bowie and I found about the stage show of 'Hair'. We both auditioned, although not on the same day, and must have been the only two people in London who didn't get chosen. Even to this day, I'm still not sure what went wrong. Let's face it, we both would have looked pretty good standing on stage starkers!

This rejection didn't stop me from regularly scouring the music papers for anything else that seemed suitable. One day, I saw a small advertisement in Melody Maker for session singers to work on a new project called 'Jesus Christ Superstar'. Tim Rice and Andrew Lloyd Webber, then virtually unknown, were looking for voices to sing on the demos of some songs, and the list of characters included the part of Mary Magdalene. I took a chance and wrote a long letter to Tim and Andrew, saying I felt I should play the role of Mary Magdalene, and enclosed a copy of my Jimmy Page-produced single, 'You Just Gotta Know My Mind'.

A week later, I got a call from Tim Rice saying he was sorry but that, on the day before they had received my letter, they had engaged a singer called Yvonne Elliman to play the part. I wasn't too disappointed at the rejection, though, as I was off to Los Angeles to have fun with Ashton, Gardner and Dyke.

During my time in California, I heard – on the grapevine – that Jesus Christ Superstar was going to be presented as a live concert in the States. The original Superstar album (featuring Yvonne, together with Deep Purple singer Ian Gillan as Jesus, and Murray Head as Judas) had been released, and producer Robert Stigwood was trying to get the concert off the ground. As I was in L.A. anyway, I thought I'd try for the part as I was convinced I was perfect for the role of Mary. Since I was not a member of the American Actors Union I was told that I wasn't eligible to audition, however, so I put everything to the back of my mind and flew off to the Caribbean island of Mustique with my mother and stepfather.

My stepfather had just broken his hip, and the doctor told him that if you've got a broken limb, the best place to recuperate is somewhere with sunshine and warm water. My stepfather had a business contact who had just finished building a house on Mustique, so arrangements were made.

We had to look up the island on a map, because we didn't know exactly where it was. When I discovered that it was in the Caribbean, and as I was currently unemployed, I immediately offered to come along to carry the luggage. As my stepfather was incapacitated, I thought it was a very noble suggestion.

This was to be the first of many trips I have made to Mustique over the last 50 years. We stayed in a house which was not exactly finished; it was more like a construction site with workmen regularly appearing. Not every day, as this was the Caribbean and everything happened on 'Mustique time', but it really didn't matter as we spent most days out on the beach. There was only a basic kitchen in the house, so we lived on whatever fresh fish was going at the time, together with banana bread and the famous callaloo and pumpkin soups.

Princess Margaret was already a regular visitor to Mustique, so it was getting the occasional mention in the press although still far from being as well-known as it is today. It really was a private, paradise island in the early 1970s, and I feel so lucky to have known it before it ever got truly famous. There were no direct flights there, so you had to fly via Barbados, then St Vincent, and – finally – a tiny plane took you to the mown-grass field which was Mustique international airport.

Much of the action on Mustique revolved around one central building called The Cotton House, and as the electricity broke down a lot, it was here that most people would meet in the evening to drink and generally socialise, often by candlelight. When I say 'action', there were probably only about six or seven houses on the island in those days, so there weren't many people there.

The island was owned by Colin Tennant, Lord Glenconner, who had bought it (totally undeveloped) for just £45,000 in 1958. There had been some speculation at the time that he was hoping to marry Princess Margaret after the collapse of her relationship with Group Captain Peter Townsend, though in later years he was quoted as saying, "I don't expect she would have had me."

Colin had given Princess Margaret some land on Mustique as a wedding present when she married Anthony Armstrong-Jones/Lord Snowdon (who ironically had been hired as a photographer at Tennant's own marriage in 1956 to Lady Anne Coke). Snowdon disliked Tennant, and only spent one night on Mustique, on his honeymoon. He called it "Mustake", and resented the fact that the wedding present had been given only to Princess Margaret, not to them both.

Whilst my mother and stepfather both knew Colin Tennant, I didn't... although I had been at school with his half-sister Katherine. He was a very dashing man, bald-headed and exquisitely dressed, and often wore a stylish Panama hat. The day I was first introduced to him, he was standing on the top of the wide steps of The Cotton House, dressed as ever in an elegant striped double-breasted pyjama suit, looking a bit like a deck chair in a hat. As my first thought was that he was wearing his pyjamas, I said to him, "You look ready for bed." He laughed and replied, "And so do you!"

That was the start of our friendship, which I have to admit did sometimes develop into the physical. It was never out in the open because he was married to Lady Anne, and he also had a mistress, so I was quite a long way down the pecking order. Colin and I would occasionally meet in London at Overtons, the fish restaurant in Victoria, then go back to the Bunker, and he would sometimes invite me out to Mustique, especially when Anne wasn't there.

I always felt a bit bad about this, and wondered whether Anne ever suspected anything. I was quite amused that, in her marvellous book 'Lady in Waiting', Anne referred to the mistress but (like me) declined to name her.

Anne and I saw each other most recently in Mustique in February 2020, and greeted each other like long-lost friends, which indeed we were. She was tickled pink that her memoirs were selling so well, and said to me that she wondered what Colin would have made of her success. "Would he have been jealous or amused?" she asked. "Probably a bit of both!" I replied.

From the moment I first visited this wonderful Caribbean island, I immediately fell in love with it. Unfortunately, nobody told me about the strength of the sun in the West Indies. As there were no people on the beach, on my first day there I went for a two-hour walk naked, and came back the colour of a lobster. I couldn't move for about two days, which taught me to be more respectful of the local climate. Other than that, I basically had an idyllic time, getting up at dawn to go to a beach where I would swim naked and be totally assured that no one would unexpectedly turn up.

There is one character on the island who remains one of my oldest friends to this day. His name is Basil Charles, and he came from the relative poverty of St. Vincent. He arrived on Mustique at a time when Colin Tennant was desperately looking for a barman for a luncheon that Princess Margaret was due to attend. Basil offered to help and changed the course of his life forever. Very quickly, this tall, black-skinned man, with an irresistible laugh and wonderful pearly white teeth, become indispensable on the island. He was soon Colin's right-hand man for many things, especially when it came to finding the right people to come to work on the island.

In those days, the roads were little more than dirt tracks, and Basil used to criss-cross the island in his pick-up truck, effectively acting as the unofficial Mustique taxi driver and gofer. Since he was the only good-looking local who was interacting with the white guests, he would also use the truck for picking up in another sense, and very soon became a huge hit with the ladies. A few years later, it was said that there was a new verb on the island, which was 'to be Basiled'. If you asked a roomful of women which ones had been 'Basiled', I guarantee most of the hands would go up, mine included.

Basil and I had a great relationship that went from physical to firm friends, and it has endured for many years. We sometimes laugh when thinking back to steamy times in the lagoon, when no one else was there and the island was ours.

Basil's name began to get known over in England when he started a well-publicised affair with Lady Virginia Royston, who had arrived on the island with two small children, Joey and Jemima, following the death of her husband The Earl of Hardwicke. Basil used to appear in the society columns of the daily newspapers, and was always described as a 'black barman'. He was far more than that.

Basil started a little business selling drinks and local food in what is now the harbour of Mustique, at a place that has become known all over the world as 'Basil's Bar'. In those early days, one boat dropping anchor in the harbour was considered a busy week. He's done well in life, and I'm so pleased for him.

Back in the day, there was a wonderfully relaxed atmosphere on the island. Colin liked to organise things for people to do, like having a picnic on the beach during the day, then in the evenings everybody would congregate at the Cotton House. Basil would be behind the bar, and Colin would be running around arranging various games. He liked everyone to be kept entertained, and would sometimes ask me to get my 12-string guitar out, and play for the guests. On one occasion, this included the rather unique combination of Sir George Solti and Bryan Ferry.

Princess Margaret was sometimes on the island when I was there. When together at The Cotton House, she would ask me to play 'What Memories We Make', which I wrote for my 'Weren't Born a Man' album, and which had been inspired by meeting a cool American hippie on the beach at Eilat, back in the sixties. It always used to please me when she described that particular song as one of her favourites.

Some evenings Colin would get everyone to recite a limerick. When each verse was finished, we all had to sing together, "That was a good little song, sing us another one, do."

One night, Princess Margaret got up to perform her limerick. As usual, she had a glass in one hand and her long cigarette holder in the other, and to the delight of us all, she sang:

"There once was a man from St. Paul's,

Who did a good turn on the Halls.

His favourite trick was to stand on his dick

And freewheel off the stage on his balls"

…after which we all came in with another rousing chorus of "That was a good little song…"

*

One of the great Mustique occasions was Colin's 50th birthday party. It was a splendid affair lasting a week, with a detailed programme for each day stating which beach we would eat on, and at what time, all carefully planned out and printed in a little booklet. Colin paid for everything; flights, accommodation, food, drink, and all the guests received a T-shirt with his 50th anniversary printed in gold. On the final night of serious partying, we were all told to wear something golden.

The sand on Macaroni beach was swept to a smooth surface, the palm trees were painted gold, limbo dancers were shipped in, and a colossal barbeque was underway as the guests started to arrive. Oliver Messel, the famous set designer, came dressed in the original costume of Nijinsky's 'Firebird', and looked simply amazing as he went round all the guests fluttering his golden wings. Bianca Jagger was dressed exquisitely in a gold 'Gone with the Wind/ Scarlett O'Hara' style gown, though looked sad, as if she and Mick had just had a marital argument.

The star of the show, though, was Princess Margaret, who decided to be different and not wear gold like everybody else. As she walked into the clearing by the beach, she looked truly regal in a silver gown, with Colin and Lady Anne at her side.

*

Although I was flitting across the globe, whenever I got back to London I had one friend who would often come to visit me. His name was John Bindon, and he can probably best be described as an entertaining rogue.

Bindon had close connections with the London underworld, and spent eight years of his life in prison before going straight (sort of) to follow his dream of becoming an actor.

For a while, things worked well for him, and he got a number of high profile film roles. He played the 'heavy' in Nicholas Roeg's film 'Performance' starring Mick Jagger, and was a villain in 'Get Carter' with Michael Caine, and always seemed to be cast in this kind of role. His problem, if you can call it that, was that he looked and talked like a thug, having obviously been one, though after a time he got frustrated about this continual typecasting.

He had a very demanding girlfriend, the model Vicki Hodge, and when things got too bad with her, he would escape to the Bunker to hang out with me and my friends. He was so funny that you would be weak from laughter once he got started on his stories, many of which were about his experiences in prison; not something my friends and I were familiar with. One time he'd been put in a cell with 'Mad Axe' Frankie Mitchell, and was desperate to get transferred out and into the psychiatric block where conditions were a bit better. He saved some sausages and lemonade from the canteen and put them in a see-through plastic potty, and when the wardens came to watch him 'slop out', he proceeded to eat what they thought was his own shit. He was moved straightaway.

Bindon, or 'Biffo' as we all called him, had a whole other world that I never saw, which involved gangsters and mobs. Names like the Kray twins would sometimes get thrown into the conversation, but I never cared much about this side of him as my world was full of peaceful dope-smoking musicians who just wanted to make music. Violence didn't come into this hippie existence at all. I think that Biffo just loved to be in a crowd where he could escape from his past occasionally. He was also very well-known around Chelsea because of his party trick, which involved hanging five pint glasses on his dick. A friend once asked me how this was done, perhaps imagining, or maybe hoping, that he balanced the five glasses on an erect cock. Sadly, I had to disappoint her by saying that, in fact, he just hooked his cock through the handles and held it up with his hand. All those years in prison obviously gave him a lot of time to practice, and he loved it when you called him by his other nickname, 'The Mighty Marrow'.

Apart from being known as a film and TV villain (as well as for having a large cock), Bindon is probably best remembered for his alleged affair with Princess Margaret. This has been much written about over the years, and as I was actually there at the time and was the one who introduced them, now it is my turn to say what actually happened.

A house in Mustique had been offered to me for a month over Christmas, so I asked loads of friends to come and stay. I knew full well that if I asked ten people who all said yes, perhaps three would actually turn up, but as it happens the only person who definitely said yes was my old mate Lionel Bart, famous for writing the musical 'Oliver', and the songs 'From Russia With Love' and 'Living Doll'.

Lionel was a great guy except when he got pissed, at which point he would become a pain in the arse. Sadly, he had lost all the money he had made through 'Oliver' by this time, and was living in a little mews house next to the painter Francis Bacon, who used to bang on Lionel's door and walls – at four in the morning – asking him why he wasn't making more noise.

When Lionel and I travelled out, my knee was really painful from my avalanche accident, and I was in a wheelchair which was pushed by Lionel. For some reason, we flew out to Mustique via Luxembourg, where we had to kill time in the tiny airport as we waited for our onward flight. By the time we headed for the plane, Lionel was so drunk that he could hardly walk, let alone push the wheelchair. He did his best, bless him.

When we finally arrived in Mustique, the house where we were to stay was still having work done to it, and – as we were short of rooms – Lionel and I had to share. Thank God there were twin beds. Lionel had just had all his teeth out, so his new dentures sat in a glass by the side of the bed at night. He was miserable about this, saying, "How can I ever kiss a young lovely again if I've got a mouth full of plastic?"

He was terribly sensitive about his toothless appearance, and absolutely forbade me to have the light on if his teeth were out.

Lionel was drinking way too much at this time, and was always nursing a monumental hangover. He spent almost all daylight hours in bed with a headache. In fact, he is the only person I have ever seen on Mustique who left the island with paler skin than on arrival.

After a few days, Bindon surprised us both by turning up, carrying nothing but a stick with a knotted handkerchief on the end, looking just like a pirate who had come off a ship, which was – in fact – how he had travelled. Although I had invited Biffo, I was quite surprised that he made it to the island, and it turned out he was on the run from the 'Old Bill'. I never found out what he was alleged to have done this time, and in all honesty didn't want to know.

Near the house was a small hillock, where Bryan Adams has his house now, and no one could get to that point without being seen approaching, so I used to go and sunbathe naked there, often taking my tapestry or beadwork so as to be industrious in the sun. One day, Biffo came up there to join me, accompanied by another friend of mine whom we all called Long-Legged Liz. After a while, Biffo asked Liz to put some sun oil on him, and after she had liberally covered most of his body he said his cock needed oiling too. Things then rather got out of hand (or not, actually!). As I sat there doing my handiwork, Biffo and Liz did theirs, about ten feet from where I was sitting. Notwithstanding what was happening next to me, I never once dropped a stitch.

There was a bush at the bottom of the hillock, and apparently three young local lads were hiding behind it having a wank while watching Biffo and Liz's hilltop performance. What they didn't know was that, back in the house, Lionel was lying on his bed looking out of the window and watching the young guys. When we all finally returned to the house, Lionel had us in stitches when he told us that he'd been having a wank, while watching the boys having a wank, as they watched the hilltop antics.

One morning, Colin Tennant said he was holding a luncheon party on Macaroni Beach for Princess Margaret, and would I like to come with my house party. As Lionel spent most days drinking rum punches, he could be quite funny till the evening when he could get a bit bolshie, so he was in. Biffo had a pair of jeans but didn't have a clean shirt to wear, so I lent him the only T-shirt I had that was big enough to go over his shoulders, emblazoned on the front with 'Enjoy Cocaine' in the style of the Coca Cola logo. Mick Liber had bought this for me in Los Angeles, and no one thought anything of it at the time.

Lionel, Biffo, Long-Legged Liz, and I duly turned up for the luncheon on the beach. As ever, Biffo was very entertaining and soon had the Princess laughing. She told him, "You must call me Ma'am, which rhymes with spam," and you could see that he was tickled pink by this… entertaining the sister of the Queen. Although Ma'am was amused by Biffo's banter, he certainly didn't overstep the mark.

At one point, Ma'am went into the water to swim, wearing a floral swimming costume with a modesty frill and a string at the back which a lady-in-waiting must have laced up for her. She was a petite woman, and her bust seemed to be balanced on what looked like some scaffolding, cunningly constructed inside the costume. She would keep her head out of the water so as not to get it wet, and swam like a swan. I'm convinced that all the Royals use some special formula sunblock to keep their skin nice and white in the sun, but she hadn't put any on the top of her cleavage which very quickly began to go bright red. Biffo found this very funny, and started singing, out of her earshot, "Marks and Spencers, Ma'am gets her underwear at Marks and Spencers". Of course, it was a swimming costume, not actually her underwear, but Biffo was just having a laugh.

Many years later, I told this story to Stephanie Beacham, and it was used in a play called 'A Princess Undone' in which Stephanie played Princess Margaret. The play was about Ma'am's life, and made reference to the 'relationship' between Ma'am and Biffo.

Anyway, back in Mustique, after we'd all eaten, I asked if I could take a photograph of everyone, and so snapped away on an ancient blue plastic Zeiss Ikon camera that I'd been given on my tenth birthday. This photograph of Bindon in the 'Enjoy Cocaine' T-Shirt and Ma'am sitting next to him on the beach was to become infamous…

The rest of the holiday passed uneventfully until Vicki Hodge, who had somehow tracked Bindon down, turned up uninvited on the island, by which time I had already left. Back in London, however, Vicki called me in a panic to ask if she could borrow the photograph, as she was trying to raise money to pay for Biffo's defence in a murder trial. Perhaps foolishly, I agreed, not really thinking about how Vicki planned to use it. She sold the photo, and to my horror it appeared on the front page of a Sunday newspaper a few days later as part of a story about Ma'am having an affair with Bindon. Having been the only one on the beach with a camera that day, I was worried that everyone would think the Bindon scandal was something to do with me, and although I was never named as the photographer, I felt so mortified that it had appeared on the front page of a redtop that I didn't go back to the island for about ten years.

There has been so much talk about whether Bindon and Princess Margaret had an affair. As far as I am concerned, they absolutely did not. Okay, she did let her hair down a bit on the island, but she was still the Royal Princess and always acted regally.

When Biffo was having fun and was in a joking mood, he would sometimes say that he'd like to give her one, but no one took it seriously. There is another story that he walked down the beach with her and she asked to see his gargantuan dick, but that did not happen either. At no time did she go for a walk with him, and I stayed close to him so I could make quite sure he didn't put a foot wrong.

Biffo and I bumped into Ma'am at the Cotton House occasionally after that day on the beach, but again Biffo was on best behaviour. Her house was at the other end of the island from where we were staying, and because there were no proper roads he would have had to go through brambles, shrubs, and swamps if he had wanted to visit her there. It simply didn't happen.

For months after we got back, Biffo used to talk about how marvellous Ma'am was. Knowing him so well, he definitely would have told me if something had really gone on. He used to say that he never denied the rumours to the press as it was good for his reputation, and it was a great story that refused to die. We'd all roar with laughter when he used to tell my friends and I that he never did anything with her due to having 'too much respect for her', knowing that in reality Ma'am wouldn't have looked twice at someone like him.

I was to have many more adventures in Mustique over the years, but in the meantime it was time for me to return to the West End stage in London.

9: SUPERSTAR AND SHAKESPEARE

Returning to London, after my latest trip to Mustique, I needed to find my next bit of work, so I once again started looking through the advertisements in the Stage newspaper. One day, I saw something that really caught my eye. A major stage production of Jesus Christ Superstar was to open at the Palace Theatre in the West End of London, and auditions were about to start.

Open auditions are a nightmare for most performers, but I've always quite liked them. Usually, people sing nice little songs and wear sensible clothes, but I decided to play it a bit differently and wore skin-tight jeans and a T-Shirt with a fist on it which accentuated my bust. My choice of song was 'Get Back' by The Beatles.

The producers were only offering a one-year contract to members of the chorus, and I wasn't keen on such a long commitment to a show which would involve singing the same notes eight times a week. Not very creative for someone like me who likes to play around with the tunes, and sing what I feel. Still, I was happy to get the job, especially when they agreed that I only needed to commit for three months.

Rehearsals were hard work but fun, and we used up lots of energy dancing and laughing a lot. We hardly saw the girl who was to play Mary Magdalene as she was in different scenes from us. She had an amazing voice, but in my opinion wasn't quite right for the part, as she was flat-chested and didn't move particularly well. She didn't look like the 'tart with the heart', and I knew I was far better suited for that role.

When the time came for them to audition the understudy for Mary, I was told that I couldn't apply as I was on such a short contract. Only a cast member on a year-long contract could apply, so the producers didn't have to keep training new people for the role. Though disappointed, I understood their reasons.

However, seven days before the show was due to open, the director, Jim Sharman, had a change of heart and said he would let me audition for the understudy role after all. I was told to prepare to sing the main song, 'I Don't Know How To Love Him' at 9.00 a.m. the next morning. Not knowing the song well, I went back to the Bunker to learn the words.

The next morning, I turned up at the theatre and was surprised to see the producers all sitting in the front row, which was odd as they didn't come in that often. Also up for the understudy part was a good friend of mine called Jean Gilbert, who had been in 'Catch My Soul' with me. Called up to perform first, even today I can clearly recall the strange but elating feeling of being on such a big stage, alone, with only a microphone and a piano player for company.

As I started singing, I felt as if something had taken over my body, and sang from deep in my heart. At the end of my performance, I had tears in my eyes and my knees were shaking. I was totally overcome with emotion. Jean then took her turn and sang very well, while I went back to the little changing room at the side of the stage to listen through the open door. The two of us then sat for half an hour, nervously waiting for a decision to be made, and when – at last – the director came into the room to tell us his choice, he didn't look at me. He just said to Jean, "You will be the understudy for Mary."

It seemed clear to me that the whole production team were deaf and crazy, and didn't know their art from their elbow, but then Jim turned to me and said, "You will be the new Mary. We have decided to pay off the original girl, and you have six days to learn the role."

It was an extraordinary moment as I had always felt that I would play Mary, and now it was coming true. Jim gave me the rest of the morning off, so I rushed home to tell my parents.

Some hours later, when I took the tube back to the West End on my way to the Palace Theatre, the train was full of people reading the afternoon editions of the Evening Standard and the Evening News. There, on the front pages, were headlines stating that – due to an illness of the leading lady just days before the big premiere – the lead role of Mary Magdalene had been given to a relatively unknown actress called Dana Gillespie. Needless to say, the reports were accompanied by photographs of me bursting out of a caveman outfit, with plenty of cleavage on show.

Not surprisingly, some of the tabloids were quick to pick up on this story, which also gave them the excuse to print glamour shots of me. Under a predictable headline, "Uplift for an unknown", The Sun reported on Friday, July 28th, 1972, "Dana Gillespie, who has a remarkable 44-26-37 figure, knows all about the old showbiz adage: stardom or bust. Until now her main claim to fame has tended to centre around the latter, but from tomorrow the 22-year-old actress singer will find herself a star as Mary Magdalene in the London production of the rock opera Jesus Christ Superstar."

As usual, I had to deal with lots of newspapers concentrating on my physical attributes. These days it wouldn't be tolerated.

The Daily Mirror printed a profile picture showing rather more than just my head and shoulders, and reported, "Maybe a 44 inch bust isn't everyone's idea of a biblical figure, but this is the girl who has been chosen to play Mary Magdalene."

All sorts of excuses were given about the late change. Tim Rice was quoted as saying that they eventually settled on me for the role of Mary after the original leading lady proved "unsuitable, not untalented but not right." Apparently, they paid her a lump sum to terminate her contract, and I felt awful for her, but know that if you're running a big show, it's the Angels – the guys with the money – who are the ones who call the shots.

Jim Sharman described me, after the audition, as, "vocally and physically impressive", and Andrew Lloyd Webber, in his autobiography entitled 'Unmasked', wrote that, "(Dana) certainly ticked the boxes for the lover of the Rubens figure," and had "an empathy with the role, but what qualified her even more was her great bluesy voice."

Some might have thought I looked a bit too sexy for Mary Magdalene, and I tried to disguise my curves by wearing a long, white, fairly shapeless caftan, which I had bought in Jerusalem a few years earlier. Because my selection was so last minute, the costume department didn't have any clothing that fitted me, so I said that I'd got something at home that might work. It was very appropriate when you think about it… it had come from the Holy Land.

One of the reasons that 'Jesus Christ Superstar' was such a huge hit, even before it had opened, was because of the subject matter. Just using the name 'Jesus Christ' in conjunction with the word 'Superstar' was quite daring. On the way to the theatre, we'd have to fight our way through people – including nuns – picketing with placards saying that what we were doing was blasphemous and that we'd all go to hell for such behaviour. It was only after the Archbishop of Canterbury came to see the show on opening night, and gave it a thumbs up, that the protests stopped. Within weeks, the show was an established hit, sold out for months in advance, and went on to run for years.

The role of Jesus was played by Paul Nicholas, who had a great singing voice. He and I had a really good relationship, though I've got to admit that at times I was a bit unprofessional. There was one scene in which I'm supposed to anoint Jesus's hair, so I would come on stage with a gold-coloured box full of 'precious oils', and Paul/Jesus would lie back against me as I soothed him. One time, I put a Tampax in the box, admittedly not used, and Paul opened it up and then had to perform the song without corpsing. Another time, I even put a rubber dog turd in the box to see if I could make him giggle. We often did the rest of the song literally shaking with laughter.

Richard Barnes, who played Peter as well as understudying the role of Jesus, had a song with me called 'Could we start again please'. We would often sing the whole song looking at each other's feet so as not to burst out laughing.

The role of King Herod was played by an American called Paul Jabara, who performed Herod's Song to huge applause at every performance. Paul was an absolute hoot, an ostentatiously gay man who camped up the part to the delight of the audience. He was also well known for having written the song 'It's Raining Men' for The Weather Girls.

Due to the Equity actors' union rules, Jabara only had a six-month contract to perform in Superstar in London, and I really missed him when he left the cast. He and David Charkham – who was totally miscast as a priest – were my great mates, and I used to hang out with them because they were the fun boys in the show.

Jabara was so popular with the Superstar audiences that Robert Stigwood wanted to cast him in the starring role of the London production of 'Joseph and the Amazing Technicolor Dreamcoat'. The British Actor's Equity did not want the part to go to an American actor, and refused to allow him to accept the offer. In protest, he chained himself to the railings outside 10 Downing Street, which made headlines in all the British papers.

Some of the people who started out in the chorus of Superstar went on to bigger and better things, including Elaine Paige, who appeared in Evita and Cats, and Richard O'Brien. The part of King Herod had always been played extremely 'camp' which really suited the role, but when the role became free, Richard auditioned for the part but decided to do things differently. He dressed as a rocker, wearing crepes, drapes and brothel creepers; the full rocker outfit. That was the last thing producer Robert Stigwood wanted, so Richard didn't get the part. In disgust, he walked out on his contract and left Superstar, deciding to write his own show in the style of music that he really liked. He did this in a couple of weeks, and is now known the world over as the man who wrote and starred in 'The Rocky Horror Picture Show'.

On the night of the premiere, Robert Stigwood held a party at his large house in Stanmore. According to Andrew Lloyd Webber, "A joyous rumour spread that upstairs in Robert's bathroom there was a peep show worth viewing. Apparently, a guest had ventured into it for a leak and discovered the not inconsiderable sight of the show's lyricist and Mary Magdalene entwined on the floor."

Much later, I discovered that Robert Stigwood had made a bet that Tim couldn't score with every Mary Magdalene (although Tim has told me that he has no recollection of this). Needless to say, I didn't know about it either. I don't mind because I've always liked Tim; he loves his music, he's intelligent, and – perhaps most importantly – he loves his cricket, big time.

On another occasion, Paul Jabara and I were invited to Stigwood's house for his birthday party. Everyone was obviously going to arrive with lavish presents, and I couldn't think what to bring. It occurred to me that if I brought a gay policeman friend to the party, he would be the perfect present for Robert. Apparently, my companion, who was a marvellous chap called Keith, was a big success with the partygoers, though I don't know whether this was to do with the size of his truncheon.

Andrew Lloyd Webber's memoir also says, "Dana Gillespie was rumoured to have organized a cock measuring contest in her dressing room. I didn't enter. Auntie Vi told me it was bad form to enter a contest you know you're going to win."

I don't recall ever doing that, as it's not the sort of thing that I would have thought of. In any case, I'm not even sure I know anyone who would want to enter it, except maybe Biffo.

When I was given the part of Mary, they asked if I wanted anything in my dressing room and I asked for a bed.

It's not what it sounds like.

As Mary, I used to do a lot of singing in the first part of the show, then there would be a long gap while Jesus was getting betrayed, tried and whipped, during which time I wasn't on stage. So, I would lie down on the bed to rest. I don't think that it was ever used for much else.

When you entered the theatre by the stage door, you would be greeted by Charles, probably the most famous stage doorman in London, as he had been at the Palace Theatre for many years. When he finally retired, the Evening Standard asked him what was the best thing that had happened in all the time that he been working at the Palace and he replied, "Whenever Dana Gillespie came in."

Thank you, Charles.

Mine was definitely the best dressing room in the house, though I'm amazed that anybody could get in the door as the room was permanently filled with people smoking dope. Sometimes, in the interval, or definitely after the show, it became the venue for a major social event. Everyone used to drop in – cast members and friends, celebrity guests – though there was one couple who didn't turn up.

It was the evening that Bowie and Angie came to the show. Ziggymania was at its peak, and David was one of the biggest stars in the country. Front row seats were reserved for them, and I told all the cast that they would be there. This proved to be something of a mistake, because they walked out during the interval. It really wasn't Bowie's kind of thing at all, and I made some comment about this in an interview once. Angie must have seen it because she wrote me an email saying, "Darling Dana, I never knew that you had been so upset that we left in the interval. I'm mortified. Please forgive me."

I replied, saying that I was sure it was Bowie's choice to leave, not hers, and that in any case I would always forgive her.

Superstar was an important breakthrough for me, and I was delighted to receive many very positive reviews. "For musical pleasure, the honours go to Dana Gillespie's Magdalene. A straight torch performance sung beautifully." (The Times), "Only Dana Gillespie manages to ride the storm, a romantic self-centred Mary impervious to all but her own problems." (The Telegraph), "The big surprise of the show is Dana Gillespie. She has a breathy vocal style perfectly suited to these questioning songs, and her positive work contributes a tremendous feeling to the musical credibility of the show." (Melody Maker).

*

The year I was in the show was spent having a roaring time, enjoying London in style, and hanging out with fun people. This ranged from high flying rock 'n' roll parties, to working during my free time with David Charkham and Joan Littlewood at the Stratford East Theatre. It was Joan who had asked me if I could keep an eye on Lionel Bart, as he only lived five streets from me in South Kensington; an area that Lionel used to call 'our draughty hallway'.

Lionel had made millions, and then pretty well lost the lot, due to riotous living, bad management, and poor judgement of character. His parties in the Fulham Road were notorious. When things got really bad, financially, he moved to a little crash pad in Reece Mews, a stone's throw away from me, and we used to meet very often for lunch at the Daquise Polish restaurant underneath the marvellous oil painting by Feliks Topolski.

Lionel once gave me a beautiful leather-bound book in which we planned to write our jointly-penned songs for a new musical. He dedicated it "To the ongoing success of the Bart Gillespie songbook", and I still have it. Sadly, it only contains one song, as it often seemed that he'd do anything rather than sit down and write more songs.

David Charkham (known affectionately to me as 'Charky'), Lionel, and I got on so well that we became a trio of pals known as 'The Three Shitters'. Hardly a day went by when we didn't meet or eat together, or generally misbehave. We used to wander around the cafes of South Kensington to pass the time until either Charky and I had to leave for the theatre, or Lionel had to keep a liaison with a young man.

Because we were seen out together so often, the press sometimes got the wrong end of the stick. Ridiculously, the entertainment correspondent in the Daily Mail asked, "Do I detect the stirrings of a romance in the bachelor breast of 43-year-old Lionel Bart? I'm told it's a case of the Bart beating fonder towards the statuesque Miss Dana Gillespie, whose splendid 44-26-37 proportions fill the role of Mary Magdalene in the West End production of Jesus Christ Superstar."

Poor Lionel couldn't come out and be openly gay. Obviously, everyone in show business knew he was gay, but the newspapers weren't about to report it. He once told me that he only slept with two women in his life – me and Alma Cogan – and that each time as he was "about to do the biz, he lost the popcorn". He said it was the smell of women he didn't like, and that he tolerated me because I always smelt strongly of jasmine oil. I felt sorry for Alma because I think she thought she was going to become Mrs Bart, and we never had the nerve to tell her he was gay. I knew all along that I wasn't ever going to be walking down the aisle with him.

Lionel hated waking up alone on a Sunday morning, so he would often send himself a telegram on Saturday afternoon, which would be delivered that evening, usually by a lad from the Post Office wearing a jaunty little hat. Invariably, the same young man would be there when I'd come over on Sunday morning for breakfast or lunch. Lionel once told me that everything he did was with love, and that he'd loved everyone he'd slept with. He had a big heart and a huge circle of friends, and his house was permanently full of people. It would be quite normal to go round to see him, and find someone like Diana Dors or Sean Connery there. Which reminds me…

On one occasion, Joan Littlewood was putting on a variety show at the Stratford East Theatre to help raise money to keep the place going, and Charky and I were both involved. For some reason, "The Canary", as Lionel used to call Connery, was there, and within 24 hours, he was round at my place. He'd just broken up with the actress Adrienne Corrie, and we became friends.

Sean would often come round to borrow books from me. Of course, once he got to the Bunker he didn't just borrow books, but at least he was between wives at the time.

Funnily enough, quite a few years later, I was performing at the Edinburgh Festival, and Sean happened to be there at the same time due to his involvement with the Scottish National Party. One day, I arrived to do the soundcheck to be told that Sean Connery had just called and left a message. Thinking they were taking the piss, I ignored it. But, the next day, he called again and this time I picked up the phone and the unmistakeable voice said "Hello". It was good to hear from him again, and after that he would meet me in London occasionally, when he was on his way to Spain or Hollywood, and had time to visit an old flame.

I'm not usually one to land up with well-known actors, but I did have another interesting interlude with one.

Mike Hewitson, Elton John's then personal assistant, took me to a party at Dave Clark's flat over the Curzon cinema in Mayfair. It was an absolutely star-studded occasion, Paul McCartney, Ringo Starr, Tony Curtis, Dusty Springfield, Nina Simone, everyone was there. Apparently, at the end of the evening, Mike was asking where I was, as he wanted to take me home, and someone replied, "Dana? Oh yes, she left with Michael Caine!"

I should explain.

The party was on the first floor, so when you entered the flat, you left your coat in the cloakroom next to the loo, then made your way upstairs to where all the action was happening. Tony Curtis had brought some hash brownies along, and these were being passed around, so the mood was pretty relaxed. At some point in the evening, I went downstairs to use the loo, and at that moment the doorbell rang. As I opened the door, standing there was Michael Caine, who gave me a passionate kiss and said, "Let's get out of here." As a result, I never went back to the party, and Michael missed it altogether.

He was staying in a flat in Grosvenor Square, and was just breaking up with one of his many girls, so it wasn't like I was poaching a man who was already taken. Anyway, I stayed for the weekend and we remained horizontal for 48 hours, almost non-stop. What can I say? He used to be known, accurately, as the "Mr Stud" of London.

Another amusing experience I had whilst in Superstar was appearing in the Christmas special of the TV show 'Til Death Us Do Part'. This was a popular sitcom, at the time, about the family of an extraordinary character called Alf Garnett – a white working-class reactionary bigot – and his long-suffering family. There is no way such a programme would be shown these days, but in the late sixties and early seventies, it was one of the most popular shows on television.

In the episode I appeared in, Alf took his family to see Superstar, and then – after the show – went to a local pub where he bumped into Paul Nicholas and me. Our sequence was filmed at The Coach and Horses pub on Greek Street in Soho, which was where the Superstar cast would often go when the curtain came down. For many years, the pub had been run by an extraordinary character called Norman Balon, known to all as 'Britain's rudest landlord'; it was also the setting for 'Jeffrey Bernard is Unwell', the play by Keith Waterhouse made famous by Peter O'Toole.

The TV programme generated a lot of column inches in the tabloids because of a piece of over-zealous censorship by the BBC. Under the headline "Censored! Alf's Big Boob", the News of the World (otherwise known as the News of the Screws because of its weekly coverage of celebrity bonking) reported on 24th December 1972, "The ample 44 inch bust of Dana Gillespie has been censored out of TV's 'Til Death us do Part' on Boxing Night... 'I don't know how the BBC censors work but they have cut out any sort of sexual connotation between Alf Garnett and myself', she says then explained how the scene was shot before the censors' scissors snipped her anatomy. 'Alf recognises me in a Soho pub... I'm wearing jeans and a tight unbuttoned shirt covered by a shawl. When I take the shawl off, his eyes pop... and what with his bald head and my tight shirt, it looks as if 3 big oranges are together on the screen. During rehearsals I thought it was very funny, but a few days ago I saw a playback of the show and I'm only wearing the shawl. It seems sad to me that the whole comic point of the scene with my bust was lost because the ending has been cut.'"

*

I had a few "stalker" incidents while doing Superstar, one being a man who said his name was Jack. He used to ring me up and say he'd got nine inches of throbbing whatever to give me. God knows how he got my telephone number, and usually I'd just hang up, but one time I agreed to meet him on Battersea Bridge. We arranged a time, and then I sent Bindon instead. Funnily enough, Biffo came back and told me there was nobody there.

On another occasion, Jack rang up and said he had seven inches to give me. I said, "Hang on Jack, what's happened to the other two inches?"

I fell about laughing and hung up on him, and never heard from him again.

For a long time in the seventies, when I was touring with my band, I used to introduce a song called 'Do the Spin' by telling the story of Jack and his nine-inch offering. I would say that I'd never met him personally, and would ask if any member of the audience was the same Jack. You'd be amazed, because nearly all the men would put their hands up. So I'd say, "Well, there is one way to prove that you really are Jack, come on up and show us your nine inches!"

Only a few times did somebody actually have the bottle to get up on stage, but I never checked out their credentials.

Not many of us in Superstar had done much theatre work before, and as it was an energetic show – which involved climbing up the side ramps of the unusual stage set – it required performers who were young, could sing and dance, and could generally leap about a lot. This increasingly became a problem for me because of my knee.

After a year in Superstar, I ultimately had to leave because the pain in my knee got so bad; it was so excruciating that I wince thinking about it even now. By the end of my run in the show, I was going on stage tightly bandaged and taking pain killers to get me through. In the end, I was given two weeks off to rest my leg because I could hardly walk, and immediately got on a plane to Mustique. The effect of walking on sand and generally taking a break helped, but within a month of being back on stage, my knee started playing up again.

I tried everything I could think of – including a faith healer – to improve my knee, but I was running out of options. Some of my co-stars commented on how unfortunate it was that the lead character in Jesus Christ Superstar was unable to help. It certainly felt as though I needed a miracle.

A second trip to Mustique was organised on medical grounds, but I hated leaving the show in the hands of my understudy. Knowing that I couldn't carry on like this, I would then sing from the side of the stage, taking only a few agonising steps into the limelight. Doctors were consulted and, in the end, it was decided I should have a cartilage operation. So, with a heavy heart, and after 13 months of being 'Mary', I handed in my notice at the Palace Theatre and went straight onto the operating table.

Recovery from the operation took several months, but my recuperation was aided by having a new man in my life, the antique dealer Leslie Spitz. We had first met at the Speakeasy in Marylebone, which was the club everyone went to in those days. Filled with pop stars, rock and Blues musicians, record business executives and good time girls, it was known as the fun place to hang out in, once the curtain came down in theatreland. At the time, I was still performing in Superstar so limped into The Speak with my walking stick. Despite the fact that I was physically incapacitated, it was not long before this short, dark, slim-built man came over to talk to me. He was very amusing, and it was one of those moments when you know that you have a really strong connection with somebody.

Not waiting for him to call me the next day, instead I called him and asked if he'd like to come and see the show. It was arranged that he would come to see me backstage after the performance and drive me home. As he helped me into the car, I knew we had some kind of future together. On our way home, we got stuck in a terrible traffic jam, and to pass the time he handed me a fruit that I'd never seen before. It was a passion fruit and I had no idea how to eat it, so when I asked him what I was meant to do with this crinkled brown thing, the size of a billiard ball, he bit a hole in it and handing it to me he said, "Now, you suck it."

And so I did.

This was the start of a marvellous relationship that was to last for over 45 years, beginning at a time when I was still young and wild. Within a week of meeting him, I had left Superstar and gone straight into hospital for my cartilage operation. Leslie was the perfect person to come and visit me in my sickbed. He was always upbeat, funny, and cheerful, and the day before the operation he brought with him as many 'sex with amputee' magazine stories as he could find, saying that he'd still love me even if they cut my leg off. What devotion!

*

One day in February 1974, I got a call inviting me to go for an audition for the National Theatre production of Shakespeare's 'The Tempest' with Sir John Gielgud. Not my usual kind of gig, but I couldn't resist a challenge. In addition to Sir John, who was to play Prospero, many other well-established British actors had already signed up to perform, including Arthur Lowe and Julian Orchard.

As I was still on the books of Mainman, I went to the audition in a limo. On arrival at the theatre, I met Sir Peter Hall, the director, who handed me the text of the Tempest and invited me to read for the role of Juno.

My reading was pretty awful, and when I'd finished, I said to Sir Peter that I was sorry that I wasn't very good. He agreed, but then asked me to do the whole thing again but this time to sing the words. So I just invented a melody, and the moment I'd finished singing it, he said, "Right, the part is yours", and suggested that all the sections where my role of Juno appears would be sung.

During the rehearsals, the limo would be waiting outside for me during my lunch break, so I would ask the driver to take me down the King's Road. There, I'd meet Bindon in a pub, have a tomato juice while he told funny stories, then get back in the limo to go back to rehearsals. Sometimes, I'd see Arthur Lowe and Julian Orchard, and even Sir John, coming out of the tube while I was poncing around like a rock star in my huge car. They must have thought I was a complete arsehole.

Sir John was famous for never knowing anyone's real name, and often called you by the part that you were playing. So he would call me Juno, or Lovey, or Darling. I understood why he did that; how could he be expected to remember such a huge cast? In any case, I wasn't a pretty young boy, so why should he remember my name?

I shared a dressing room with two other actresses, Julie Covington and Jenny Agutter. Julie went on to star in 'Rock Follies' and to have a hit with the original version of 'Don't Cry For Me, Argentina' from the musical Evita. Jenny was already well-known for her roles in film adaptations of 'The Railway Children' and 'Walkabout', the latter directed by Nicholas Roeg, whom I would work with a few years later.

Every night, Julie and I would sway above the stage out of sight for the first 30 minutes, sitting on and strapped into elaborate thrones suspended by ropes. Mine was built like a huge peacock, and I was dressed up in a ridiculous corsety thing. There I would be, dangling high above Sir John as he ponced away in his best Shakespearian voice. Now, I hate heights, and so every night I was scared shitless as we oscillated around above the stage. Eventually, we 'Goddesses' had to come down from the heavens, and we would be slowly lowered to the ground. Sometimes, I was quite queasy by the time I got down to terra firma.

After the opening night, Micky Feast had (probably) been celebrating so heavily that he completely overslept and missed the second night. Just before the show was due to start, there was total panic because we had no Ariel. He was supposed to fly on stage with one leg in a sort of metal stirrup, but he wasn't there. The poor understudy was pretty well thrown into the harness and pushed out onto the stage. I have no idea how he got through it, because you don't expect to be stepping in for a leading character on the second night! Luckily, they let Micky off, and he never did it again. Actors are all quite fragile people, so it was nice that they didn't sack him instantly. I had good reason to be grateful for their forgiveness, myself, a few weeks later…

Sometimes, there would be a break in the run, to allow different productions to be performed at the theatre. Whenever this happened, and we had a few days off, I'd leap on a plane to go and join the Mainman circus, either in New York or wherever Bowie

144

was playing, to do some serious hanging out, plus a lot of shopping with Angie.

I'm afraid that I did something which, to this day, I am very embarrassed about. When you have a contract with the National Theatre, you're not meant to leave the country once the show has opened, but on one occasion I did not tell them I was off to Toronto for the weekend to see Bowie. My understudy was called Judith Paris, and I thought it would be OK to go, and for her to take my place in the show. What I hadn't allowed for was that poor Judith was involved in a car accident while I was away. The producers contacted me and said that I was needed, but I couldn't get back from Toronto in time for the next performance, so Judith being a real trooper, and professional, managed to make it through the show. The producers can't have been happy with me, and I had to own up and admit that I was not in England so was in breach of my contract. They didn't say anything, but I knew everyone just thought that this was what to expect from some rockstar twit. The National Theatre never hired me again, and I can't really blame them.

10: THE MAINMAN YEARS

From the moment we first met, Angie and I were like soul sisters, and it was great to have another really good friend that I could hang out with. When I was in Superstar, she and Bowie were in a rented house in Oakley Street, Chelsea, only a short stroll down the road from me. There wasn't much special about the house except that the bed was in a sunken section of their bedroom, named 'The Pit' by Angie. People would sit around and carry on talking while David and Angie lay on the bed, and it was almost as though visitors were being granted an audience. Of course, other things used to sometimes happen in The Pit, but I'm not saying any more.

Marc Bolan would visit, and I remember David and Marc often being together, sometimes at my place or at Oakley Street, lying on the floor cutting up magazines or books to create ideas for lyrics. This was William S. Burroughs' cut-up technique, famously demonstrated by David in the Alan Yentob BBC television documentary, 'Cracked Actor'.

The basement flat underneath David and Angie's place was occupied by David's clothes designer Freddie Burretti and his girlfriend, Daniella Parmar. This was very convenient for David, who could pop downstairs to get his clothes fitted, and often when I arrived at the house, I'd find David being measured by Freddie for a new outfit. Many of the costumes for David and the Spiders during the Ziggy period were made by Freddie. Angie would go down to Liberty, the high-end fashion store in Soho, and would come back with brightly-coloured materials for Freddie to create the costumes with. On the famous 'Top of the Pops' appearance, when David sang 'Starman', Freddie made David's quilted jumpsuit and the costumes for the Spiders, and he also made David's ice-blue suit which he wore in the 'Life on Mars' video.

David had wanted to promote Freddie as a singer, in a band called Arnold Corns, and gave him the stage name of Rudi Valentino. They issued a single featuring early versions of 'Hang On To Yourself' and 'Moonage Daydream', both of which were to appear on the Ziggy Stardust album, and a follow-up single on which Mick Ronson, Trevor Bolder and Woody Woodmansey all played. The basic problem with the whole project was that Freddie couldn't sing. He had the looks but sounded awful, and the project was soon abandoned. David still, however, liked the idea of having his songs performed by an alter ego, and everything changed for him on the 6th of July 1972 when he performed 'Starman' on the aforementioned 'Top Of The Pops'.

In August 1972, I went to see David and the Spiders rehearsing with Lindsay Kemp at the Rainbow Theatre in Finsbury Park, and stayed on to see one of the shows. The stage was covered in scaffolding, with ladders leading up to different levels from where David would sing whilst Lindsay's mime troupe contorted their bodies around the set. You can see moments from the show in Mick Rock's promo video for 'John I'm only Dancing', which he was filming while I was there. In January 2020, I was invited to perform at a Bowie tribute event in Rome, and shared the stage with two dancers who replicated the dance moves of the Kemp group all those years earlier.

My Superstar commitments meant that I wasn't able to see more of Bowie's shows on the Ziggy Stardust/Aladdin Sane tours. His touring schedule was intense, taking in trips to the States and Japan as well as around the UK, and I would sometimes go a couple of months without seeing him. However, I was with him and Defries the day before the famous Hammersmith show on 3rd July 1973, so I knew in advance that David was going to kill off the character of Ziggy.

Whilst my understudy sang the part of Mary at the Palace Theatre, I joined the crowd in Hammersmith to see Ziggy's last stand, and count myself lucky to have been there to witness it. Poor Woody and Trevor didn't know what was going to happen until they were on stage and heard the 'This is the last show we'll ever do' speech, which must have been awful for them. The concert was filmed by D.A. Pennebaker, the same guy who had made the Dylan 'Don't Look Back' film in 1965.

A party was held at the Café Royal off Piccadilly Circus straight after the 'retirement' show. The evening became known as 'The Last Supper', and there is now a cocktail bar at the Café Royal marking the event, appropriately named 'Ziggy's'. It was a star-studded affair, which included the McCartneys, Mick Jagger, Lou Reed, Peter Cook and Dudley Moore, Elliott Gould, Tony Curtis, Ryan O'Neill, Rod Stewart, Keith Moon, Jeff Beck, Cat Stevens,

Barbra Streisand, Sonny Bono, and many others. There is a nice photo of 'me and my mates' taken that evening, where I am sitting with Mick Jagger, Lou Reed, David, and Ronno, together with Jeff Beck, who had played a couple of songs with the band at the Hammersmith show. Allegedly, he was so unhappy with his performance that he insisted that those numbers were deleted before the show was released as a record and video.

In the previous 18 months, David and the Spiders had performed almost 200 shows, starting in small venues such as the Toby Jug, a pub in Tolworth, Surrey. After crossing the States twice and playing nine shows in Japan, they finished an extended tour of England and Scotland by regularly playing two sold-out concerts a night. David was knackered, and it was agreed that a planned tour of the States would be cancelled.

A few months later, when David was recording his 'Pinups' album, Angie and I flew over to France and stayed with him at the Chateau d'Hérouville. It was an extraordinary old place, not too far from Paris but in the middle of nowhere. Chopin and George Sand had lived there in the past, and Van Gogh had painted it (well, pictures of it to be totally accurate), and in the sixties, it had been converted into a residential recording studio. Elton recorded several albums there, including 'Goodbye Yellow Brick Road', and it was getting a great reputation in England as the place to go and record. Bowie went back, a few years later, to record his 'Low' album. There had always been a rumour that it was haunted, but I didn't see anything while I was there.

Angie and I flew in on a Sunday morning and stayed for about 36 hours, as I had to be back on stage – with Jesus – on Monday evening. Although we weren't there long, Angie and I managed to act outrageously, with the result that music journalist Charles Shaar Murray, who was reporting for New Musical Express, assumed (wrongly) that we were lesbian lovers. Yes, we did walk around with our arms around each other, or with arms linked, but that was to stop me falling over whilst tottering around on the high heels Angie insisted I wear. We were dressed to the nines, with Angie looking like a whippet and me dressed at my most voluptuous, and were having a whale of a time. Lesbian lovers? No, that's not true.

While we were at the Chateau, we hung out with the band and ate with them, and even sat in the control room for a bit, but I can't remember which songs they were recording. The album was a collection of hits by David's favourite musicians from the 60's: The Who, Pink Floyd, The Easybeats, Them, Mojos, and other great bands from that time. The story was that David simply didn't have any new material to record, having just completed his breakthrough 18-month Ziggy Stardust/Aladdin Sane tour, but still had to satisfy his contractual obligation to produce another album.

Getting David together with Twiggy for the 'Pinups' album cover shot was a great idea. The picture was taken by Justin de Villeneuve, who was Twiggy's husband at the time, and was originally intended for the cover of Vogue until David said he wanted it for his record sleeve. David and Twiggy's 'masks' for the photo were done by a really good friend of mine called Pierre La Roche. He was responsible for a lot of David's makeup in the Ziggy Stardust/Aladdin Sane period, including the golden sphere David wore on his forehead, and the iconic red-and-blue lightning bolt painted across Bowie's face on the cover of the Aladdin Sane album. Later on, he did the makeup for the Rocky Horror Picture Show.

Pierre lived near me, in Edith Grove, and I used to go and see him a lot. He was a very striking-looking guy with long hair, and he spoke with a strong French accent. Men didn't have makeup artists like Pierre at that time, so what he and David did was quite ground-breaking. So much so, that Mick Jagger hired him to do his makeup on the 1975 Rolling Stones tour.

On the back of the 'Pinups' album were photos taken by Mick Rock, along with David's handwritten notes, "These songs are among my favourites from the '64-'67 period of London". This was the time when the two of us would spend hours hanging out together in the coffee bars of Soho, listening to the latest hits.

My favourite song on the album was the single 'Sorrow', originally recorded by the Merseybeats, or the Merseys as they later became known. I saw David perform it at the Marquee in what was known as 'The Nineteen Eighty Floor show', a TV special made for American television, in which he sang it to his friend, Amanda Lear. She was a very glamorous blonde who was a regular in the gossip columns due to her well-publicised friendships with several rock stars. There had always been a rumour that she had been born a man and had undergone a sex-change in 1963, allegedly paid for by Salvador Dali. Angie once told me that she had some kind of fling with David, but I can't confirm or deny this.

I always liked Amanda. The story I heard was that she had been born Alain, but had changed her name to Peki d'Oslo after the operation, before finally adopting the name Amanda Lear with which she had a successful modelling and singing career. She never confirmed or denied the sex-change story, saying, "It makes me mysterious and interesting. There is nothing the pop world loves more than a way-out freak."

Some might say that would be a good description of Bowie at the time.

Bowie always had something of a penchant for the exotic, if that is the right word for Amanda. A couple of years later, in Berlin, he hooked up with her friend, the transsexual Romy Haag. That was about the time when Angie went out there to try, unsuccessfully, to salvage some kind of friendship with him when their marriage was falling apart.

Going back to the Marquee show, it was filmed over three days, but I only went to one of them. Lionel Bart was my escort for the evening, which once again got the press hopelessly confused. Melody Maker reported, "Showbiz romantics of the year Lionel Bart and Dana Gillespie made their dramatic entrance."

Much more interesting was David's duet on the old Sonny and Cher song 'I've Got You Babe', which he sang with Marianne Faithfull. She wore a nun's outfit that was open at the back, showing everything. It is not obvious, when watching the show itself, though it was clearly very distracting for Aynsley Dunbar, who was trying to play the drums behind her.

People have often asked me what it was like to be around David in 1972/3, when Ziggymania took off, and he became one of the best-known pop stars in the country. The strange thing is that, at the time, I didn't see any real change in him at all. He was just a good friend who happened to be doing rather well. Admittedly, I wasn't with them every day, but when I used to visit most Sundays, both David and Angie were the same friends as before. While it was obviously an exciting time for David, who was at long last finding fame and success after many years of failure, to me he was still the same David Jones that I had known for the last nine years. It was as if David Bowie/Ziggy Stardust was an alter ego who would appear when he was out in public or performing, but who would be left outside when he came home.

A lot changed when he moved to America, but not yet.

*

One of Tony Defries's sayings was that if you wanted to do anything in the music business, you had to go to America and make it there. David was obviously more ready to go than me, as he'd had several big hits and was fast becoming one of the top stars in Britain. My Superstar commitments meant that the 'Weren't Born A Man' album hadn't yet been released, as there would be no time for me to promote it. As a result, it was agreed that David would go ahead, and I would follow on later.

He moved into a huge suite in the Sherry Netherland Hotel overlooking Central Park, one of the top hotels in New York, together with Angie, Zowie, and his nanny Marion. Things were hotting up in America for Mainman and Bowie, and I began to feel left out and stranded while all my pals were raving it up in the Big Apple.

In 1973, Defries finally arranged for me to go to New York to sign my contract with RCA Records. RCA was then one of the biggest record companies in the world with Elvis Presley on their books, amongst many others, and I was looking forward to meeting the head of the company.

When I was finally presented to Rocco Laginestra, President of RCA Records, I told him how pleased I was to be signing to his label, as they had three artists I greatly admired under contract. Naturally, Elvis was one, but I mentioned how much I also liked Jerry Reed and Charlie Rich.

Rocco looked rather surprised because, although he knew that Jerry Reed was a wizard country and western guitarist, he hadn't heard of Charlie. This was quite shocking to me as Charlie had recorded one of my favourite songs, 'Mohair Sam', and it seemed odd that the boss of the company wouldn't know the name of one of his artists. Rocco called in his secretary and asked about Charlie

152

Rich, and she returned some minutes later to say, "I'm sorry, sir, his contract ran out three weeks ago, so he is no longer on the label."

This was maybe a warning sign that RCA weren't going to give my new album the promotion it needed. Nevertheless, I felt pretty confident that Mainman would always be there to give them a push. As for Charlie Rich, the moment he changed record label, he had a huge smash hit with 'Behind Closed Doors'. Sometimes, a change of record label can make all the difference, but it does help if the man at the top knows what is happening at the bottom…

Rocco was kind enough to give me all of Elvis's RCA albums, and arranged for me to see Elvis perform live at the Nassau Coliseum, just outside New York City. It was the early seventies, and he was starting to get a little bit bloated, but it was still good to see him in fine voice. Somebody from RCA took me, and we had really good seats. Towards the end of the show, Elvis said something like, "I'm staying in the Holiday Inn round the back."

He didn't actually say his room number, but he definitely let it be known where he would be later, maybe hoping that all the girls would rush round there after the show. It could have just been a ploy, of course, and he might have been staying at another hotel, and said it just to get them to go to the wrong place. Knickers were constantly being thrown on stage while he was singing, though I didn't throw mine. In fact, I never wore knickers if I was wearing a skirt, unless they were Janet Reger's best.

When 'Weren't Born A Man' was finally released, it was agreed that I should initially promote it back in England. 'Andy Warhol' was chosen as the first single, and I was sent off around the country to appear on local commercial radio stations, with Angie alongside me. I was quoted in one of the music papers at the time as saying, "We will be touring Britain, then Europe for six weeks, before going to America for another two months. Angie will make sure I avoid all the pitfalls. I'm such a sucker. I will have to be guarded, in case I meet the wrong people."

Saying I was a sucker does seem a rather unfortunate choice of expression.

Mainman had to find things to keep Angie busy, and to stop her spending too much money. The idea of sending her out on tour with me was to keep her out of David's hair, so he could carry on getting up to mischief in America. He certainly became pretty wild when fame arrived, and like any new rock star, he took every opportunity to satisfy his sexual appetite.

Angie and I set off to tour the UK and Europe, armed with copies of the 'Andy Warhol' single. It was just the two of us on the road, occasionally accompanied by a man from the RCA promotions team. A series of appointments was arranged for us, and all we had to do was to be at the radio station at the appointed hour. What an absolute hoot. We would walk in, both dressed provocatively, and would literally see the disc jockey thinking, 'Holy Shit!'.

We would egg each other on to be naughty, and could see the DJ worrying about what we might say on air. It was lots of fun and we really enjoyed it. Unfortunately, I don't think it helped to sell many records.

Although she called herself Angie Bowie, she was – of course – actually Angie Jones as David never legally changed his name. I remember once, when she wanted to do some modelling, she called herself Jip Jones. She was very elegant and could look stunning if you like that boyish whippet-like figure, but she was never really cut out for the discipline of modelling. Being a model, you've actually got to be on call the whole time; you can't just be swanning off because somebody is having a party or doing a concert down the road. So she gave it up.

It was then time to go back to New York. Mainman had moved most of its operations Stateside, and had very swanky offices on Park Avenue. Defries encouraged Bowie to behave like a star, with a personal assistant and a 24-hour limo, and he took to it like a duck to water. Many of the people who joined Bowie's entourage and worked for Mainman came from Andy Warhol's 'Pork' show, which had absolutely captivated David when he had first seen it in New York. When the show transferred to London, David and I – together with Angie, Defries and Freddie Burretti – went to see it at the Roundhouse in Camden Town, and once the run was over David suggested to Defries that they hire some of the people who had been involved, which is how Tony Zanetta, Cherry

Vanilla, Leee Black Childers and Wayne County came to join Mainman.

Tony Zanetta, who played the Warhol role in Pork, went on to become Defries's right-hand man, and was road manager on David's American Ziggy/Aladdin Sane and Diamond Dogs tours.

Cherry Vanilla was, and still is, a fabulous woman. Loud and sassy, you couldn't miss her as she had bright red hair, which was very unusual in those days. Officially, she was Bowie's 'publicist', and her marketing technique famously involved offering a blow-job to any disc jockey who would play his records. She was bubbly, effervescent, and had a mad horizontal life, maybe even more mad than mine. Not many people had tattoos in those days, but she had cherries tattooed just above her boobs, and she made sure that the tops of her dresses were low enough so you could see them. She is a total original.

Leee Black Childers was a peroxide blond who was also a member of Warhol's Factory. He was appointed Vice President of the Mainman office in New York, as well as being David's 'personal photographer'. He also got involved in organising some of David's tours. Sadly, he is no longer on this planet.

Wayne County was one of the more extraordinary characters who used to hang around the Mainman offices, and that is saying something. He is known as the first transgender singer in rock, and I got to know him quite well. He was always outrageous and outspoken, and once said, "I used to work for David Bowie, and we had a very brief fling, but he was ripping me off like crazy. He took my song 'Queenage Baby' and changed it around to 'Rebel Rebel'. Then he took my 'Wayne at the Trucks' show and changed it to 'Diamond Dogs'. Oh, it goes on and on. Plus, he's a horrible kisser!"

Wayne later became known for recording songs that could never be played on the BBC, such as 'Fuck off', 'Toilet Love', 'Fucked By The Devil', and 'Goddess Of Wet Dreams'. In the late 1970's, he changed his name to Jayne, and I saw him a few years later when Steve Strange put on a show in Islington which Wayne/Jayne performed at. He came on stage wearing a red nylon Baby Doll see-through shortie nighty, showing his recently acquired tits. There was a party after the show, and as I was chatting to him, I said, "Excuse me, but I have never felt false tits before, so may I?" and he said yes fine, so I had a quick feel. Rock solid, they were, absolutely rock solid.

Tony, Cherry, Lee and Wayne/Jayne were all part of the Mainman circus, but were by no means the only ones. The more quirky and weird and wonderful they were, the happier everyone was, especially Defries. Image really mattered, and the Mainman logo became iconic. We had T-shirts, postcards and stickers made up, and we were all busy getting the name out there, putting stickers up wherever we went.

David and Angie invited me into their spacious suite at the Sherry Netherland Hotel, and I stayed with them for a couple of months. Their three-year-old son Zowie and his nanny, Marion, were also there. In his teenage years, Zowie called himself Joey, but now calls himself Duncan Jones and has become a successful film director. David, Angie and I all had our own rooms, but didn't usually sleep in them; it was a bit like musical beds!

Mick Jagger would often come over to hang out when he was in town alone, as he was staying across the road at the Plaza Hotel. David had a grand piano moved into the living room, and on one occasion while David played guitar, Mick and I accompanied him, duetting on piano. We were just mucking around and having fun, and played until we saw the dawn come up.

Angie didn't mind if I slept in David's bed, because we were best friends, 'so what's mine is yours'. You have to remember that she met David when they were both having an affair with the same guy, Calvin Mark Lee. They were both very open about who they saw, and slept with; Angie once said that jealousy doesn't enter into her life.

There is a story in Angie's 'Backstage Passes' book, which begins with the wonderful line, 'I was there the time Mick got his pecker up...', in which she describes in graphic (and somewhat imaginative) style what happened when Mick Jagger came round to the suite at the Sherry Netherland one evening when she and I were there. I won't go into detail, suffice it to say that Angie describes Mick as, "...a billy goat... He's like David, he'll fuck anything!"

According to Angie, "Dana and Mick were having an affair at the time."

Okay, my memory is a little hazy of what went on then. So maybe we did sleep together a few times, but that's not what I call an affair, that's what I call a bit of a fling. And, then again, who didn't sleep with Mick? It was no big thing, though for the avoidance of any doubt, I am NOT making any comment on Mick's equipment here, or Keith Richards' famous description of it.

As mentioned, Mick was staying across the road at the Plaza, and he did come over to visit quite often. Everyone was so out of it, then, that I'm amazed anybody remembers anything. Mick would normally come round to see David, but sometimes he wasn't there (he'd be out clubbing), so if Angie and I were in the suite he'd hang out with us girls.

There was nothing unusual about Mick coming round. Just because he's a rock star, he's no different to anyone else. If you're sitting in your luxury hotel and have mates staying just around the corner, you'll go and hang out with them. So over he came to the Sherry Netherland, we'd order up some room service, and everyone would get stoned, and then whoever was still able to function at the end of the night would end up in bed together. That's just the way it was.

There is a famous story that Angie came in once and found David and Mick naked in bed together, and the press made a huge fuss about it. The erroneous rumour at the time was that Angie had promised to keep quiet about it if Mick would write her a song, and that resulted in 'Angie', the then-current single by the Rolling Stones. Mick once said that it wasn't about her, and Keith Richards (who wrote most of the song) said in his autobiography 'Life' that the song "was not about any particular person." That sounds fair enough, but if someone had written a song as good as that called 'Dana', I would – of course – have claimed it.

In any case, as far as I'm concerned, David and Mick were probably both recovering from a late night and had just crashed in the nearest bed. They were probably too out of it to do anything.

Angie really loved shopping, and when we went out, she used to buy me several pairs of Manolo Blahnik shoes, in different colours. She was the same with clothes. Sometimes, she'd buy me six outfits, same design, different colours. She also bought me about 20 pairs of Janet Reger French knickers, which were made out of the most fantastic coloured silks, edged with bits of white lace. They were kind of horny for those that wanted to push the gusset to one side.

It didn't matter if it was day or night; there was always lots to do. It was shopping all day with Angie, then up all night partying, with everything being bankrolled by Defries and Mainman. God knows how we ever got any sleep. Everything was paid for: first-class airline tickets, 24/7 limos, store cards, the lot. RCA must have given Defries an advance, but neither David nor I bothered to question where the money was coming from; we were too busy having a great time.

After several months living with David and Angie, Mainman finally got me a flat on 58th Street, between 2nd and 3rd Avenues. Moving in was delayed because Iggy Pop and Wayne County had been living there, and the cleaners complained that the place was left in a truly disgraceful condition. It took them three days to clear up the poppers, the shit, the syringes, and all the drug paraphernalia before it was okay for me to move in.

Once I had settled in, I quickly discovered that there was another flat opposite my front door that was occupied by some very busy hookers. Sometimes, I'd find clients waiting on the stairs for their turn to be let in for some action. What they didn't know was that there was a grill in the wall between the two flats, so that if I stood on the edge of my bath I could see into their bathroom. The view was sometimes quite eye-opening.

Mainman was such an exciting company to be with, and there seemed to be no shortage of money. I was put on a weekly wage, and all my expenses, including travel, were covered by the company. Defries really cotton-woolled my life from the daily grind. All I had to do was produce good songs, and so I spent much of my time at the piano or on the guitar.

I was now spending a lot of my time commuting between New York and London.

*

I'd gathered a lot of instruments in the Bunker: a full drum kit, a bass guitar that Bowie had given me, several John Bailey hand-built acoustic guitars, a Martin D41 guitar with abalone shell, and an early Stratocaster bought in Manny's Music store in New York. I had replaced my old Vortexion machine that could record on two tracks with a more modern Revox. As so many of my friends were musicians, they would often drop into the Bunker to hang out and just play, or I'd use it as a rehearsal room. One thing I regret is that I lost the tapes I recorded of Marc Bolan and David Bowie jamming together and knocking out some new songs. They would probably be worth something these days.

I have always disputed the fact there was friction between Bowie and Bolan. They were friends, and I never saw any tension between them. Marc was the first to have real success, when 'Ride A White Swan' reached number 2 in the charts in early 1971, but he had recorded it only a few weeks after playing guitar on David's 'Prettiest Star' single. Mick Ronson followed Marc's guitar part when the track was re-recorded for Aladdin Sane. David even did a light-hearted impersonation of Marc's voice on 'Black Country Rock' on his 'Man Who Sold the World' album. There was always a kind of friendly rivalry between them, but it was other people who invented the alleged bitter competitiveness, presumably just to sell newspapers.

Bowie was much more taken by the New York scene than I ever was. I'm far too European to ever want to live in America, but he was fascinated by the whole shebang, which in many ways had led to the establishment of Mainman. Although I wasn't there when Bowie first met Warhol, because of the connection with all the Pork people – such as Tony Zanetta, Cherry Vanilla and others working for Mainman – someone suggested that we get Warhol's Factory to do the cover of my next album, 'Ain't Gonna Play No Second Fiddle'.

The Warhol Factory was a bit like the Walt Disney studios. Stuff went out under the name of Warhol, but there were several people in the Factory actually producing the artwork. The final screenprint was done by an artist called Richard Bernstein, based on a photograph taken by Terry O'Neill. There were two versions; Tony Defries has one with a blue background, which was the version used for the cover of the album, and I have the other one which is dayglo pink and sickly yellow; not at all the kind of thing I would ever hang on my own walls.

I was at my slimmest, tottering around in my Manolo Blahniks, and everyone was dressed in their wildest outfits as we swung through New York. I was having such an amazing time; I love five-star hotels; I love room service; I love Bloomingdales; I love spending a fortune on home-made Li-Lac Chocolates, and essential oils from Kiehls; and I loved padding around hotels in bare feet when people were dropping in all the time and nobody was paying any bills. Well, obviously, Mainman was, but I wasn't. It must have cost an absolute fortune for this entourage to stay for weeks and weeks and weeks in the Sherry Netherland. It's such a shame that David could never, in later years, admit that he had been having fun; instead he blamed Defries for everything when things started to go wrong.

Angie made pretty disparaging comments about Defries in one of her books, too. In this, I have to differ from her because I instantly adored him, especially when he used to say, "You can have whatever musicians you want, and you can rehearse whenever you want."

Any problem I had to do with the music business, I could ask Defries, and he would sort it out.

Defries had already said that I should get a band together, to tour with, after my knee operation. So the moment I knew I was leaving Superstar, I had asked Simon Phillips, the drummer in the show, if he would leave the show at the same time as me, and happily he said yes. That was the start of him being in my band for the next two years. I had noticed that, on the nights when he wasn't playing in Superstar, the show somehow lacked the fire that was there when he was drumming, and it was amazing that a 16-year-old could have such an impact.

I've always been lucky with the musicians I've used, but the band I had then was *exceptional*, mainly because of Simon. He is an amazing drummer, who has gone on to have a spectacular career, playing with everyone from Asia to Zappa and pretty well everybody in-between.

When he agreed to join my band, he told me that he didn't have a passport, had never tried any drugs, and that he hadn't slept with a woman. I told him to come over to my place after the Saturday night show, and by the time he crawled out on Monday, I had taken care of most his needs. Once he'd got a passport, something that I had not been able to provide for him, he was ready to take on the madness of touring with a Blues band in America. There is a saying in the Music Biz that 'a band is only as good as its drummer', and with Simon onboard our band was definitely flying high.

Travelling with musicians in America was very different to touring in Europe. For example, we had to watch out for Simon, who was still underage, and therefore not meant to be in some of the venues where we were playing, as the drinking laws were very strict. In the end, Defries decided it was more economical to get an American band to work with, as it was costing too much to bring in the British guys constantly.

Once we were on the road, it became clear that we needed a tour manager, and through an introduction from Mainman, I got one, a marvellous gay guy called Darryl Peck. English musicians in America were known for their sexual conquests, as the English accent seemed to turn American girls on, but no one could compete with Darryl's exploits. Every morning at breakfast, I would be falling about with laughter hearing about his nightly sexcapades, which usually seemed to involve truck drivers. Sadly, Darryl is now in that gay funfair in the sky.

One of the band did manage to get lucky during that tour, well almost. I can't now remember which band member it was, which in hindsight is probably a good thing. Anyway, we were playing in a club in New York, and as the evening progressed he became increasingly friendly with a dubious local bird in the audience. When they left the club together, he obviously thought that he was finally going to get a shag, and the rest of us went back to our hotel, looking forward to hearing a report over breakfast the next day.

Apparently, she drove him back to her place, which was in a huge block of flats, and when they arrived she said that she'd really get turned on if he'd tie her up. She had some sort of manacles at the back of her bed, and being the gentleman that he was, he agreed to her request and chained her up. This, however, was not enough to satisfy her because she then requested some coke and amyl nitrate, saying that she had some in the glove compartment of her car. Our intrepid band member set off with the car keys to get the poppers, but when he got in the elevator to go back to her flat, he realised that he didn't know the flat number. Worse still, he couldn't remember which floor it was on, and didn't even know her name.

As you can imagine, we all roared with laughter when he told the story, which certainly made a change from hearing about Darryl's sexploits with guys who looked like members of the Village People. We were, however, more than a little concerned about whether the poor woman was still manacled to the bed in her flat.

While in New York in 1974, I had a residency at a club called Reno Sweeneys, playing ten nights in a row. Reno's was a club a bit like Ronnie Scott's in London, and in the seventies was known as one of the trendiest places in the city. Whilst there, The New York Times gave me a great review, describing me as "a pulsating performer... Mainman artiste, the Baroness Dana Gillespie, made her American debut at Reno Sweeneys... attracting one of the trendier crowds of recent weeks. Leading the list of stellar personalities was none other than Raquel Welch... On the second night of Dana's engagement David Bowie himself was there, entertaining Bob Dylan and Bette Midler at his table."

That was the night I mentioned, earlier, when I had lost my voice, and Biffo wouldn't let Bob Dylan visit me in my dressing room.

After Reno Sweeney's, I went on an American tour with my band. On a few occasions, when I was playing but David didn't have a show, Earl Slick and Michael Kamen from his band came and played with us. Earl played with David a lot in subsequent years, including on his 'Serious Moonlight', 'Heathen', and 'Reality' tours. Many people may remember Michael for co-writing '(Everything I Do) I Do It For You' – the song that Bryan Adams had a huge hit with – but during his career, he played with pretty well everybody, from Aerosmith to Kate Bush, Eric Clapton to Pink Floyd. He also wrote loads of film scores and he should have lived longer, but sadly died of a heart attack in London in 2003.

One gig that wasn't organised too well was in a large venue at Washington University. I got there for the soundcheck and found that I was due to perform in a huge gymnasium, where they probably played basketball. Just before we went on, I remember thinking how quiet it seemed, so I peeped through the curtain and there were only about 20 people there. I'd been mistakenly booked at a weekend when all the students had left for the holidays, and only stragglers who couldn't get home were in the audience. So I'm thinking 'Holy Shit', when my wonderful keyboard player, Larry Luddecke, whispered in my ear, "You know, when this happens, what you do is you go out, and you say to people, 'Please don't worry that there are so few people here. Just remember, in life, some of the best times you will ever have is when there are only two people.'"

So I went out and said that; after which, it went swimmingly. It was a really great concert, with some of the audience almost sitting on stage with the band.

Whilst in Boston, on that tour, I was lucky enough to see my hero, Muddy Waters, with Pinetop Perkins on piano, in a small joint that doesn't exist anymore called 'Paul's Mall'. Clubs like this are a joy as you get to see the performer up close. The ceiling was so low that I could almost put my hand on it, and I got to sit very near to Muddy's feet. The vibe was the same as you used to get in all the great smokey clubs, which provide an intimacy you never get in a big venue. It was a wonderful experience, and one I'll never forget.

On one occasion, we arrived in San Antonio to find a huge banner saying 'Welcome to Dana Gillespie', but immediately above it was another sign saying 'V.D. Seminar starts today'. The two signs weren't connected, but I've always wished I'd taken a photograph of them.

The first time I went to L.A., I had stayed in a cheap motel in Santa Monica, but when I came back at the end of my 1974 tour, I moved into the Hyatt House, known by all musicians and groupies as the 'Riot House'. On the rooftop was a swimming pool where the musicians would recover from the night before. For amusement, people would sometimes ask the Reception to put a call out for 'Alan Wanker', 'Mike Hunt', or 'Isaac Hunt', and everyone by the pool would then piss themselves laughing when the call came over the tannoy.

*

back to those days, I probably drove with him five or six times, and he would usually just sit quietly in the corner of the back seat, looking out of the window. He was hardly eating anything at the time, surviving on a diet of milk and copious amounts of cocaine, and so he used to have very little sleep.

Despite doing loads of coke, he somehow never once did a bad show. He did get thinner and thinner and thinner, and by the time he got to the end of the tour, he was really twitchy and not at all relaxed. How he kept going for the whole tour, and how his voice held up, I have no idea. The show was so exhausting that everyone was worried that David's lifestyle would knock him out before the tour ended. Somehow, he survived it, but by the end of it, he had become so worryingly pale. This was ideal for his role in Nick Roeg's film, 'The Man Who Fell To Earth', and for his next stage character, the Thin White Duke.

In later years, Bowie was reasonably honest about his coke involvement during this period. The cocaine certainly changed him once he got to America, not his basic character but physically. He was tired, he was wired, and he often seemed to have his mind on other things. Defries once said to me that one of the main reasons he and Bowie split was because he could no longer handle Bowie's intake, though I had already seen signs of friction between them. David and Angie always rented homes, but after he was riding high in America, David told me that he wanted to buy somewhere permanent to live but had been told by Defries that he couldn't because there was no money. It had all been spent on recordings, promotion, and running the Mainman company. This was when I first started to see clashes between the two of them, which in time led to the total collapse of their relationship.

It was certainly true that everyone in Mainman was spending money like water, as we all had 24-hour limos at our disposal and personal assistants, whilst all our expenses were being taken care of. Obviously, it couldn't last, and slowly things began to crumble. The gradual demise of Mainman was beginning, and Defries had decided it was time to pull in the financial reins. Sadly, it all came too late for the company to be saved.

The cracks started to appear when bills weren't getting paid, as Mainman was living far beyond its means. The office on Park Avenue was the first to go, together with most of the staff. It had always employed too many people in the office – and I certainly didn't need a personal assistant – but like so many other things, it was an expensive extravagance. One by one, the employees were dropped from the payroll until, in the end, there was just a skeleton staff in London.

By this point, all David seemed to want to do was escape; from his wife, from his manager, and even from his band. He wanted to break free. He was becoming a bigger and bigger star, and I think he started to believe some of the people who had been coming around and saying, 'We can get you a better deal'. His assistant, Corinne, was increasingly being used as a barrier to anyone who tried to get through to him. He needed peace and he needed sleep, but he didn't get much of that either thanks to the cocaine.

By this point, Defries couldn't talk to him, and couldn't deal with his drug madness. The cocaine use was by now out of control, and when Defries came out to Mustique, I was with him when he made his final telephone call to David. Defries said that this just can't go on anymore, and from that point on, whatever legal fights they had were done through lawyers.

Although I'd had loads of fun in America, made lots of friends, and spent a lot of my time partying in-between working with great musicians, I knew that the party was over and it was time for me to come home. As Mainman collapsed, and America became a bittersweet memory – as I always knew it would – it wasn't the end of my world, and I didn't even miss America too much. The sad part for me was when I realised that the people I'd known and loved dearly, in the five years of Mainman's existence, were all going to be scattered across the globe.

Many of them I never saw again.

Bowie headed for Berlin, and Defries moved to Zurich. Angie was having a terrible time too, as she could see that her marriage to David was over, and that left the problem of divorce and custody of their son Zowie. It is always sad when two people can't even talk anymore. At least David always had his music to keep his life together, but it was really hard on Angie as she was losing not just her husband, but her son, her job, and what she thought was her best friend. I felt very sorry for her, but there was nothing I could

11: AIN'T GONNA PLAY NO SECOND FIDDLE

I decided that my next album for Mainman should be in more of a Blues direction, and I called it 'Ain't Going To Pay No Second Fiddle'. People might have thought, from this, that I was complaining about being number two to Bowie in the Mainman stable, but that was not the case. I simply loved the song, which had originally been recorded by Bessie Smith in 1925, with Louis Armstrong on trumpet.

Not feeling quite ready to do a pure 'Blues-only' album, it was certainly more Bluesy than 'Weren't Born a Man'. My view is that Blues is a musical way of life, and it really only works if it can be backed up by years of experiences, both good and bad. Only then can you really *feel* what you're singing from the bottom of your heart. It's when you've been to heaven and hell quite a few times, and you've got some life lesson notches on your belt, that you can start to truly sing the Blues. I still had a long way to go, but at least I was making a start.

Whilst the title track was an old Blues standard, all of the other tracks on the album – other than two – were written by me. One of them was a mad song called 'Get My Rocks Off', by Shel Silverstein, who used to write a lot of the material for Dr. Hook, including 'Sylvia's Mother'. He also wrote 'A Boy Named Sue', a rather unusual hit for Johnny Cash.

No expense was spared for a Mainman artiste, and the LP was issued in a gatefold sleeve with the lyrics of my songs printed inside, together with details of where they had all been written: London, Lisbon, Klosters, and the West Indies. This was something Defries told me to do for some tax reason, having told Bowie to do the same on his Aladdin Sane album – though, in his case, the place names follow the song titles on the label of the record itself. The cover picture was the screenprint of the Terry O'Neill picture of me, done at the Warhol Factory.

Mainman was heavily promoting Mick Ronson as a solo act at the time, as Defries probably felt quite bad that Ronno had been left out in the cold when Bowie killed off Ziggy, and wanted to give him every opportunity to become a star in his own right. There

There was always a fun crowd around me in the studios, and even though it was all quite drug-fuelled, I don't remember anyone getting out of control. However, there was the one time when Phill snorted some PMA thinking it was cocaine – not realising that you had to swallow it – and he ended up doing the whole session with a mighty hallucinogenic headache. Being a real professional, he somehow managed to keep it all together. Remember, nearly all of the great classic rock albums of the sixties and seventies were written while under the influence of some drug or other.

Phill tells stories in his book about our trip to New York to mix the album. Being welcomed at the door of the Bowie suite, at the Sherry Netherland, by a totally naked Angie was clearly not something he was prepared for. He also found having dinner with Angie, Jagger, and me to be a somewhat more extreme experience than he was used to. As he says, "This was high rolling rock 'n' roll."

The album was finally released in November 1974, and got some really positive reviews. Billboard described it as "a vast improvement", and said that "the instrumental backing she receives on this record plays a major part in its success. She sounds more and more like a vocalist in the Bonnie Raitt mould on this record." High praise indeed.

Once the album came out, I went on a promotional tour of the UK. The New Musical Express reviewed my show at Dingwalls in Camden Town, saying, "Her set took away my breath. She rocked, jazzed and bluesed through an hour without a flicker of suspender or sub-Bowie campery. I never looked at the much vaunted tits, being too busy listening to her voice which is strong and very fine, and which she knows how to use. She studied her roots and is confident – and with good reason."

Part of the tour took in some RAF bases where I was playing to people who had no idea about the kind of Blues I was doing, but did get some media attention. One newspaper wrote, "Dana Gillespie is the new forces favourite. Army officers have been ringing Mainman offices in London, asking for as many photographs as possible so that they can send them to troops in Ireland to help keep up their morale. Know what we mean eh?!"

This was a marvellous era for good music venues, some of which are sadly no longer with us. My favourites in London were the Golden Lion, the Nashville Rooms, The Dublin Castle, and – later on – the Hope and Anchor (which everyone called The Grope and Wanker), which is where Punk and Stiff Records really kicked off. There was great music every night, and you could build up a good following. I played regularly at all these places as well as many others around the country.

I accept that I used to dress quite provocatively on stage in those days, though I never really got used to everyone remarking on my shape. One short newspaper article, accompanied by a large photograph of me, was simply headlined, "Dana's Knockers". Why didn't people just listen to the music? There was always a little voice in the back of my head saying, 'You're going to have to get much older, and *then* people will listen to your voice.'

As it happens, things were actually going pretty well for me. I was getting a lot of positive reviews and was voted Number 10 in the Record Mirror poll for the top female singer in 1975. In case you want to know, the nine voted ahead of me were: Olivia Newton-John, Lynsey de Paul, Suzi Quatro, Kiki Dee, Cilla Black, Lyn Paul from The New Seekers, Lulu, Maggie Bell from Stone The Crows, and Polly Brown from Pickettywitch.

I had always wanted to do a more raunchy form of music, but in those days the record companies didn't want their female singers to be too outrageous. They wanted middle-of-the-road girls wearing pretty little dresses. I would certainly never have been able to do a television show singing 'Weren't Born A Man' wearing the outfit from the album cover. How times have changed; nowadays, one is considered to be overdressed when just wearing dental floss.

*

Movie offers were still occasionally coming my way, and the next project was quite an interesting one.

Ken Russell was making a film called 'Mahler', a biopic of the great composer, and I was invited to meet Ken to discuss the role of Anna von Mildenburg, an opera singer and sometime mistress of Mahler. Extraordinarily, I didn't have to audition for the role; I just had to turn up at his house and chat to him. Knowing that the role was to play Mahler's mistress, I decided to dress appropriately: black rubber skirt, little green embroidered top, green suede Manolo Blahnik shoes with very high heels and wraparound ankle straps. I looked quite exotic, and think that's why I got the part.

Ken Russell films are never straightforward and normal, and this was no exception. There was lots of abstract stuff, Nazi symbolism, and crucifixes. It was a very unusual experience, and it proved a weird sort of film. There's not much of a story: the Mahlers take a train journey, and – while on the train – Mahler looks back over his life, as imagined by Ken Russell. Perhaps surprisingly, being that it's a Ken Russell film, there are no lurid bed scenes, even though I'm supposed to be Mahler's mistress.

Robert Powell played the title role, and some of the filming took place in the Lake District, where it was often rather grey and bleak. It was certainly bloody cold, and I felt very sorry for poor Robert, who – for one scene – had to dive into a lake and pretend he was enjoying himself.

In the film, I have to sing a piece of opera which – bearing in mind I was playing an opera singer – was, I suppose, to be expected. Now, I know nothing about opera, and after about a week of training to sing something called 'Das Lied Von Der Erde', it became patently obvious to Ken that I could never sing it as a proper opera singer. In the final production of the film, they actually dubbed my voice. If you ever see the film and wonder why I sound so strange, now you know.

Mahler's wife, Alma, was beautifully played by an actress called Georgina Hale, and she seems to spend the whole film trying to keep the noise down so Mahler can concentrate on writing music. Alma had aspirations to become a composer herself, and in one of my scenes she arrives to deliver a piece that she's written, hoping that Mahler will say it is marvellous. However, Mahler and Anna (me) reject it as being too childish, and make Alma feel small, left out, and unappreciated.

The song that Alma presented for me to sing seemed far too complicated to be called childish, and so I said to Ken that he needed something simpler. He gave me 24 hours to come up with something more suitable, so I rushed home and – that night – wrote the piece of music ('Alma's Song') that was used in the film.

The good news is that I still, occasionally, get some royalties for this.

Ken Russell had a fearsome reputation and I wondered whether I would be overawed working for him. In fact, I found him really easy going; as long as you treated him the same way as everybody else, you'd be OK. I have to admit that I found filming rather boring, as most of the time you would be sitting around waiting for everything to be ready for the next shot. To keep myself occupied, I took to embroidering tapestries; not very rock 'n' roll, but it helped to pass the time.

When the film finally came out, it got mixed reviews, and that is possibly a generous description. It was soon overshadowed, anyway, by Ken Russell's next film, 'Tommy', featuring Elton in his big boots, Ann-Margret swimming in a sea of baked beans, and Tina Turner appearing in a coffin full of syringes!

Once the filming of 'Mahler' was out of the way, my then-boyfriend Leslie and I decided to drive across Morocco from top to bottom in an old VW minibus. The van had no seats in the back, so we were able to sleep there on blankets, robes, kaftans, and other things we'd picked up en route.

On the trip, we decided to take the long scenic route from Tangiers to the south via Ketama, which was known as the hash-producing area. We weren't actually looking for hash (known locally as 'kif'), we just wanted to see the beautiful landscape. With pine trees and small, isolated houses dotted about, it looked rather like rural Switzerland. There were no cars around at all, but every now and then a lone man would leap out from the side of the road holding bags of fresh kif, and would get in the way of the van to make us stop to buy some. After five of these men had nearly fallen under the wheels while trying to wave us down, Leslie said, "Right! The next guy who comes along will get a shock as I'm not going to slow down."

Sure enough, after a few minutes, there was another vendor and, as promised, Leslie put his foot down on the accelerator. The man was so surprised and angry that, as we sped by, he threw the bag of hash at the van in his rage. Unfortunately, my window was wide open, and the whole thing flew in, then burst and spilled the contents all over us. We were totally covered in the stuff, and some of it blinded me for about 20 minutes and stung like crazy. It was in our hair, clothes, all over the place, but we drove on until it seemed safe to stop.

On surveying the mess, we realised we had some top quality pollen-like hash onboard, so fresh it was like a thick powder and the colour of mustard. There was so much of it that we knew we had a bit of a problem. What to do with it all? Well, first we smoked some, but there was a lot, and we realised that taking it all back to Spain, on the ferry, would be far too risky. So we decided to keep a small bag to last for the rest of our journey, and dumped the rest by the side of the road. We then tried to clean up the car as much as possible but, every day for the next two weeks, we kept finding more of it in what were increasingly impossible places to reach. We cleaned and cleaned until we thought it was finally all gone, and slowly made our way back to Spain. This we did with no problem, after which we drove across Spain and France to Calais, from where we took the ferry to England.

We were the first on the boat, and the first off at Dover, but one glance at the van by a customs officer was enough to get us pulled over. I don't blame him, I would have done the same myself if I'd had his job. The van was covered in dust, was full of Moroccan goods, and we probably looked like two hippies who'd been driving for months on a diet of drugs.

A sniffer dog was brought out and got pretty excited as he came near the van, so the customs officer must have thought he was on to something. Two men searched everywhere while the dog kept jumping up and down, and finally the only place left to search was under the driver's seat. We'd never bothered to look there as it was firmly rusted on and was impossible to move. This didn't stop the customs officer, who went off to get a wrench. Thinking quickly, Leslie said to him that if he broke the seat it would be his fault, but if he let Leslie do it, then it would be our fault if it got damaged. Fortunately, the customs officer agreed.

So Leslie climbed into the driver's side and, after a lot of effort and a few choice expressions, he managed to prise the seat free with the wrench. As he lifted it out, he saw – to his horror – that a large lump of kif was sitting there. He handed the seat out of the van and, while the customs officer turned to put the seat down, Leslie swallowed the lump. The dog then climbed into the van to have another look around, but he found nothing. Eventually, they had to let us go as there really was no kif in the van now, but as we drove out of the customs shed and on to the normal road, Leslie pulled over and said, "You'd better drive the van home. I have a feeling I'm going to be out for the count very soon."

Within minutes, he was unconscious, lying in the back of the van among the carpets and pots, while I drove back to the so-called civilisation of London.

12: MARC BOLAN, MARDI GRAS, AND MOVIES

When Mainman was still flying high and money was no object, Defries gave me a BMW, saying that it was a birthday present. It never occurred to me that it was, in fact, only bought on hire purchase, so still had to be paid for. I subsequently discovered that the monthly payments had stopped being made because of Mainman's financial difficulties.

The first time I realised something was wrong was when I noticed that someone was following me. At first, I thought it might be a stalker. Could this be Jack with his nine inches, I wondered. Whoever he was, he never actually approached me, but after a few days, I was contacted by somebody telling me that I had to hand the car over.

For the first time in years, I had no wheels, but help came almost immediately from an old friend, Marc Bolan. He was so upset when he heard that my BMW had been repossessed that he immediately offered me a vehicle of his own. It was an Austin Mini Van, but I was grateful for anything with wheels, so I didn't mind. In fact, I've always loved vans, and even now I drive a van when I'm in London.

For some reason, his van was in Ross-on-Wye near the Welsh border, about 130 miles from London, so Leslie and I set off by train to collect it. When we arrived, I have to say that it really looked like a wreck from the outside; it was all rusty and beaten up, so a major refurbishment was called for. By the time it was finished, the inside was completely covered with shagpile red carpet; the ceiling, the floor, even the inside roof and dashboard, everything was done in red shagpile. Our friend Trevor, who'd tarted it up for us, was as high as a kite for days because of his proximity to the large amounts of glue needed to do the job. At least the van had an engine that worked, and it was certainly a lot better than nothing. It was very sweet of Marc to give it to me, and I was most grateful.

The only time the MarcMobile broke down was when I was driving through Soho with the head of EMI records, Leslie, and my dog, together with loads of stuff in the back. We got out of the van and were pushing it out of the way of the traffic when I noticed a minibus full of policemen had arrived, and I thought, "How marvellous, they've come to help me push my car." What I didn't know was that the police had apparently been tipped off that somebody was transporting a load of drugs through London in an old van; when they saw my rust bucket, they thought that I was the smuggler. The next thing I knew, I was being held up against a wall and told I was to be taken away to the police station. So, I was carted off to Vine Street police station and strip-searched. Fortunately, it didn't take long for the police to see that I was innocent and to release me.

As I left the police station, my situation finally hit home. I had been highflying for five years, and suddenly all my mates were in America. Things seemed to be literally crumbling all around me, and I remember thinking, "This shouldn't be happening. I shouldn't be in a car that breaks down. Everything has literally been taken away from me."

*

The financial collapse of Mainman inevitably led to lengthy legal wrangles, and – as I was contracted to them – I got caught up in it. Bowie wanted his freedom, and Defries wanted paying for his efforts; in the end, it seemed as though only the lawyers made money out of matters. Frustratingly, I didn't get a say in what I wanted, and I was not contractually free to record for anyone for several years until the mess was finally cleared up.

Bills still needed to be paid, though, and I was once again looking for work. Somehow, I was given a role in a short film called 'Sink or Swim', alongside Roy Kinnear (The Beatles' 'Help!', 'The Three Musketeers'), and Chris Langham ('The Pink Panther Strikes Again', 'Life of Brian'). It was a rather strange documentary-style film which was produced by The British Overseas Trade Board and was intended to 'demonstrate in a humorous fashion the value of exports during Export Year'. Whilst I can't say whether or not it achieved its objective, I somehow suspect that not enough people saw it to make much of a difference.

Shortly after that, and following an introduction from my friend Marsha Hunt (who had already been promised a part), I was invited to an audition for another West End musical. The show was called 'Mardi Gras', with the words written by Melvyn Bragg and the music done by two guys called Ken Howard and Alan Blaikley. At the time, they were probably best known for writing the hits for Dave Dee, Dozy, Beaky, Mick and Titch, including their number one single 'The Legend of Xanadu'. They also wrote for a young band called Flaming Youth, who had released a prog-style concept album called 'Ark 2' which came out in 1969, in a really extravagant gatefold LP cover done by Gered Mankowitz. The album launched at the London Planetarium, and Gered and I were invited to attend. This involved sitting in darkness for half an hour watching the stars until the lights suddenly came on, and there were Flaming Youth. They were all about 16 and 17, and the drummer was a young chap with long hair – called Phil Collins. Who knew then that he would go on to become a global star.

'Mardi Gras' was set in a bordello in New Orleans in 1917, and the main character was a hooker called Celandine. Originally, the part was meant to be played by a black singer, but there was a stumbling block: she had to sing the Blues. There were many good British black singers who could sing, but none of them really did the Blues convincingly. Even now, as my ex-drummer Chris Hunt, might say, they are 'as rare as rocking horse shit'.

When I went to the audition, I didn't know what they wanted me to sing; I just knew that I needed a job. My knee was pretty bad at that time, so I hobbled in on my walking stick and said to the director, "I'm so sorry I don't have any sheet music, as the sort of music I do is not really written down. Also, I'm sorry I'm hobbling, but my knee should get better soon."

That last bit was not entirely true, but I spent much of my life trying not to make my disability show, and most people didn't notice it. Thank goodness for performers like Ian Dury and Dr. John; they didn't seem to care if they went on stage with a walking stick. At the end of the day, it's the music that matters.

Anyway, I asked if I could sing sitting down and – when they agreed – went to the piano and told them I'd play something myself. With nothing to lose (except of course getting a role in the show), I decided to sing one of my favourite songs, 'Organ Grinder Blues', written by Clarence Williams around 1915, with marvellous lyrics like,

'Organ Grinder, your sweet music seems to ease my mind,

But it's not your organ, it's the way you grind!'

If there is one thing I know I can do well, it's singing the Blues in the good old style from the 20's and 30's – when it first started. This has been second-nature to me nearly all my life, and I've been doing this since I was 11. Well, of course, this was just what the producers of the show were looking for, and I was offered the lead role. I felt a bit sorry for Marsha as I think she may have wanted this part too, but she was given the role of a crazed gypsy woman who practised voodoo and danced about in juju feathers. She'd just had a hit with the Dr. John song 'Walk on Gilded Splinters', so the producers must have thought she was well suited for that part.

My leading man was Nicky Henson, a lovely guy who had a long and successful career in theatre, film, and television. Shortly before he died, he commented that, despite his 50 years of professional acting, his tombstone would probably read, "Here lies Nicky Henson, he was in one episode of Fawlty Towers."

Other than me and Nicky, the rest of the cast were predominately black. There had been some complaints from a couple of militant cast members to the actors' union, Equity, that a non-black had got the lead role, but the producers got around this by saying that I was playing an octoroon (which means one-eighth black), and eventually the fuss died down.

The show opened in March 1976 at The Prince of Wales Theatre in London's West End, and it felt good to be treading the boards again. The setting was the fleshpots and bars of New Orleans, where "you can get everything you want, but only for money." Celandine, the top hooker in town, meets a young musician who tries to persuade her to give up her low life, which she doesn't do, with tragic consequences. It was another 'tart with a big heart' role, not too far away in spirit – if not in style – from Mary Magdalene in J.C. Superstar.

There was a great moment in it that featured the choir singing the hymn 'Immortal Invisible' in the background, whilst I sang 'From now on' as a counter-melody over the top of their voices. It had originally been written for Flaming Youth and had been performed by them at the Planetarium, but the writers then decided to include it in 'Mardi Gras'. It's a beautiful piece, and I have often thought about re-recording it myself.

The show got a lot of good publicity and some great reviews. Of course, I had to put up with the usual boob references, such as, "Lovely Dana's busting back into the West End in a new musical called Mardi Gras." (London Evening News). A more sober review came out in The Sunday Times review on the 20th of February 1976, "It is splendidly sung and danced, with Nicky Henson and Dana Gillespie playing with panache the hero and heroine buffeted by the passions of carnival, organised prostitution and violence."

Some nights, there seemed to be more stars in the audience than on the stage. Marc Bolan and Gloria Jones, Linda Lewis, Cilla Black, Susan Hampshire, Leslie Anne Down, and Prunella Scales all came in the opening weeks.

It's all very well being a leading lady in a West End Show, but nobody could imagine the financial troubles I was in. Defries had obtained a court order requiring the producers of the show – the Delfont Organisation – to freeze my earnings while the Mainman litigation was going on. So, I didn't actually get any money for the whole run, which was about nine months. The theatre has a tradition that you must tip the doorman and your personal hairdresser every week, and soon I hadn't enough money to tip anyone because I was totally broke. This was such a bizarre situation, as I was a leading lady in a West End production who didn't have any money and was driving around in a van that looked ready for the scrap yard. Also, my knee was playing up again. All in all, it was a pretty miserable time.

*

One of the best ways to see the world is by going off to sing in different countries. A two-week residency in a hotel in Hong Kong sounded very appealing, in 1977, even though it meant singing with pickup musicians who originally all came from the Philippines. Thankfully, I didn't have to do this gig alone, as John Porter came along as my musical director. Usually, the booker would want a cabaret singer doing corny pop songs – definitely not my style – but a gig is a gig. At least I was learning something new, as well as confirming in my own mind what I *didn't* want to do with my life. Sometimes that is just as important as knowing what you *do* want to do.

On another occasion, I was booked to sing in Dubai, and the agent decided to send me on to Oman to perform in one of the top hotels there. Unfortunately, he'd booked me to perform during Ramadan, so the place was deserted, and there were only a few drunk expats in the audience. I didn't really mind, as I loved being in the Arab markets; the landscape thrilled and soothed me, and the hotels were outstanding. A million times better than some grim bed and breakfast in the north of England.

Just when I was wondering where on earth I could find some more work, I got a call to go for a screen test for Hammer Films. They were casting a film called 'The People that Time Forgot', though I always jokingly called it 'The Film that People Forgot'. It was a sequel to a movie entitled 'The Land that Time Forgot', which had been released a couple of years earlier. It had enjoyed a certain amount of commercial success, notwithstanding its puppet dinosaurs.

Hammer Films were looking for a female lead with a large bust, and I seemed to fit the bill. They sent me off to the famous theatrical costumier Bermans, to get fitted out for the role, who put me into a revealing jungle girl outfit, complete with spear and bouffant hairdo. This was 1977 – still in the days of plunging necklines, but certainly no more than that. The producer John Dark must have been impressed, as I was immediately offered the role. I was also pretty chuffed to hear that some of the filming would be on location.

The destination was La Palma, one of the smaller of the Canary Islands. In those days, the airport couldn't take very big planes, as the runway ran out into the sea. Once the actors and crew were on board the plane, I found myself sitting next to the executive producer, Steve Previn (brother of the famous conductor Andre). As we were coming in to land, I couldn't help noticing that he had an agonised look on his face and was gripping his seat tightly. Asking him what the problem was, he said that as this was the first time a plane this size had ever attempted to land on La Palma, the insurance company would only provide cover if Steve showed his faith by flying with the rest of the cast.

Filming on location can be heaven or hell, and much depends on whether you have a cast that gets on well with each other, or not. Luckily, we all got on famously. The star was Doug McClure, who had also starred in 'The Land That Time Forgot'. At the end of that film, his character gets stuck on an island populated by prehistoric animals and cavemen, so the plot of 'The People That Time Forgot' was that Doug's friend (played by Patrick Wayne, son of 'Big John' Wayne) led a search party to go and find him. Doug, whom we called 'Glug' as he was a bit of a drinker, had found fame in the television series 'The Virginian', a popular American Western programme from the sixties. Although it was no longer being shown in England, it was still running in Spain, so Glug was greeted as something of a hero everywhere we went.

Of course, in a film like this, it's sort of obligatory to have a busty native girl bouncing around, and this was where my character – Ajor – came in. I didn't have to do much in the way of acting, but I had to be agile and fight prehistoric animals that moved around menacingly. When I say 'menacingly', I am using rather a lot of artistic licence. In reality, the 'animals' had men hidden inside them, who were controlling the arms and legs. 'Jurassic Park' it most definitely was not!

Some of the newspapers gave the prehistoric creatures better reviews than the actors. "The scaly beasts on view look real enough, even though the human beings, played by Patrick Wayne, Doug McClure and Thorley Walters are unconvincing. Lots of explosions, fire and smoke make the adventure exciting and the sight of Dana Gillespie's boobs makes one regret the invention of the bra."

As usual, I had long flowing locks, and was dressed in chamois leather with the obligatory cleavage to make me look like a cave girl (or perhaps just to encourage more men to see the film). The trouble with the skimpy outfit was that every time I ran to escape a volcanic eruption, or a dinosaur, my tits would fall out of the costume. After the poor director had yelled 'Cut' one time too many, and whilst the rest of the crew yet again doubled up in laughter, the costume department decided to preserve my modesty with double-sided Sellotape. This had the advantage of ensuring that my breasts didn't make an unexpected appearance during a thrilling chase scene. Unfortunately, every night when I undressed, the tape took a layer of skin off, and I had to spend every evening rubbing cocoa oil over my chest.

When the film was finally ready to be released, the censors were worried by the amount of flesh on show (they should have seen the outtakes!), and gave producer John Dark quite a bit of grief. Ultimately, after much debate, it was decided that it was all in good taste, and nothing was edited out. When the film hit the cinemas, I got what must be one of the funniest reviews I have had in my entire career. Thank you to The New Musical Express, who wrote, "For the lads, Dana Gillespie strides through the film like some over-endowed inflatable doll, her halter top revealing twin attributes as wobbly as most of the set."

These days I'm pleased to say that 'The People That Time Forgot' has acquired something of a cult status, and turns up at film fairs and on late night television from time to time.

A lot of the interior filming was done at Pinewood Studios, and while we were there, a casting call went out for the female lead role in the second Superman film. Sarah Douglas, my co-star in 'People', and I both screen-tested for the part of Ursa, but Sarah won out. Years later, I was surprised to find that my screen test was included amongst the 'extras' on the DVD for the first Superman movie. I don't think I would have made nearly as a good villain as Sarah did; indeed, I've never been too good at looking stern. To be honest, that was usually the last thing the film producers wanted from me.

*

I can still clearly remember the words Marc Bolan said when he gave me the minivan a year earlier, "I have a feeling that if I get into a mini and drive a mini, I will die in a mini."

And, extraordinarily, he did indeed die in a mini; albeit not the one he gave to me, and not with him at the wheel. The accident occurred, late at night, near a bridge in Barnes on the 20th of September 1977, and even now, you can still see flowers at the spot where it happened. It was so tragic, as his life was really going well then. He was happy, living with his partner Gloria Jones, the mother of their son Rolan, and he had just completed filming his comeback TV show when he was killed.

The final episode of the 'Marc' TV Show, which was broadcast after his death, ended with Marc and Bowie playing a duet called 'Standing Next to You', which Marc was… until he fell off the stage. There is a reference to this performance in Kevin Cann's excellent book 'Any Day Now', which suggests that Bowie and Marc may have written the song in the Bunker and that I had taped it. They were there together jamming and composing on a number of occasions, so I guess it's quite possible.

Marc's funeral was a pretty awful occasion. Loads of fans, often with mascara running down their tear-stained faces, waited for the hearse outside the Golders Green crematorium. There was a huge swan made of white flowers to remind us all of his hit 'Ride a White Swan'. The worst moment was when the coffin was brought in, as it was so small; Marc was quite petite, and it almost seemed like a child's coffin. As it headed for the flames, someone started screaming.

Obviously, you shouldn't laugh at a funeral, but there was one rather funny moment. Leslie and I were sitting in the pew behind Bowie and Rod Stewart, and Rod was trying, not entirely successfully, to balance a little black Jewish kippah on top of his spiky hair.

There is a sad footnote to the story of Marc's minivan. One year after his death, I drove to the Rainbow Theatre in Finsbury Park (another great venue which is no longer there) to see a Little Feat concert. As I was hanging out with their drummer Richie Hayward at the time, I offered to drive him to a studio somewhere near Leicester Square after the show, where our friend John Porter was doing a recording session. When we came out, at about five in the morning, my little MarcMobile was missing. It had been stolen, and a few days later, the police contacted me to say that it had been involved in a fatal car crash and was a total write-off. Spookily, this had happened on the anniversary of Marc's death.

*

Early the following year, I got the call to appear in the stage musical of The Who's 'Tommy', and I jumped at the chance. The show played at the Queen's Theatre in Hornchurch, East London, for a few weeks and was due to be transferred to the West End, but that never happened. Or, to be more accurate, it did go to the

West End, but with a completely different director, a completely different cast… and with much worse reviews.

Who guitarist and Tommy writer, Pete Townshend, came down to the rehearsals, and saw the show once it opened. The run lasted just a few weeks, but I enjoyed it while it was on, and – unusually – it gave me the chance to play a couple of the characters. First, I was the Mother, which was Ann-Margret's role in the Ken Russell film of 'Tommy', and then I got to play the Acid Queen. The stage show was quite different from the film, with no baked beans for Mother, and no drug paraphernalia either.

The role of Tommy was played by a guy called Allen Love, who was not only a great singer but also had the considerable advantage of being a Roger Daltrey lookalike. My friend Richard Barnes, who co-starred with me in Superstar as Peter, performed as Tommy's Mother's Lover.

Around that time, I found myself doing some television shows, including the 'Little and Large' show, on which I had to sing music that really was not my style. After all, Blues was not the sort of thing that was wanted for this kind of show, so I felt rather like a fish out of water. Another television show at the time was 'Seaside Special', a BBC variety show filmed (not surprisingly) by the seaside(!), on which I appeared three times, including once as compere. I was described in a newspaper as "the female equivalent of Bruce Forsyth.", though I don't remember having to do a twirl!

Some episodes of 'Seaside Special' were filmed in St. Malo, and we all had to travel over to France by ferry. One bright spark decided to film me miming to 'Trains and Boats and Planes' while we were on our way over, which would have been fine if I didn't suffer from seasickness. Before we left, I had taken some anti-nausea pills to avoid throwing up in front of the Geoff Richer Dancers – a sort of poor man's version of Pans People, who were dancing about on deck – but must have taken one pill too many. As a result, I did the whole thing completely out of my head, looking at the horizon and trying to keep the nausea at bay. Fortunately, the director had told me to look moody and sing, so I don't think my zombie state was noticeable in my performance.

When we finally got to St. Malo, they filmed a couple of shows in a circus tent, and one featured Grace Jones who – quite amazingly

– appeared on roller skates in a long evening gown. Naturally, I was asked to sing 'I Don't Know How To Love Him', as well as 'Love Potion No. 9', and got what I suppose were quite good reviews. The Daily Record dated the 12th of August 1978 described me as, "A lady with a strong personality, an excellent voice and of course an awe-inspiring frontage. Compering 'Seaside Special' should give her a boost towards her goal of being a singer, rather than a lady with big boobs."

I'm afraid I was still getting more comments on my infrastructure than my singing. One compere even introduced me with the words, "Here they are… Dana Gillespie."

These types of variety shows were absolutely not the kind of thing I was aiming for in my life, but I needed the work to stay in the public eye. Without doing television, you are totally forgotten, and whilst I didn't want to be thought of as a cute girl singer, I was happy that I was still getting noticed. The Record Mirror poll of the top pop ladies in August 1976 put me first, ahead of Lyn Paul and Eve Graham (the two girls in The New Seekers), Olivia Newton-John, and Eurovision Song Contest winner Dana. Quite an improvement on my tenth place finish in the 1975 poll.

I even recorded a duet with Tony ('Is This The Way To Amarillo') Christie around that time. The song was called 'Magdalena' and it had been written by Tim Rice and Andrew Lloyd Webber, not for a musical but as a standalone single. It was a big production number with a full orchestra in which Tony croons away about a girl he met on holiday, and was clearly destined for the top of the charts. Sadly, it got nowhere. Andrew probably got it right when he wrote in his autobiography, "Could it have been a mistake that this blatant attempt at a summer hit was released in the iron wintry grip of February?"

Back in the land of TV, I also 'starred' in the last episode of the second series of ITV cop show 'Hazell'. I got to play a prostitute catering for 'unusual tastes'. Nicholas Ball, who played the lead role, was married at the time (but not for long) to Pamela Stephenson, and I remember her visiting him on set when we were filming. This was, of course, some time before she married Billy Connolly.

Soon after this, I landed up in a film called 'The Hound of the Baskervilles', based – extremely loosely – on the book of the same name by Sir Arthur Conan Doyle. This seemed to have enormous potential because it had the most wonderful cast. Peter Cook played Sherlock Holmes, Dudley Moore was Doctor Watson, and the other characters were performed by the cream of the British comedy world: Denholm Elliott, Joan Greenwood, Hugh Griffith, Irene Handle, Terry-Thomas, Max Wall, Kenneth Williams, Roy Kinnear, Jessie Matthews, Prunella Scales, Penelope Keith, Rita Webb, and Spike Milligan. What could possibly go wrong?

For a start, the director was an American called Paul Morrissey whose previous experience had been to direct films for Andy Warhol. He really was not equipped to deal with all these great British actors and, dare I say it, never got to grips with British humour.

Peter Cook was drinking heavily and hardly left his dressing room except to come on set and say his lines. The script was disjointed and included, for no obvious reason – at least as far as the plot was concerned – a number of Pete and Dud's well-known sketches. One of them featured Dudley, as a one-legged man, auditioning for the role of a runner on the moors. It was pretty well a word-for-word repeat of a sketch Pete and Dud had first performed on 'Beyond the Fringe' in the early 1960's, which they continued to use – with Dudley auditioning for the role of Tarzan – for the rest of their careers together, and which ended with Peter saying, "Your right leg, I like. It's a lovely leg for the job. I've got nothing against your right leg. The trouble is neither have you!"

The whole thing was filmed at Bray Studios. I was supposed to look like a gypsy girl, so they put me in a corset with my tits up under my chin. An observant reporter from The Sun visited the set while we were filming, and his report included this splendid line, "'I seem to be cast in all the big, busty parts", says big, busty Dana.'

In the film, I played the partner of a very sloshed Hugh Griffith, a guy with a bulbous nose, which I fear he may have acquired from overdrinking. He's dead now but was a fabulous actor who had made his name in the 1963 film 'Tom Jones' starring Albert Finney. We had a scene together which was supposed to take place in a swamp on the moor, but which was actually filmed in the studio.

The 'swamp' was a hole in the ground, about as big as eight bathtubs. Because we had to be in the water up to our necks all day, we were put in rubber suits to keep out the cold. They also heated up the water, so we weren't cold at all. Quite the opposite, we were like boiled lobsters, getting redder and redder in the face as the hours passed.

My rubber suit stopped at the waist so that my cleavage was showing over the water. Hugh, who loved a drink, was given rubber bootees that were meant to keep his toes warm, but he got air in them, which meant that they kept rising to the surface, and his head kept flipping backwards into the water. I spent the whole scene trying to keep his feet down and his head above water, while he got increasingly furious with the amount of time the shot was taking. This resulted in a lot of brandy being consumed. The only one who didn't seem to notice this was Paul Morrissey, and when Hugh finally passed out from excessive heat and alcohol, it didn't help that Paul called for some more brandy, hoping that would revive Hugh. He came round long enough to have another tipple, and then passed out again.

In another scene, Denholm Elliott had a chihuahua under his arm, which never stopped peeing. The dog was assisted in its 'performance' by a guy with a tube and a bucket of water hiding behind Denholm, whose job was to squirt water everywhere. That pretty well illustrates the level of humour in the film.

I'd drive to Bray Studios every day and would lie down by the river in-between takes because the corset prevented me from sitting up. Filming my part took about a week, and sadly I didn't see some members of the cast, such as Max Wall, as we weren't all working in the same scenes. Everything seemed to go over-budget, over time, over the top; in fact, over everything.

Dudley Moore and I appeared together in one scene, in which he somehow lands in my cleavage. He kept everyone entertained off-camera, so much so that the make-up girl had to work overtime because he would reduce me and some of the other actors to uncontrollable laughter. Dudley was a very, very funny man, and I got to know him quite well but only after the filming was over…

It was a lovely film to be involved in, because of the cast, but somehow it was doomed from the start. It has since become *another* cult classic. Some people think it's hilarious; others find it painful.

*

While all this was going on, I was dealing with the Mainman litigation, which seemed to be never-ending. At the beginning of 1979, I still wasn't free from my contract, so I couldn't look for another record deal. As a result, I didn't release a record for five years, which was extremely frustrating.

Thankfully, another film came my way. Directed by Nicholas Roeg, it was called 'Bad Timing' and starred Art Garfunkel, Theresa Russell, and Harvey Keitel. The storyline is of a rather doomed and gloomy love affair, though it might be more accurately described as a love story with a hint of necrophilia thrown in.

There is a lot to admire about the films Nicholas Roeg has directed, such as 'Performance' with Mick Jagger and Anita Pallenberg, as well as Bowie's first major film 'The Man who fell to Earth'. He is probably best known for making films in which the action doesn't always follow a chronological order, leaving the viewer to try and work out what's going on. He also used to film *far more* footage than he needed, with the result that a lot ended up on the cutting room floor, and in some cases whole characters were chopped out. This meant that large sums of money were effectively being thrown away, which must have been a nightmare for the producer, the very amusing Jeremy Thomas.

It was well known that Art Garfunkel had fallen out with Paul Simon, whom I'd known a few years earlier, so I was slightly worried about what he would be like. When we were about to start filming, I said to Nick Roeg, "I've never met Art Garfunkel, and now we are going to do a sex scene. Could you at least introduce me to him?"

Art was standing on the side of the set looking rather uninterested. Anyway, Nick introduced us and we put our arms around each other, at which point I said to him, "We've got to get to know each other because I'm going to be sliding all over your body shortly."

I told him how I'd met Paul Simon years ago, before 'The Sound of Silence' became a hit. He didn't respond much, and I found him quite reserved and moody.

After we had talked for about 20 minutes, it was straight onto the bed, surrounded by film crew, lights, hair and makeup people. We started the scene fully dressed, but soon I had to pull my dress off and do the rest of the action with nothing on top – no bra – and just a pair of purple suede Spanish riding boots and purple Janet Reger French silk knickers. It's strange to have to kiss someone passionately as a job of work. I enjoyed it for the first few times, but hours (and many kisses) later, being filmed from different angles, my face was red and raw from Art's five o'clock shadow, and the whole thing just became like hard work. This was the first time I had ever been in bed with a man whilst surrounded by cameras, lights, microphones, and a guy shouting 'Cut' just when we got going.

In the film, as I'm sliding down his body to give him a blow job, the telephone rings, and it's his girlfriend played by Teresa Russell. She had taken a load of pills, so he leaves me and goes off to do the business with her overdosed unconscious body. Yes, you read that right.

There is another sequence in the film where Harvey Keitel is sitting, fiddling with his radio in the car, listening to some of my Blues music which I recorded specially for the film.

Some of the filming took place in Vienna, and apart from a three-day visit with Leslie, a few years earlier, I really didn't know the place, but I definitely grew to love it. Within a year, I was to find myself spending much of my life there.

13: INTO THE EIGHTIES

As Christmas 1979 approached, I did something very ill-advised.

Normally, I would have expected to see out the year skiing in Klosters with my mother and Tom, or go to Davos to hang out with my father and Lorna in the wonderfully old-fashioned Hotel Schatzalp, where you had to dress up for a five-course dinner every night.

Not this year.

Instead, I had foolishly agreed to do a Christmas pantomime in Eastbourne, and can honestly say it was one of the worst experiences I've ever had in my professional life.

It's not that I've got anything against Eastbourne. In fact, I grew to love it a few years later, when I went there to record two albums in a curious Christian studio near the seafront, filled with Billy Graham tapes and daily prayer meetings. God only knows what they thought of my devil's music. No, Eastbourne was OK; it was the panto that I loathed.

The show was 'Cinderella', starring Jimmy Edwards, Norman Vaughan, Avril Angers and 'the lovely Aimi MacDonald'. Dressed as the Principal Boy, I played Dandini and sang Barbra Streisand's 'Don't Rain on my Parade' every night. In typical panto fashion, my role involved a lot of thigh-slapping.

Jimmy Edwards, a man with a huge handlebar moustache, was a well-known comedian at the time. He was perhaps best known for a show called 'Whack-O', in which he played a school headmaster who was always threatening to cane the boys. That would definitely not go down well these days. I didn't spend any time with him backstage as we had no reason to bond, and he certainly wasn't interested in me.

The rest of the cast were largely old troopers whose careers had seen better days. Norman Vaughan, whose oft-used catchphrases were "Swinging" and "Dodgy", accompanied by a thumbs up or down, is probably best remembered for telling you that "Roses grow on you" in a TV advert in the sixties. Avril Angers had been a well-known actress in the past, but was quite elderly by then. The poor dear seemed to play the fairy every year in Christmas panto in places like Scunthorpe and Skegness. Aimi MacDonald lived up to her nickname by being lovely, and probably saved my sanity.

When I got the part, I thought – Eastbourne, it's by the sea, and not too far from London, so why not? Big mistake. It was freezing cold and rained all the time, which made the place seem pretty grim. Attendances were low, and I felt as if I was on a sinking ship every night. My accommodation was a bleak dump on the top floor of a boarding house near the seafront, and my only friend and consolation was my dog Sneezi. Together, we'd brave the arctic conditions while out on our daily walks, and even now I shudder when I think back to how depressing it all was. Christmas was about as miserable as it could be, with me living on rice in an attempt to save money, as I didn't know where the next bit of work would come from.

It was all utterly dreadful.

God knows how I got the role as I'd never done panto before. Some agent must have called me, and maybe I auditioned? No, I wouldn't have needed to audition for that. Certainly I will never do panto again unless it's with Julian Clary, whose style of camping it up would have made things bearable. Maybe I would have survived it if it had been 'Dick Whittington' with those immortal lines: "6 o'clock, and no Dick" and "10 miles to London and not a sign of pussy". Sadly, I was in the wrong show, it was 'Cinderella' and I loathed it. Ghastly songs, corny as anything, and I felt I'd fallen about as low as you can get.

Mainman, the closest family I'd had (apart my real family) was lying shattered across the globe because the financial house of cards had collapsed. Defries and Bowie were no longer available at the end of the line, I no longer had a 24/7 limo service or personal assistant, and I couldn't record for anyone because of the Mainman litigation.

*

1980 really was a year of change for me. My parents had decided it was time to get out of South Kensington as my mother yearned to go back to her Norfolk roots, close to her brothers and sisters, and my father wanted to return to the one place in his childhood that he'd adored… Italy. As a result, our house on Thurloe Square was put up for sale, which – of course – meant the end of my beloved Bunker. It had always been my refuge to come home to after lots of travelling, and suddenly I was about to be homeless.

Just when I thought things couldn't get any worse, fate intervened in the form of a marvellous Swedish lady called Mai Zetterling. She had been quite a big film star in the fifties, and had recently re-invented herself as a film and theatre director. Mai was auditioning for a new show just up the road from me in Chelsea, and we hit it off really well together. Within minutes of meeting, I knew she wanted me for the production.

It was a very odd piece called 'Playthings', written by William Saroyan with the stage set done by Andy Warhol, and it was scheduled to open at the English Theatre in Vienna in the spring. I say it was odd because all the characters in the play were inanimate objects that spoke, so I was a 'Ceiling' and a 'Floor', and some of the other actors played objects like 'Cup and Saucer'. It was scheduled to run for two-and-a-half months in Vienna before transferring to England. We did ultimately perform it at The Half Moon in Stepney, and although Mai thought she was going get it to a bigger theatre, it never got any further, probably because it was too avant-garde and weird.

As usual, I was in a body-hugging catsuit that left very little to the imagination, and I had to get into lots of contortionist positions, which I could do well thanks to my many years of dance classes. I would come on doing the splits or putting my foot behind my head. The instructor, who was very 'in' when I used to go regularly to the Dance Centre, was a great man called Matt Mattox. He'd played one of the Seven Brothers in the film version of 'Seven Brides for Seven Brothers', and looked amazing for his age. All the girls in his classes, and probably the men too, had a bit of a crush on him. Every time the film was shown on the television, usually around Christmas time, I'd watch just to see him do his dance routine, perilously balanced on a wooden plank.

The whole cast was dressed in skin-tight body stockings on stage, as Mai wanted to accentuate our different shapes. We had a very fat man, a thin one, a fat lady, a normal girl and a very small man played by a guy called Peter O'Farrell; all our body imperfections and bumps were there to see.

The cast were all given rooms in a Bed and Breakfast place near the theatre in the 8th District of Vienna, and although I didn't know it then, this area was to become my second home for many years. As far as I knew, I had a three month summer job that would keep me busy until I could finally move into my new place in London, just around the corner from where I'd lived before. Thankfully, I could still remain a South Kensington girl.

Once I got into the swing of Vienna life, I spent my time walking around town by day and going to perform by night. When the curtain came down, and each performance was over, I used to go into a small cafe around the corner called the Cafe Lange, and there I'd have a hot chocolate nightcap before retiring. It was on one of these evenings that I heard – across the crowded room – some great bottleneck Blues being played on an acoustic guitar, and I started to sing along with it. Slowly, the people stood aside as I sang my way through the crowd to come face to face with a young man with a big afro-style hairdo. Once the song was over and the applause had died down, I sang some more with him, enjoying every note he played, until we called it a day and he introduced himself in very good English, "Hi, my name is Erik Trauner and I'm in a band called the Mojo Blues Band. We are playing in a place called Jazzland in three days' time. Would you like to come down there and sing with us?"

Explaining that I wouldn't be able to make it until late as I would still be on stage in 'Playthings', I assured him I would be there as soon as I could. Three days later, I headed off with Peter O'Farrell to Jazzland. It was everything that a Jazz and Blues club should be – packed with people, all drinking and smoking (the air used to be pretty bad), and enjoying the music.

Jazzland is situated in cellars underneath the Ruprechts Kirche in the 1st District, and I went there to meet the man who ran the place, Axel Melhardt. Once I had finished singing my numbers with the band, Axel offered me a gig, and 40 years later I'm still going back there to sing.

This was the start of my life in Vienna, and I juggled my time between there and London, where I was still working with my English Blues band. The problem with being on the road with a band from another country is that I could never really integrate with them, as so much of their conversation and jokes just went above my head. It was only after spending three years of commuting between London and Vienna that I had a sort of breakthrough with the language, and things started to make sense.

The Mojo Blues Band were all about ten years younger than me, but there was no problem with the age gap because we had the Blues in common. These guys were very dedicated to their music, especially Erik Trauner who later took over the band by himself after splitting from the co-founder and pianist Joachim Palden. Whenever I was in Vienna, I would stay at Erik's rooftop flat and we would listen to Blues, buy Blues LPs, talk Blues, learn new Blues songs, and go to Blues gigs. In other words, we'd eat and sleep with the Blues. It was pretty intensive training but I'm so glad I had three years of this; it put me back on a track that I loved, and it gave me a lifeline when everything else seemed to be sinking in my world back in London.

When I reminisce on my time with this band, I only remember the good times which were all to do with the music. Sometimes, I felt lonely and out of place in Vienna, and was still scarred from the Mainman collapse, but I kept my heartache to myself and eventually the Mainman legal battle resolved itself. It had taken nearly five years, caused a lot of stress, and cost a lot of money. Defries and I had one last meeting in Los Angeles and then – finally – it was all over and I was free to record again.

Although some people have said nasty things about Defries, I don't actually feel badly towards him. No matter what anyone else might think of him, I still had a great time. OK, the fact that I couldn't record in the late seventies was really frustrating, but looking back now on the Mainman years, I wouldn't have missed them for the world.

*

Being prevented from recording, just when I had been starting to do well, was a big stumbling block, particularly as it had lasted for five years, so now I had to think about how to re-build my name and reputation in the fickle world of the music business. Looking back, this is where the Blues most definitely saved my life. Most performers in the pop business have a short career, but I was looking for something *more* than that. It was the genre that touched my soul; it was definitely the way forward for me.

The year was 1981, and I knew I had to get myself a Blues recording deal, so what better label to go to than Ace Records. The boss of the company, Ted Carroll, had started up his business selling second-hand records from a stall in Camden Town, and from this he expanded to a small shop called 'Rock On'. It was his choice of music that attracted me, because he sold all the Blues that I listened to myself. Talking to Ted, in his little office, which was stacked high with LPs, I told him that I had the musicians, I had the songs, I had the studios, and all I needed was the deal. My idea was to record a collection of the rudest old Blues I could find and call the LP 'Blue Job'. Thank God Ted had a sense of humour and roared with laughter. He said "Sign here", and I did.

A number of top notch musicians played on the 'Blue Job' LP, including Dave Rowberry on piano, with a guest piano spot by Diz Watson, Erik Trauner on guitar, Pete Thomas on sax, and Dr. John's favourite English drummer, Kieron O'Connor. Kieron was slightly crazy, often turning up for rehearsals having forgotten his drums, but when that happened he'd still beat out a strong rhythm on some empty beer cans and it was almost impossible to get angry with him once he started playing. He was also part of my then-favourite band, Diz and the Doormen, who were also signed to Ace; a band that managed to perfectly recreate the New Orleans sound of Professor Longhair. I was very honoured to have them all on my album. All it needed was a good Gered Mankowitz photograph on the cover and I was back in the swing of things.

Having a really great band meant I was getting more and more gigs in and around London. In those days, there were a lot of venues to choose from, and I once again became a regular in places like the 100 Club, the Golden Lion, the Kings Head, the Nashville Rooms, and the Dublin Castle. Some of these were pub gigs, but there was a circuit to be done and all the best bands played them.

All these years later, I'm still with Ace Records. In the days of LPs, I went on to make two more for them, called 'Below the Belt' and 'Hot Stuff', but with the birth of CDs the three LPs were merged into two CDs called 'Blues it Up' and 'Hot Stuff', featuring lots of naughty rude Blues songs. It wasn't 'nasty' rude, but 'funny and risqué' rude, with lyrics to make you smile as only the old Blues knows how. With titles like 'Organ Grinder', 'My Man Stands Out', 'Come On (If You're Coming), 'Big Ten Inch', and 'King

Size Papa', you can't help but be cheered up. I still play many of those songs at my gigs today.

*

Back in Vienna, I was playing more gigs with The Mojo Blues Band. Originally they were a scruffy lot, often appearing on stage in jeans and T-shirts, so I used to tell Erik Trauner that musicians must always look smarter than their audience. Slowly, the whole band took on a look of professionalism, and even their choice of songs was becoming more mainstream and popular, rather than just sticking to Chicago or Country Blues. They had already done one LP on Bellaphon Records and were preparing to do a second one, and I became their lead singer on this next bit of vinyl which was released in 1982. The title track on the album was 'Rockin' Pneumonia and the Boogie Woogie Flu', which was an old Huey Smith song, and the record also included another Huey Smith classic called 'Sea Cruise'. This style was far more commercial than anything the band had done before, and the album sold well, leading to more gigs and appearances on television in Austria, Germany, and Switzerland.

Whenever there were gaps in our touring schedule, I would fly straight back to London as I really missed my friends, the English language, and the British sense of humour. Occasionally, I would pick up some work while I was at home, which happened in 1982 when Mai Zetterling cast me in her next film. It was called 'Scrubbers', and was a gloomy tale of life in a women's prison. As you can imagine, it wasn't a comedy. And probably not a first date movie, either.

A year earlier, a film about life in a boys' prison had been made called 'Scum', and 'Scrubbers' was meant to be the female equivalent. Mai had met an ex-prison warden who had told her harrowing tales about the cruelty that goes on in women's prisons, and as she was always one to fight convention and stand up for what she felt was right, this seemed a perfect vehicle for her.

The building used to represent the prison was the old Holloway Sanatorium, just outside London. Mai had hand-picked the cast, using a combination of ex-offenders and actresses, so that the whole thing had a real gritty feel to it. The main colour was grey to represent the depressing conditions, so all clothes, food, buildings, and furniture were various shades of grey. The only colour in the film was red, which was used whenever blood was shed (which was often). We'd all turn up at dawn to sit in the makeup chair, and instead of the usual transformation of being made to look wonderful, we were all made to look grim and, you guessed it, grey. This went on for seven weeks, and I have to say that, after a few weeks, it started to affect the mood of the cast and crew. We all seemed to occupy our time under a cloud of depression.

My role was quite a sympathetic character called Budd, who was the prison warden, and in the storyline, I take pity on one of the inmates and help her escape. There were some great people in the cast, like Kathy Burke, Miriam Margolyes and Robbie Coltrane, and some really good performances, but it didn't have the feel-good factor and I guess the public didn't want to sit through such grisly stuff. Time Out described it as "an entertaining washout", which was one of the better reviews it got. It never did well at the box office, and so disappeared without trace.

George Harrison's company, Handmade Films, produced the project, and there was always a buzz of excitement whenever he came down to watch the filming. He was such a polite and decent person, and it was always a pleasure to talk to him.

Mai Zetterling and I stayed in touch once filming was over, and a few years later, I went on to do two more productions for her. One was an episode of a TV series called 'Crossbow', which was filmed in France and told the story of William Tell; in fact, the title of the show was later changed to 'William Tell'. I saw some of it recently, and was astonished to see that I had been in episode 18 of Series 3, so the programme must have been popular, though God knows why.

My character, Hanka, offered some very banal lines, which included,

"Don't you dare do that again, little man."

"Now I've started it I just can't stop it."

"I'm sorry I blow so hard."

"I'll see if I have any puff left. I'm going to blow into a more comfortable place."

Sounds like the lyrics from one of my more 'adult-themed' Blues numbers…

The other project I did with Mai was a television show called 'Sunday Pursuit', from a series called 'Love at First Sight'. It starred the wonderfully funny Denholm Elliott and Rita Tushingham, and I played a woman called Maureen. My character responded to a 'lonely hearts' advertisement placed by Denholm, and they agreed to meet on a Sunday at The Palm Garden. When I turn up, I find Denholm and Rita together after he has mistakenly thought she was the woman he had spoken to. I kick up a stink though it doesn't do me much good, as Denholm chases off after her.

Apparently, it was shown on Swedish television, but other than that I never saw it or heard of it once it was finished. I've no idea what became of this epic; answers on the back of a postcard, please!

Soon after that, Mai became unwell. She would often disappear to her converted monastery in France and would sometimes invite me to visit, but sadly I never had the time. Once, when I did finally find a gap in my schedule allowing me to go, she was too ill, and she died soon afterwards. What a great and wonderful lady she was.

*

Another mad venture that I took on was a one woman show at the Edinburgh Festival called 'Cora', which was about the famous French courtesan Cora Pearl, also known as 'La Grande Horizontale'. To this day, I'm not really sure why I agreed to do this as it wasn't the sort of thing I normally do, but – hey ho – I never could say no to a challenge, and this was definitely one of those. It involved me being alone on stage from start to finish. The subject of the songs and dialogue ranged from Cora's lovers to people whom she knew before she died destitute, having been reduced to begging outside the Monte Carlo casino. Another case of Good Girl Gone Bad.

I'd been invited to take the role by the director Julian Sluggett, but should have realised that it was ill-fated when he agreed to give me a lift to Edinburgh and his car blew up before we'd even left London. In the end, I had to do the driving, all the way up to

Scotland in my pea green Citroen 2CV, together with Julian, and two others, plus my costumes. An inauspicious start.

This was my first trip to the Edinburgh Festival as a performer, and I simply had no idea what to expect. Our venue was a large white tent, and you could hear other productions through the canvas which didn't help Cora's tender moments of love or death on stage. It also happened to be one of the rainiest and coldest Augusts for years, so the tent was more like a fridge full of mud. As I had to wander about on stage in various bits of underwear and night attire, I spent my entire time there freezing.

One of my costumes had been made by Natasha Korniloff, who had made many clothes for Bowie including his Pierrot outfit in the 'Ashes to Ashes' video. Mine was a huge fluffy boudoir dressing gown, which was see-through except where the frills covered important bits, and as I wore nothing underneath you could see the crack of my arse if I stood with my back to the audience. One night I got so fed up about how badly the show seemed to be going that I threw open my black frilly costume to expose myself – full frontal – just to see if I'd get any reaction. Not a ripple from the audience, not a gasp, nothing. I guess everyone was either bored stiff or frozen stiff – or most likely both! Anyway, I think I can safely say that it's the only time I've ever showed my pubes on stage.

At one point in the production, Cora announces that she had once served herself up naked on a silver salver on a dinner table, decorated only with parsley. One evening this caused a walkout by a bunch of Scottish feminists, but it wasn't my fault; the show was historical drama, and that's what she actually did.

My time as 'Cora' was saved by the music, which had been written by Alastair Collingwood. He really did write lovely songs, one being called 'Paris Is For Lovers', though as far as I'm concerned Paris is for eating because it has the best souffles in the world. Alastair played 'live' with three of my Blues musicians who (like me) were also wondering what they were doing there. To make matters worse, I agreed to transfer with the show to the small Lyric Theatre in London, where it died yet another death in front of scant audiences. As I was still suffering from the horrors of panto, this put me off anything to do with the theatre for a long time. Would I never learn?

Fortunately, my music career was beginning to go well again, and I was busy doing gigs in England and around Europe. In 1983, I did quite a few shows with the Mojo Blues Band supporting Chuck Berry in Austria and Belgium. He would always use a local pickup band when on tour, and he never rehearsed them because he assumed that every musician knew all his songs, which of course they always did.

At one Festival, the wives of the two organisers turned up at his caravan in Festival T-shirts, knocked on his caravan door and asked for an autograph. Chuck misunderstood their intentions and thought they wanted a threesome, so was horrified when they ran away. He then threw a hissy fit, and wouldn't leave the caravan for several hours.

Chuck was famous for not going on stage until he'd been paid upfront, and would always play exactly the number of minutes he had agreed to perform, and not one second more. Under the terms of his contract, he was given the use of a Mercedes-Benz to drive around when he had some free time, so he would sometimes disappear and only come back just in time for the show.

At one Festival, near Dendemonde in Belgium, he turned up very late. The crowd was getting restless waiting for him, and the organisers were so angry that they refused to pay him before he performed. 'Discussions' between Chuck and the promoters became very heated, and the police had to be called before he eventually agreed to go on. He then played exactly 59 minutes and 59 seconds, came off stage, took his money and stormed off. That was the last show of the tour, and he was due to return to America the next day. It was only after he had left the country that somebody asked what had happened to the Mercedes-Benz. It was never seen again.

Chuck was always quite flirty with me, and I was pretty sure that if I'd told him my room number, he'd have nipped over. I never did tell him, however, because he was absolutely not my type. Sometimes, I'd chat with him backstage before we went on, but I never hung out socially with him. Whatever else you could say about Chuck Berry, there is one thing that is without doubt true: he was one of the greatest songwriters ever.

Memphis Slim was another great Blues piano player who sometimes appeared at these festivals, and he was definitely 'touchy-feely'. He would often tell me his room number in case I was interested, though once again I wasn't. I did love his music though.

One of the best musicians I ever shared a stage with was Bo Diddley. He had his own distinctive sound when he played on that cool oblong guitar, and is one of the few artists who has left a legacy behind. When his music is played, it's impossible to sit still, you just have to get up and dance. What great rhythm and beat he had.

Somehow in the middle of all this I managed to persuade the Austrian record label Bellaphon that I had a song that I thought would be a hit. This was completely different to anything I had done before, and was based on something that I had heard a few years earlier. One day, when I had been walking through the souk in Dubai, I had come across an old Arab sitting on the sand, who had a scratchy old song blaring out of his ancient cassette player. There was something about the melody that made me stop, and I sat down by him and asked if he'd play the song again. This he did several times, and eventually I asked him if I could buy the cassette, which he agreed to. As I said goodbye to him, I had an incredibly strong feeling that I had found something that I could turn into a hit. When I got the cassette home it fell to bits after about three plays, but that was enough for me to work with to develop a song.

I went into the studio and recorded the song, 'Move Your Body Close To Me', which was released in Austria, Germany, and Switzerland. This was a time when synthesisers were very popular, and the recording had a very hypnotic, oriental feel to it.

Although I had expected the song to go straight to the top of the charts, it lay gathering dust in record stores for 11 months because no one was buying it. Even though it wasn't selling, I still believed in it, so I decided to enter it in a song festival in Austria. It was a sort of local Eurovision thing, and the prize was something called the Golden Carinthia, which was a large gold-coloured statue of a singer holding a microphone. Everyone said I was mad to enter an oriental-style song in a festival that was obviously going to be full of pop music, but nevertheless I put a band together to play it 'live' on the show and called them the Cobras.

We were completely different to everyone else.

I was dressed in a silver sequin top and black jeans and the band all had long-hair, whilst all the other performers were very short-haired and rather straight-looking. Maybe it was the very fact that we looked and sounded so different that helped us to win first prize; whatever the reason, I had the satisfaction of knowing that an inner hunch of mine had been right. Even better was the fact that it was performed on television, which meant that it finally started to move up the charts.

Suddenly, the song was being played everywhere. The newspapers in Austria called me 'Dana Move Your Body Close To Me Gillespie' for many years, which made a pleasant change from 'Dana 44-24-36 Gillespie'.

'Move Your Body Close To Me' became a big hit in Austria. It was in good company, with other songs in the top 10 at the time including, 'She Drives Me Crazy' by Fine Young Cannibals, 'Something's Gotten Hold Of My Heart' by Marc Almond, 'You've Got It' by Roy Orbison, 'Especially For You' by Kylie Minogue and Jason Donovan, and 'Angel Of Harlem' by U2. It also charted well in Switzerland and Germany.

Sadly, even though I approached several record companies in England and told them how well the song was selling in Europe, I couldn't get anyone interested to release it at home.

Having a hit meant that my diary quickly started to fill up with gigs, and so The Cobras and I went out on the road to promote it. The single was put onto an album called 'Solid Romance', which was soon followed by another LP called 'It Belongs To Me' featuring a marvellous keyboard player called Tim Cross. Both albums stayed with the oriental feel, and incorporated some Arabic styles too.

It's a well-known fact in the music biz that following up a first hit is a tricky thing to handle, and this was the case with me. (Don't forget, it took David Bowie three years, and several flops, to follow up 'Space Oddity'.) I kept the same oriental influences for 'It Belongs To Me', but not everyone is as crazy for this sound as I am and it didn't do as well as I had expected. This resulted in gigs drying up and ultimately meant that the Cobras were disbanded.

My success with 'Move Your Body Close To Me' led to Erik Trauner, the leader of the Mojo Blues Band, telling me that I was not being true to the Blues and that it would be better if we didn't work together anymore. Looking back on it, this was just the thing I needed to hear, as I really wanted to get back to London and work more with my English musicians. I'd had enough of being in a situation that wasn't much fun for me, due to the language and humour differences. Thinking that my time in Vienna was over, I headed back to my beloved South Kensington. As it happens, I was wrong in thinking that it was a case of 'Goodnight Vienna'… circumstances got me back there again quite soon.

*

Whilst London (and in particular South Kensington) was very much my home, I continued to spend a lot of time touring around Europe. Of all the places that have been close to my heart, Vienna comes second after London. I know one is meant to say something romantic about Paris, but I always had a miserable time there. It's meant to be for lovers, but the sun never seemed to shine on me when I was there. It's got a bit better now, thanks to my doing gigs with one of my favourite piano players, Julien Brunetaud, at 'le Caveau de la Huchette', a basement dive in St. Michel.

Zurich has always been another city I'm fond of, much to the surprise of people who find it boring. For starters, they had the High Temple of Chocolate – called Sprungli – right on Parade Platz, where I would happily gorge myself in the eighties, exploring the town by day and playing gigs at night. The place that booked me and the Mojo Blues Band was the '82' Club, right on the river front, called the Limmatquai. The venue no longer exists, but it stays strongly in my memory as the band and I used to do five sets a night. Yes, five! Each one was 45 minutes long, and the engagement was always for ten days. Towards the end of the last set in the evening, I sometimes used to forget what song I was doing, I was that tired.

But Vienna is the place that has given me the most pleasure, outside home, and where I still love returning to. I first went there when I was broken down and unhappy, but once I had got over the language problem I felt the city nurturing me and making me strong. The city gave me a hit with 'Move Your Body Close To Me', and the opportunity to sing with good musicians in a great club like Jazzland, so I am always happy to go back there.

*

Although things were going well for me, I missed having a companion and kindred spirit, but luckily Vienna had another gift for me. This appeared in the shape of an artist called Jorg Huber.

I had asked my agent, Karl Scheibmaier, to tell me who were the most famous painters in Vienna, as I was looking for someone to do a painting of me for my next LP cover. Girl singers usually had boring photographs of themselves on their record covers, and I wanted something very different. Karl told me there were three artists worth checking out: Hundertwasser, Helnwein, and Huber. When combined like that, they sound like a firm of Viennese lawyers.

Well, I knew that Hundertwasser was no good for me, as he only did abstract stuff. Helnwein had done a painting for the Rolling Stones in a photorealistic style of a man in agony, so I didn't think he was suitable either. When I asked about Huber, Karl replied, "Jorg Huber is a strange painter, whose style is very psychedelic and full of fantasy, but he hardly ever is seen out and about as he lives in a large crazy apartment in the 8th district and tends to stay hidden there."

Of the three, Jorg Huber sounded the most promising, but my agent didn't know how to track him down so I put the idea of meeting him on the back burner. However, fate took a hand three days later as I walked in to the Metropole, a music venue where I was due to perform, and Karl said to me, "You remember that painter I was talking about, called Jorg Huber? Well, there he is, standing by the bar."

This tall, good-looking man was propping up the bar surrounded by women. That didn't deter me, so I walked up to him and asked if I could see some of his paintings, as I was looking for someone to do the cover for my next album.

He told me that would be no problem, so I left him at the bar and went off to get ready for the gig. At the end of the night, when most of the audience had gone and I had changed out of my stage gear, I saw that Jorg was still standing by the bar – and was still surrounded by women. Not knowing if any of them was his wife or girlfriend, I nevertheless went to say goodbye to him, looking to remind him that I really was serious about seeing his work.

"You can come to my studio now if you want," he said.

I didn't need to think twice, so I just said, "Right! Let's go, if you're sure it's not too late for you."

It was two in the morning, but for artists that means nothing.

Without saying goodbye to the women he was with, he pulled his green Tyrolian hat lower down on his head and the two of us headed out onto the heavy snow-covered streets. I walked behind him in his footprints and had this strong feeling that our lives were going to be entwined somehow. As we walked to his car, I instinctively knew that the huge black jeep with a skull and crossbones painted on the bonnet was his. Not so unusual in this day and age, but in 1983 it was a rare sight!

To my amazement, when I got inside his apartment and looked around, I saw that most of his decor was exactly the same as mine in London. All very oriental; walls covered with art, Indian and Arabic artefacts hanging everywhere, and the old familiar smell of incense. I felt as if I'd found a soulmate who shared the same tastes as me, and when his Siamese cats came out to greet him, I knew I'd found a real home from home.

We sat talking till seven in the morning, and I also got to look at his truly amazing paintings. As I was leaving, he asked me to choose one as a gift, and I selected a painting of a demented piano player which I carried back to my hotel under my arm. Funnily enough, he told me later that this was one of his most expensive pictures, and I'm happy to say that it still hangs above my own piano at home. Jorg was due to leave for Peru later in the week for a very long trip, but he cancelled everything to be with me, and within a couple of days we were an 'item'.

When I look back on this time, I have great memories. OK, perhaps I am wearing the old rose-tinted glasses, as in reality it wasn't always a bed of roses. Two artists living together can sometimes result in both interesting and explosive times, but we certainly had great adventures together, and this included lots of travelling.

One of our favourite haunts was Turkey, especially Istanbul. My father had always told me that the place to stay, back in the thirties, had been the famous Pera Palas Hotel where he'd drunk raki with Kemal Aturturk, so I was determined to stay there too. It never entered my head to book a room in advance as it was April, so not a particularly busy month. Ringing the hotel from Istanbul airport to reserve a room, I said, "Hello, this is Dana Gillespie and I'd like to reserve a room from tonight."

When they told me that they were fully booked, I was devastated, but I refused to take no for an answer so I hung up and rang them again, and this time I said, "Hello, this is Baroness de Winterstein, I'd like to reserve a double room for tonight." To my great pleasure, they said no problem, that was fine. So we leapt into a taxi and off we went to see what my father had always been talking about. That's the only time I've done such a thing – pulling rank with a title – and it amused me how well the ploy worked.

This was in 1983, and it was obvious that the decor hadn't changed much in the 50 years since my father had stayed there. Everything was run down and tired, a bit like an old British Rail sandwich curling up round the edges, but it was right in the centre of town and you always had the feeling that Agatha Christie might walk down the black marble staircase at any minute. This was where she got the inspiration to write 'Murder on the Orient Express', and the hotel had actually been built to accommodate the passengers that got off the famous train when the line was first opened. So many well-known people had stayed in the place, but it was definitely sliding into disrepair when Jorg and I were there. I've since heard that it has had a mega facelift and makeover, returning it to its former glories.

Another place we visited in 1983 was Marrakesh in Morocco, and whilst there I had a most extraordinary experience. To tell the story properly, I need to go back to my teenage years, briefly.

When I was 15-years-old, I started having strange visions. They occurred about every two months, and slowly escalated to about two a week. They would last between ten and 20 seconds, be accompanied by a curious smell, and an odd sensation as if I was falling off a cliff, and would leave me drenched in sweat. The visions themselves were nearly always the same: a row of men dressed in long flowing robes, all with beards and blue turbans on their heads, and all holding an instrument in their hands that looked a bit like a large tambourine. There were always nine of these men, standing with lighting from below, and they appeared to me as clear as anything in the real world. I could hear what was going on, but my vision was completely obliterated and I could only see the row of men.

I lived with this in my head for nearly a year, and didn't tell anyone as I was worried that maybe I'd smoked one joint too many. One day, I was driving my little car through the underpass at Hyde Park Corner and the nine men suddenly appeared in front of me. It was only my inner automatic pilot that stopped me crashing into a wall as I couldn't see the road, only the row of bearded men. This was when I realised that I had to tell somebody, as I could easily have killed myself and others. When I told my father, he was marvellous about it, and within a few days I was in the Queen's Hospital having electrodes put on my head and a huge syringe stuck in my neck to shoot coloured dye into my brain.

After lying absolutely still in hospital for two days, I was taken to see the top neurologist. He asked if I'd ever been dropped on my head as a baby, but the only thing I could think of was when I fractured my skull when I was five. He told me that I had a mild form of epilepsy called 'petit mal', and that sometimes pubescent girls get this but usually get over it. He then handed me some potent pills and said I should take them for six months, promising that this would stop the visions, though warning me that most people seemed to miss them.

How true this was. I did miss my visions, and no, they never came back, but the medication turned me into such a zombie that after three months I threw them away. I never forgot the row of men though; the image is as clear in my mind as if I'd seen them today.

Now, fast-forward 20 years. I'm in Marrakesh in 1983 to film a pop video for two songs, 'It Belongs To Me' and 'In Danger Tonight'. I was there with a professional film crew, headed by an Austrian director called Wolfgang Lesowsky, but also with me were two of my best friends, Jorg and Leslie. In fact, it was Jorg who directed the film for 'In Danger Tonight', whilst Leslie was put onto crowd control.

One evening we had tickets to see a big folklore festival at the Palais Badi. One of the reasons for going was to allow me to check out the sort of costume I wanted to be filmed in at the next day's shooting.

The festival was huge, with about 450 participants from all over Morocco, complete with dancers, musicians, camels, and horses. We had front row seats and I settled down to watch the show, but halfway through something happened that totally shocked me. Onto the stage walked the nine men from my visions, all wearing the same blue turbans and all holding the same musical instruments. I was amazed, as I was seeing something that I had seen 20 years earlier, the *identical* scene; even the lighting from below was the same.

To this day, I have no real explanation for what happened, but it made me realise that there are things going on in this world that are inexplicable. Could reincarnation be the answer? Had I been there in a different life? It would possibly explain why I felt so 'at home' in Morocco, and why I'd always felt drawn to this country. I could find my way around any back street in Marrakesh, whereas I'd often get lost in England if I moved away from my usual haunts. Although most Europeans get hassled just walking through the Djna el Fnaa main square, I used to walk through there as if I owned the place, and nobody ever troubled me for money or wanted to be my guide.

This whole episode opened my eyes to the possibility of rebirth and transmigration, and somehow it was also connected to my fractured skull when I had 'seen' the whole universe in a split second.

*

In 1984, I made another film appearance, this time alongside Bryan Brown, Cheri Lunghi and Tom Wilkinson in a British crime movie initially released as 'Parker' but subsequently renamed 'Bones'. I played a character called Monika, and one of the other actresses involved was another star of Hammer films, Ingrid Pitt. In the film, a successful businessman (Brown) disappears whilst on a trip to Germany, and later he claims that he had been kidnapped. It was directed by Jim Goddard, who had rather more success with his next movie 'Shanghai Surprise', starring Madonna and Sean Penn.

Following 'Bones', and another version of the life of Mahler (this time for Wolfgang Lesowsky), acting seemed to totally vanish from my life. The Mahler project was 'different', mind you, as it was a dramatized documentary in which the music – Bernard Haitink conducting the Berlin Philharmonic Orchestra – was probably a lot better than the acting. It was made in German and never really made the grade, but if you are really into Mahler you can find the DVD (with English subtitles), which is called 'To Live, I will Die'.

At the end of the eighties, my life was strolling along quite peacefully, and I wasn't on the lookout for any major changes in my world, but they say that God laughs when you make plans. He was certainly laughing now, as the biggest change *ever* was about to pick me up, throw me around, and dash me to the ground! All in the most positive sense.

14: INDIA CALLING

When the Sixties were going strong, and the Beatles were hanging out with the Maharishi, I never seemed to get the opportunity to go to India myself. So many of my friends were going off with rucksacks on their backs, but the moment was never right for me, though – if I'm honest – I probably wasn't really the type for sleeping rough. Finally, in the mid-seventies, I did manage to go. I went with Leslie, and visited Rajasthan to do the tourist triangle of Jaipur, Jodhpur, and Udaipur. We had such an amazing time that I fell in love with the country and vowed to return, though I didn't know when or with whom.

In the mid-eighties, I was back in Vienna to sign a new recording contract for my more commercial (in other words, not Blues) music with Gig Records. The boss of this company was Markus Spiegel, and he ran it from a swanky office right in the centre of town. He had done astronomically well with a hit called 'Rock Me Amadeus', which had been sung by a guy called Falco who had been on Spiegel's books for seven years. It's always a good sign if a record manager sticks by an artist over a long period. I felt confident in having Markus on my side, and went on to do three LPs for him, 'Hot News', 'Amor', and 'Where Blue Begins'.

Like the Bellaphon albums, these three Gig Records LPs were only released in what is known in the music biz as the 'GAS territories', namely Germany, Austria, and Switzerland. Much as I wanted people in my own country to hear my new music, I could never get any UK label interested. Even now, I am sad to say that what I consider to be some of my best work has never been heard by English ears.

Occasionally, I took a break from living with Jorg in Vienna, and went to Switzerland to meet up with my father in Davos. It meant being back in the wonderful Schatzalp Hotel, where I had nothing to do all day but walk in the snow, eat too much, swim, and read. My father was there with Lorna, and also staying with them was a wonderful Indian lady called Mukunda Kumari, who had decided to join them and breathe in the clear, clean Davos air. Mukunda was one of four children of the Rajmata of Navanagar and Jamnagar, and after leaving India many years earlier now lived around the corner from me in London.

My time in Davos was running out, and I had to take a 12-hour night train journey back to Vienna. To while away the hours, I asked Mukunda if she had a spare book to lend me as I had nothing to read. The only one she had on hand was a slim copy of something called 'Man of Miracles', written by an Australian called Howard Murphet. The book had a lot of pencil marks in the margins, as Mukunda was editing it with a view to publishing it in England. As this was the only thing on offer, I thanked her for it and took it gratefully with me onto the train. At the time, I thought that I'd probably get through it in a very short time, and then what would I read? How little I knew.

As soon as I opened the first page, I was hooked. My heart beat faster as I turned the pages, and instead of speed-reading at my usual galloping pace, I lingered over every word and slowly read through the book that was to change my life forever.

The book was all about an Indian guru and spiritual leader called Sri Sathya Sai Baba. Now, I thought I was pretty well up on my knowledge of spiritual Masters, having happily ploughed through everything on Yogananda, Vivekananda, Mehr Baba, and Ramakrishna, so I was surprised to see a name I had never heard of. It had always seemed odd to me that all the Spiritual Greats in the past – Jesus, Muhammad, Krishna, and Buddha – had lived over a thousand years ago, and yet where was a Saviour and Spiritual Teacher when we needed one in this day and age? I had assumed that nothing would ever come now and save us, me especially.

I didn't know what an Avatar was, and especially not a Purna-Avatar, which is what the book said Sai Baba was. When I researched this, I found that an Avatar is an incarnation of the divine consciousness, whilst a Purna-Avatar is the highest form of Avatar, someone who has a complete, comprehensive overview of everything and everyone. In other words, He is omniscient, omnipotent, and omnipresent, able to be anywhere at any time, do anything for anyone, and be in any form. This seemed an outrageously tall order, but the more I read, the more my heart kept telling me that this was no illusion.

Just as I came to the last page, the train pulled into the Westbahnhof in Vienna, and as I stepped onto the platform, I decided that I must return to India as soon as possible. Something had happened to my heart, and it was almost as if I had got off the train a different person. I would not be content until I had seen Sai Baba with my own eyes.

It was amazing how fast everything went from there. On returning to London, I applied for the first of my many Indian visas, reserved my ticket, and three weeks later I was on a plane to Mumbai (then Bombay), where I had to change to get a flight to Bangalore. From there, I had to take a five-hour taxi ride over pretty bad roads before finally reaching a small village called Puttaparthi. Nowadays, everything is so much easier, as you can fly direct to the modern Bangalore airport (now renamed Bengaluru), and the roads are so good all the way to Puttaparthi that the car part of the journey can sometimes be done in just over two hours.

I didn't notice or care about any discomfort on my first trip though, and looked forward to reaching my destination where I was sure Sai Baba would be waiting with open arms to welcome me. That was not how things panned out. I didn't know it then, but He never actually spoke to me for 12 years.

Although the place is called Prashanti Nilayam, meaning the Abode of Heavenly Peace, it seemed so crowded to me that peace was the last thing going. Forty years later, I am still going there once a year, only these days the thousands have become tens of thousands.

Because I knew no one there, I did what everyone must do when entering the Ashram; I registered at the accommodation office to get somewhere to sleep. In those days, there were many huge buildings known as the Sheds, a bit like small aircraft hangars, with hundreds of people sleeping on bedrolls with all their belongings stashed around each bed space and a mosquito net hung from above. Each Shed had about ten lavatories and showers, but with so many people it meant that one had to get up at the crack of dawn to get in line to use the facilities.

The first time I was shown inside one of the Sheds, I gulped with horror. I had never even slept in a girls' dormitory, so it was quite a shock to see so many ladies resting in various states of undress due to the heat. They were all waiting until it was time to go to Darshan, the word used for when Sai Baba would come out to talk and walk among the people, which would happen twice a day. Thinking that if all the other ladies could stand this lifestyle, I just had to knuckle down to make the space around my bedroll as habitable as possible, though I did wonder how I was ever going to get to sleep.

Life in the Ashram was very disciplined, with lights out at nine in the evening. Everyone got up between four and five in the morning in order to do Omkar, which meant walking in silence around the temple area, known as the Mandir. This you would typically do nine times, in keeping with the nine planets, but some people would do it 21 times, and others would even get to 108 times – as that is a holy number for many Indians.

On my first night there, I had no idea what I was doing, and at ten minutes before lights out, a man stood at the entrance of the Shed and called out my name. Oddly, he shouted for Dana Gillespie, and I wondered how he knew this name as I had registered in the name of Richenda. He told me I could have a room in the modern Round House, but I couldn't be in the room alone and must find some ladies to share it with me. Not knowing a soul there, I told him that I would try to find some companions the next day, as by then it was too dark to do anything. Grabbing my bedroll and bags, I followed him to the building that was considered the best place to stay.

He opened the door to show me a concrete-floored bare room with nothing on the walls. The loo was the usual hole in the ground, with one tap over an ancient sink and another tap where you put a bucket to wash with. At least it was quiet. In fact, it was too quiet.

Laying down on the concrete floor, I somehow drifted off into a deep sleep, being dead tired due to the long journey. Strangely enough, two ladies turned up the next morning without me even having to search for them, one English and one German, and having established that they too needed somewhere to sleep, I looked on as they made a little altar by their respective beds on the floor, putting flowers around a photograph of Sai Baba. I realised I had nothing to build an altar, and didn't even know where to get a photograph of the One I had come to see.

Getting up at dawn has never been a problem for me, so I ventured out of my room to join the crowds that were all heading for the Mandir. In order to get a place at the front, one had to join lines of women who were all waiting patiently for what can only be described as a sort of lottery. The person at the front of each line had to a draw a number out of a little bag to determine which line they would go in. Everyone would be hoping to get number 1, which meant the front row.

While the ladies were conducting this seating lottery, the same would be happening on the men's side, as Sai Baba was always very particular that the sexes should sit segregated.

The moment I had been waiting for – that magic time when Sai Baba came out at 6 a.m. – was not at all like I had imagined. For starters, He didn't even look at me as I was sitting quite far back. He walked through the crowds as if inspecting His flock. With a mass of curly black hair, almost afro-style, He wore His trademark orange robe that went down to the ground and covered His feet. Occasionally, He would stop and allow someone to touch His feet, or even kiss them, which is a mark of the highest respect. No such thing happened to me as I got no hello or recognition, but I felt an extraordinary peace in my heart, and I knew that this was what I had unknowingly been looking for all my life. This was where I was meant to be, even if it was in the back row.

There was gentle music playing as He seemed to float around His devotees. This was the only sound to be heard, as otherwise there was pin-drop silence. My immediate reaction, when I got my first look at Sai Baba, was that I must give up eating meat. I hadn't gone to India with the intention of becoming a vegetarian, but it became clear to me that this was what I must do, and from that day on, I have never eaten meat.

To go into the temple area, all the ladies had to cover their shoulders, either with the pallou if wearing a sari, or with a scarf or shawl if wearing a full-length skirt or shalwar kameez (a sort of baggy trousers and long top). No flaunting of the female body was allowed, and the rule still stands, as discipline and decency were, and are, the order of the day.

The men would all dress in white, often a kurta pyjama, which makes sense from a practical point of view as it kept the wearer cool in the heat.

In a way, my first trip to Puttaparthi was pretty uneventful, and looking back I can see I was just learning how to survive an ashram existence. I left the place very uplifted, full of the joys of spring, and determined to be a better person.

Back home, some lifestyle changes had to be made. First up, I stacked all my diaries in a tin bucket and burned the lot. Having written a page-a-day diary since the age of 11, there was quite a bonfire as many of my old 'encounters' literally went up in smoke. When I told my friends what I had done, they were shocked, and there is no doubt that the diaries would have been very useful whilst writing this book! Still, what's done is done.

As one of the main sayings at the Ashram is 'Love all, Serve All', I decided to enrol as a volunteer at the Royal Marsden Hospital, around the corner from where I lived. This is probably the most famous cancer hospital in Britain, and like every hospital, there is an organisation called the League of Friends that provides a small shop for patients to purchase things, and a trolley service which visits the wards for those that are too ill to get out of bed. I was happy to join them; at last, I had found something useful I could do.

Many people come out of this great hospital totally healed, but some do not, and I made it a point of chatting to the patients as I was doing my rounds. It was always heartbreaking to see some of them, so skeletal and thin, and just about clinging on to life. In the 11 years that I volunteered as a League of Friends helper, I can honestly say that I learnt and got far more from the patients than I ever gave of myself, and it gave me a good insight into what can easily be the end place for many of us. Eventually, I had to give it up as I was doing so much travelling that I was never in one place long enough to be counted on to do my allotted shifts.

Having experienced and seen with my own eyes all that Sai Baba was doing in India, I really wanted to spread the good news to all my friends and family. To my dismay, no one was interested; in fact, some were even hostile when I tried to tell them what I had seen. More of a shock to me was that my absolute closest friends, like Jorg and Leslie, didn't want to know and thought I had lost the plot. Luckily, Tom and my mother wanted to see for themselves, and so too did my father's partner, Ingrid. Dadster said that he felt he was too old to take such a long journey, but he knew Ingrid wanted to go and so he bought us both air tickets to go four months after my first visit.

Since returning from my first trip to the Ashram, I had been feeling so good, as I'd cleaned up my life by renouncing sex and drugs and rock and roll. How naive was that? The night before I was due to fly to India with Ingrid, I had a riotous evening with an old friend from the sixties, Richard Cole, who had been Led Zeppelin's road manager. All the things I had previously renounced I managed to squeeze into one night, and so the next day I felt like death; I could hardly walk as I staggered on and off the plane to Bangalore, and walked around the Ashram like a zombie for three days, feeling mortified that I had broken all my promises.

There is one aspect of Ashram life that consists of singing Bhajans, a type of devotional song. This was done twice daily, and I loved these songs, even though it took me a while to get the hang of them. On my third day of feeling wretched, I sat in the Bhajan Hall, about 20 rows from the front, and watched as everyone around me was singing and clapping to the music and looking so happy. I just sat there and cried. Not a loud sobbing cry, but silent and aching, and the worst thing was that I couldn't stop my tears from flowing. Up on the stage sat Sai Baba, merrily beating time to the music with His right hand, whilst His left hand rested on His knee and didn't move at all. Occasionally, He would look sympathetically at me as if to say, 'Calm down, don't cry'.

After 20 minutes of this, my dress was soaking wet, and I asked Him silently in my heart, "If You really are all that they say You are, and You can really see into my heart, then I want a sign from You *now*. I want You to beat time for me once with Your left hand."

Without taking His eyes from me, He beat time once with His left hand, and then never moved His left hand again till He finally left the stage. This was my first clear example of His omniscience, and it shook me to the core. It was also a relief, as I felt as if all my later, the rumour doing the rounds was that I had once been a stripper. That was never the case.

I was still recording other kinds of CDs and not just Blues, and was writing a lot of songs with one of my favourite men on the planet – David Malin – the stepson of actor John Le Mesurier of 'Dad's Army' fame. Malin and I would often spend days and nights writing together, and when I look back now, I can see that he was by my side for some of the best songs that I have ever written. Having collected enough material for an album, I booked the studios, and – together with Nick Hogarth – Malin and I started work on the 'Methods of Release' project.

Some albums have a very special place in my heart, and this is one of them. All the musicians were great; they included Guy Pratt (bass player in Pink Floyd after Roger Waters left), Mel Gaynor (drummer in Simple Minds), Mel Collins (sax for King Crimson, Camel), Tim Cross on keyboards (more of him later), Bill Sharpe from Shakatak on piano, Durga McBroom (one of the backing singers for Pink Floyd), and Tim Renwick (Pink Floyd touring guitarist, Eric Clapton, Elton John, David Bowie, and others too many to mention). Also on these sessions was Pandit Dinesh playing tablas and percussion, who has been in my life ever since we met – years earlier – at a song festival in Sopot, Poland. I first saw him playing there with a group called Blancmange, and he has since played on about 15 different CDs with me.

One song, called 'Still around', was written as a duet for Gary Glitter and me to sing, but he didn't turn up for the session so I sang it solo. This was after his seventies/eighties heyday, but before his ignominious fall from grace in the late nineties.

Another song on the album was 'Sun Arise', made famous by Rolf Harris, another who has sadly been in the news for the wrong reasons in recent years. He played on quite a few of my CDs, and even joined me and The London Blues Band at what I still think of as the Hammersmith Odeon when we performed at the Mick Ronson memorial concert in 1994. Rolf, who was still really popular then, got a huge roar from the crowd when he stepped onto the stage and did a wobble board solo on my song, 'A Lotta What You Got'.

Showing how loved and respected Ronno was, the show drew a star-studded list of performers. The surviving Spiders from Mars, Trevor Bolder and Woody Woodmansey, played some old Ziggy-era songs, with Joe Elliott from Def Leppard deputising for Bowie and Phil Collen standing in for Ronno on a stunning 'Moonage Daydream'. Roger Daltrey (The Who), Roger Taylor (Queen), Steve Harley (Cockney Rebel), Gary Brooker (Procol Harum), Mick Jones (The Clash), Bill Wyman (Rolling Stones), and Ian Hunter (Mott the Hoople) were amongst the many musicians who took part. It was a very emotional evening and when, towards the end, Ian sang his tribute to Ronno, 'Michael Picasso', there wasn't a dry eye in the house.

Mick Ronson was a truly great human being as well as being a hugely talented musician, and I just wish he had lived longer. He was hurt when he and the Spiders were sacked by Bowie – they had been like brothers when they were on the road together – but it was time to move on. Nothing lasts forever.

The cover of the 'Methods of Release' CD was a painting by Jorg in which I'm riding a tiger and have eight arms, a bit like the Goddess Durga. It was just one of Jorg's fanciful psychedelic paintings, and it was clear to me that I was not trying to appear as Her.

As I was doing some concerts in India at the time, The Times of India interviewed me for a big story for their Sunday magazine. I was to be on the front cover, and they said they would send a photographer over to take some pictures, but he didn't turn up. The newspaper was going to press that night, so with no photograph available, they used the first picture of me that they could get hold of, which was Jorg's album cover painting.

Once the newspaper hit the streets, all hell broke loose.

Shiv Sena, the Bombay-based Hindu nationalist political party which used a tiger as their emblem, was very strong and militant at the time, and they thought I was being disrespectful by sitting on a tiger. On seeing the offending picture, they contacted the Times saying that if an apology was not immediately printed, they would blow up the newspaper building and eliminate me. This was even reported back in England by Reuters.

15: DIRTY BLUES

The nineties was a decade when I seemed to be busy all the time, mostly with music, which is the way I like it. As well as doing a lot of gigs with the London Blues Band, I had now got onto a good circuit working with the Viennese boogie-woogie pianist Joachim Palden, playing Blues venues all over Europe.

We recorded our first 'Live' album together from December 7th to 9th 1990 in Jazzland, and released it as 'Boogie Woogie Nights'. Our follow-up album was called 'Big Boy', and was recorded in England with Mike Vernon as producer, with the added bonus of having Magic Slim and the Teardrops from Chicago on some of the tracks. This was also the first time I got to work with a great sax player called Martin Winning, who was to join my band a few years later but then left after a couple of years when Van Morrison offered him a higher profile and more money. Of course, I forgave him, and we still work together occasionally; Martin co-wrote, with me, most of the songs for my Ace Records CD called 'Staying Power'.

The 'Big Boy' album included a song called 'Fine and Fancy Free', which due to a printing error on the CD cover was unfortunately called 'Fine and Fanny Free', thereby giving it a wholly unintended meaning. To add insult to injury, their promotional material for the album called it 'Bog Boy'. That's what can happen when an Austrian record company releases your music.

Joachim Palden is a very easy-going guy, and when I was offered the chance to do some concerts in India – working primarily for the Taj Hotel Group but sometimes the Oberoi in Mumbai – he said he'd be happy to come along and play. Even though we got very little money for performing, we did have the great pleasure of staying in fabulous five-star Hotels, eating well and living like kings – or maybe I should say, Maharajahs.

For both of us, it was a way to get to know the country better, but I had an ulterior motive for going. The Taj also sent us to their wonderful West End Hotel in Bangalore, where we only had to play for an hour every night. After the last note of the performance, I would take a taxi (preferably an Ambassador car) all the way to Puttaparthi, arriving at about five in the morning and ready for Sai Baba's first appearance of the day. When that was over, I'd get in the cab for the long return journey, and go back to catch up on sleep at the hotel.

*

Something rather unusual happened to me during 1991; I was interviewed for Austrian television company ORF by film producer and director Rudi Dolezal. What is unusual about that, you may be thinking. The answer is that the interview took place in the bath, with both of us starkers!

It wasn't the first time this had happened. When I first came to Vienna in the early 80s, I was invited by ORF to appear on one of their programmes with Rudi. It was he who suggested that – "to make things more interesting" – we should conduct the interview naked in the bath. Of course, I said yes, on the understanding there would be plenty of bubble bath and foam. Sadly (or maybe not), the footage from the 80s programme has been lost, but Rudi still has a copy of the 1991 interview.

During his colourful career, Rudi has made music videos for many of the world's leading rock stars, including the Rolling Stones, Bruce Springsteen, Michael Jackson, Whitney Houston, David Bowie, and U2. However, he's probably best known for having made many iconic videos and documentaries for Queen and Freddie Mercury. And maybe for interviewing me in the bath three times.

Yes, three times.

In 2016 Rudi decided to make a documentary about me for his film company DoRo called '25 jahre danach, damals heute' (25 years later, then and today), so yet another naked bath interview was set up, involving even more bubbles than before. This has to be one of the craziest ways of doing an interview, but I just remember it being great fun, even if we fought even more than before over the diminishing foam, as neither of us wanted to expose too much. Funnily enough, the documentary ends with me telling Rudi – in the bath, of course – that I was going to write my memoirs.

*

The 24th of May 1991, was Bob Dylan's 50th birthday, and one of the British newspapers asked 50 of his friends what they would give him as a birthday present. Marianne Faithfull suggested a leopard-skin pillbox hat, and Judy Collins proposed a Francis Bacon painting, but I said I'd give him a ticket to India and show him a good time so that he'd smile more. It occurred to me, later, that people might have misunderstood what I'd said… I meant that he ought to come with me to see Sai Baba.

*

It was soon time to go back into the studios to record another Blues album called 'Where Blues Begin', again produced by Mike Vernon. He and I travelled daily from London to Portsmouth to work in a studio owned by Bob Ross, and I was quite happy when the title track was 'covered' by a well-known Danish singer called Sanne Salomonson. It always makes you feel good when someone else likes one of your songs so much that they record their own version. This was actually a co-write with Mike Vernon, David Malin, and Mo Whitham, and I'm pleased to say that the royalties still roll in.

I was also doing quite a few European tours with the sax-playing legend Big Jay McNeely, who had actually started recording in the year I was born. The fact that he was then in his seventies made no difference to the great sound he and his tenor saxophone could make, a real old-style honking Blues with all the right licks. We co-wrote some songs and made a CD of duets called 'Cherry Pie', recorded it at Pete Thomas's studio in London, and used many of the musicians I regularly worked with: Ed Deane on guitar, Dave Rowberry and Ben Waters on piano, Steve Lima on bass, Chris Hunt on drums, and David Malin on tambourine and backing vocals.

Looking back, things were going well on the music front. I was voted leading British Female Blues Vocalist by the British Blues Connection and Blueprint Magazines between 1992 and 1996, and was later elevated into their Hall Of Fame.

I must have forgotten how grim and exhausting it can sometimes be at the Edinburgh Festival because I agreed to do another new show there. It was the idea of an old friend of mine called Kevin Williams, whom I had first met when he had rather appropriately played 'Cousin Kevin' in the musical 'Tommy'. The idea was to call the show 'The Dirtiest Blues In Town', and I guess in a way it was. On the song 'Sweet Meat' I had to get on my knees and sing into the crotch of singer/guitarist Earl Okin, and on 'My Man Stands Out', Mike Paice the sax player had to raise up his instrument from behind the piano, so it looked like it was... standing out!

As part of the show was sponsored by a condom company, I even had to hand out condoms to the bemused audience as they left. This was the Aids era when people were being advised to use condoms, and there were slogans all over London saying things like "Don't be iffy, come in a Jiffy".

I talked my Blues Band into joining me – together with two beautiful, young, black jive dancers to liven things up – and we all set off for a two-week stint in the Gilded Ballroom. The show was very scripted, involving me talking about little episodes of my life between songs, and I couldn't deviate too much on stage as there were dance and lighting cues to be considered.

The show included a saucy old song called 'Meatballs', and Kevin suggested that I went and fed meatballs into the mouths of the audience. I was going to put my foot down and say no until he assured me that the 'meatballs' were actually vegetarian.

The production did well in Edinburgh, so Kevin said that we must bring it to London. He booked us in at the little-known Boulevard Theatre, bang in the heart of the red-light district of Soho, in a small alley surrounded by sex shops behind the legendary transvestite nightclub Madame JoJos. There was a big sign outside the theatre with the name of our show on it, and everyone said we'd be sure to get passing trade. This was true, but probably only because the punters thought they'd be seeing a real dirty strip show. They must have been somewhat disappointed. There were Blues fans there too, but not enough to make the show the success that we all thought it would be; yet another mad venture bit the dust.

Around this time, I was given a role in a short made-for-TV feature film called 'Byron's Mine', featuring Leslie Phillips. It was a rather strange production in which Leslie played a vicar who, over a hundred years after Lord Byron's death, decided to dig up

Byron's body as part of a wild scheme to raise funds for the church where the famous poet was buried. His partners in crime in this plot are a psychic medium (my role), together with another woman played by Tricia George. Their purpose in digging up His Lordship was to confirm the longstanding rumour that he had been extremely well-endowed.

The film includes what is probably my only front-page newspaper headline, in which Tricia and I (showing as much cleavage as was permitted those days) appear under the heading "Dirty Dames in Ding-Donger over Byron's Big Organ" in a spoof newspaper called 'The Sunday Spank', which prides itself on containing "All the sex that's unfit to print."

'Byron's Mine' was broadcast on ITV in 1993, and the director, Nick McCann, included several songs from my 'Blues It Up' compilation album on the soundtrack. The songs chosen were 'Come On (If You're Coming)', 'Organ Grinder' and, somewhat appropriate in view of the storyline, 'Big Ten Inch'.

*

For most of the Nineties, I spent a lot of my time commuting between London and Vienna, where I hosted a weekly radio show called 'Globetrotting with Gillespie', specialising in Indian, African, Arabic, and Blues music. This was transmitted on an English-speaking station called 'Blue Danube Radio' and was syndicated across most of Europe every Saturday night. I didn't do it 'live' as I was never in town on a regular basis, so often would go into the ORF building and pre-record a month's worth of shows.

One day, during one of my few 'live' shows, before playing a Ray Charles record, I offered up this old chestnut. "Someone once gave Ray Charles a cheese grater, and he said it was the most violent book he'd ever read!" Of course, I got a bollocking for saying that, although it still makes me smile now.

Having this programme also meant that I was part of the World Music Jury, that had the great task of voting which CDs should be in the World Music Hit Parade. The CDs were voted on by various disc jockeys across the world, so I used to get sent loads of CDs and would listen to every single one, even if it meant sitting up till four in the morning.

Sadly, after 11 years, ORF decided to close the whole station down, so my show got the chop. I was philosophical enough about it but sorry to see it go. Ah well, nothing lasts forever, and anyway I had things to do in India.

In 1996, it was Sai Baba's 70th birthday, and huge celebrations were planned to run for the week leading up to the actual day of November 23rd. No one was more surprised than me when – two months before this date – I got a call asking if I'd like to perform. Of course I said yes, and as I had just done my first Indian-style Bhajan CD, I assumed that this would be the sort of music that was wanted. In fact, Sai Baba Himself had said that I should do my Western music. This presented me with a real problem as the only Blues songs that I really knew and performed were ones with totally unsuitable lyrics, often very bawdy and risqué, and Sai Baba's Ashram was definitely not the place for that.

The next problem I had was finding the musicians to come with me, as this would involve a week in India with no alcohol, no smoking, no meat… and no money. Although it was relatively easy in later years to persuade them to come out to Mustique, I wasn't exactly overwhelmed with positive responses for a trip to India on these terms, so I had to look elsewhere. To be fair, Ed Deane, who was my great Irish left-handed guitarist, said yes and so too did the bass player, Adrian Stout. That still left the problem of the pianist and drummer, so I asked Joachim Palden who straightaway agreed to come, and he found the drummer Harry Hudson (who plays with a wonderful old-style Austrian Blues singer/guitarist called Al Cook), to come onboard.

Even I was not prepared for the hundreds of thousands of people who had travelled from all over the world to celebrate Sai Baba's Birthday. The organisers had told me that I'd be well looked after, but I was concerned in case they put the musicians into one of the communal sheds. I needn't have worried, as they were given two rooms with beds in them, and I was in the height of luxury as I had a room of my own, with a proper bed to sleep on.

The other surprise for me was that I didn't have to sit at the back. There were music performances every day for a week, with posters everywhere saying which musicians were playing on which day. Many of the Indian performers were very famous, but right down at the bottom of the list – scheduled for the final night of the 23rd

– it just said, "Dana Gillespie, London". No one knew who I was, and definitely no one knew I was about to perform Blues, as this type of music had never been done there before.

Because Adrian Stout had arrived late in India, just in time to make the concert, the band and I didn't have an opportunity to rehearse together. What little time we had for a soundcheck was pretty useless as the grand piano was so badly out of tune that Joachim spent all of our allotted time trying to make it sound better. Thank heavens he'd bought a tuning fork with him.

The stadium is about ten minutes' walk from the main Ashram area, but due to the incredible swelling crowds, it took about an hour to get there. I had seen some Japanese walking around with masks covering their faces, and I remember thinking that I was not going to walk around looking idiotic like that, no matter how dusty it was. Big mistake!

In all the heat, dust, and crowd, there was a strange feverous bug going around, and naturally, I got it within one hour of arriving. Twenty-four hours before the scheduled time of my performance, I had a burning fever, running nose, and worse still, no voice at all.

On the actual day of the concert, all the artistes were gathered up and ferried to a waiting area behind the stage, which had been constructed like a huge sun, out of which we would each appear at the appointed time. It was far too crowded to get back to the rooms to lie down, so we had to stay in this area all day in the baking heat. To make things worse, as men and women were segregated, I didn't have a chance to tell my musicians or anyone else that I felt like death. Whilst I could cope with feeling bad, the fact that I had lost my voice was a different matter altogether.

Looking out at this sea of humanity – a crowd of a million – I wondered how I'd ever get through the day. Half a before the band and I were scheduled to go on, I looked ac Sai Baba who was sitting about 30 yards from me. He was g out over the enormous crowds, and I said a prayer to "Dearest Baba, You have got me all the way here, and I'm mess, and I need Your help, so if You want me to sing well, t please look at me and help me NOW."

He immediately turned His head and stared into my eyes, and I had a feeling that I would somehow survive. Within five minutes, a stranger came up to me and offered me some cloves to suck, saying that his father had been a singer and that this would help the voice. A minute later, another person came up to me and gave me some vibhuti (a kind of grey ash often 'materialised' by Sai Baba) to eat.

Before I started to sing, even a whisper was agony, and I simply had no idea what would come out of my mouth. Fortunately, once I started, about 60 per cent of my voice seemed to be working, and although I was sounding rather gruff it didn't matter; in fact, it was ideal for singing the Blues.

There were about 200 cameramen and television crews there, all busy recording the event and also putting it up on the huge screens that were positioned around the stadium. As I started to sing, Sai Baba got up from His chair and went and sat on His jhoola, which is a kind of swing, and began to rock back and forth in time with the music.

My short set was only three songs, not a lot compared to my normal two or three hours at a Blues gig, and I'd written suitable lyrics which I'd hoped were uplifting but still in the Blues genre. The first song was 'I Sigh For You', Chicago Blues in style but with the added bonus of having a double meaning: Sai and Sigh. This was followed by a slow Blues number called 'Big Daddy Blues', as that was my nickname for Baba. We finished on a fast boogie-woogie, which is Joachim's forte and it was simply called 'Happy Birthday Baba'.

After the show was over, I made my way back to my room. My shoe had broken, and my knee was aching from standing on it all day, so I limped barefoot through the streets. This was a good lesson for me, as one minute you can be singing for the Avatar of the Age, and the next minute you can be nearly crawling on your knees. It is most important to treat both situations as equal.

After 12 years of going to Puttaparthi, I'd still never experienced a private interview with Sai Baba, and I was starting to accept my fate. My hopes were raised when I was told that He always calls in the artistes for an interview the day after they perform for Him, and so it was with great expectation and excitement that I sat with all the other performers the day after His Birthday, waiting for Him to come out for the morning Darshan. He walked slowly along the line of performers, and picked every single person to go in for a personal interview – except for me. As everyone else stood up to go into the interview room, I sat on the floor alone, in front of a huge crowd, and I don't think I have ever felt so small and unloved. I had been deliberately ignored, and was absolutely shattered by it. Worse still, I was aware that most people might have loathed my Blues music, and I wondered if this was the reason I hadn't been chosen.

Now I had the awful task of standing up and walking out of the Mandir area, with my head held high as if I didn't care and without breaking down in tears. Of course, I did care, and it hurt me so much. Even as I write this now, I can almost taste my own blood in my mouth as I bit my gums so hard to stop myself from crying until I got back to the privacy of my own room. Once there, I burst into tears and howled into my pillow.

It was while I was crying that I realised Sai Baba had, in fact, answered a prayer I had made five years earlier. Someone at the Russell Square Sai Centre had been explaining that the real significance of Krishna, often swinging on the jhoola, is that the Lord should swing in our heart, and I remember thinking, 'Hmm, I like that. Please dearest Baba, will You swing whenever I sing?' I thought back to the previous day, and this is what He had done at the concert the moment I had started to sing. Never in a million years did I imagine He would answer my prayer in such a way!

It wasn't until four months later that Sai Baba actually took me to His private interview room and spoke to me. I wish I could say exactly what He said to me, but my memory of this is erased. In fact, I'm told that many people remember nothing when first confronted by Sai Baba's mesmerising eyes, and having waited 12 years for this moment, my brain had gone blank.

Years later, Sai Baba asked me if I wanted to ask Him a question, and as I couldn't think of anything too earth-shattering, I just said, "Swami, what is the meaning of this thing called Life?"

He looked at me sweetly and said five important words.

"Play the Game. Be happy!"

Anyway, I said to Basil, "You love the Blues, and I do the Blues, so if you get a real piano here then I'll find some musicians to come out and play."

This was the night that Basil and I came up with the idea of starting the Mustique Blues Festival, which in 2020 celebrated its 25th consecutive year.

The harbour bar is a perfect place for a gig, as the stage, dance floor and dining area are three-quarters surrounded by the ocean, and at night all you see are the lights of the yachts bobbing on the water. It's a stunning setting, and the Festival has become one of the highlights of the year for those lucky enough to attend.

We decided that the festival should be organised to raise funds for the Basil Charles Education Foundation, a charity which arranged educational scholarships for the children of St. Vincent. It does so much more than that now, to such a point that Basil was awarded the OBE by the Queen in 2005, and was invited to attend the wedding of Prince William and Kate Middleton in 2011. Although St. Vincent is only ten minutes away on a little hopper plane, there are still many children in need and places of real poverty on the island, even though Mustique is so near and is rolling in money.

A few weeks later, after Jorg and I had returned to Europe, Basil flew to New York and bought a white upright piano, and the following January, the first Mustique Blues Festival took place.

My job was to find the musicians and ask them to come and play for 15 nights. There was no payment involved, but I knew full well that if we offered free tickets to the West Indies in January to a bunch of English musicians, nobody would say no. We started very small but grew organically, and every year it got bigger and better with more and more people coming to enjoy the music. In the early days, we had well-known British blues musicians performing, then – after a few years – we started to get the Americans to come. Nowadays, a great enthusiastic crowd is there every night.

Basil and the Mustique Company organised the airfares, food, and accommodation for the musicians, and I was responsible for making sure everyone got on and off the stage at the right times, as well as checking the recordings that I was overseeing every night. At the end of each Festival, I would take these recordings home to London, have the best ones mixed and mastered at Wolf Studios in Brixton, and put them onto a compilation CD. Over the years, I have taken so many CDs to be mixed and mastered there, by the quiet Frenchman Dominique Brethes, that this studio has become almost like a second home for me. The proceeds of the CDs all go to the charity, sometimes augmented by donations given by people who happened to be in the audience or who had heard the show from their yachts.

Princess Margaret was in the audience in the first year of the festival. My band and I performed the song 'King Size Papa', which was originally recorded by Julia Lee, who was famous for singing songs with very naughty/suggestive lyrics. While I was singing, I saw to my amazement that Princess Margaret was mouthing the words of the risqué song. At the end of our set, she came round the back of the stage and, although I knew full well that Royal protocol means you can't ask a member of the Royal Family a question, on that occasion my enthusiasm overcame me and I asked her how she knew the song. She smiled and told me, "When I was a little girl, my father used to sing it to me. He was, after all, the King."

When you think of it… that made perfect sense.

A year or two later, when I was on Mustique, Colin Tennant rang me up and asked if I would like to attend a luncheon party which he was hosting for Ma'am on Macaroni beach. She was there with her son David Linley and daughter-in-law Serena, together with fashion designer Carolina Herrera, and she looked so unhappy. Whether she was on some pills or something I don't know, but she seemed very lonely and distant. My heart really went out to her because she used to be the life and soul of the party, and clearly, something had happened.

That was the last time I ever saw her alive.

When I read some of the negative things that have been written about Princess Margaret, I do get very upset. She was always far nicer than she is ever portrayed in books.

Since those early days, Mustique has become a famous celebrity hotspot, and is sometimes described as 'Billionaires' Island'. Mick Jagger bought a piece of land quite early, and you can rent his house 'Stargroves' if you want to, provided you can afford it.

Ridge Mountain Train', 'Blue One Too', 'Out of the Blue', 'Who's got the Blues to Blame', 'Too Blue to Boogie?', 'Blue Night', 'Baby Blue', 'Blue Water', 'Back to the Blues', 'Travelling Man Blues', 'Guardian Blue Angel', 'The Sky Will Still Be Blue', 'It Makes Me Blue', 'Turning over a Blue Leaf', 'Queen of the Blues'.

The great thing about the colour Blue is that it lends itself to so many emotions and situations where another colour could never do. Black is too dark and moody, pink is too gay, red is too political, green is too environmental, brown is too boring, yellow does nothing to me (and I'd never wear it as a colour), orange doesn't rhyme with anything so that only leaves BLUE, the perfect colour for a Blues lyric!

*

After the first Mustique Blues Festival in 1996, I went to Mustique every year for the next 20 years. This would always involve several weeks' work before and after the Festival; telephone calls and emails to make sure all the performers knew their travel plans, a week of mixing time in the studios to complete the CD, and getting the cover finished by Jorg in time for it to be printed and shipped out to be sold in Mustique. Once this was done, I could relax until July, when I would start trying to pin down the musicians for the following year.

Only I don't relax. This was when I would take off for Vienna to do some regular gigs with Joachim Palden, drummer Sabine Pyrker and sax player Tom Muller. Wherever we did festivals, I would always keep my ear to the ground to see which musicians were hot, thinking of who would fit in well at the Mustique Festival. Being on a small island and dealing with the same musicians every night could get fraught if the wrong attitude creeps in, or if someone freaks out. I had to be sure that all the participants would gel well together.

On one occasion, in the late nineties, I was in America doing some gigs with Big Jay McNeely, and while there I stopped off to see Keith Richards. Roy Martin, who used to go out with Angie Bowie and who was now working as Keith's minder, drove into New York to pick me up and take me out to Keith's house. At the time, Keith was recovering from an accident which had caused the postponement of the European leg of the Rolling Stones' 'Bridges to Babylon' tour. He told me that he had been standing on some library steps to reach for a Leonardo da Vinci book on the top shelf, put his weight onto another ladder that had wheels on it, went flying and broke two ribs. Keith was famously reported as having said, "I was looking for Leonardo da Vinci's book on anatomy. I learned a lot about anatomy, but didn't find the book."

When we arrived, Keith said that he couldn't offer us anything, explaining that all his dealers had left town because they thought he was going on tour. He had a little pile of grass, and rather apologetically said, "I'm sorry, but that's all I've got for now."

Keith was never as out of it as people used to think, and that becomes clear when you read all the stories in his excellent autobiography, 'Life'. Perhaps he shouldn't have mentioned the size of Mick's private part (and I can't even remember if it's true or not!), but I do know that, even if a guy is hung like a donkey, the effect of too much cocaine is that he will have a tinier todger.

One further memory involving Roy and Keith was in 2006, when Roy phoned to say he had backstage passes for the Rolling Stones concert at Twickenham, and would I like to see the show. This was on the Stones' 'Bigger Bang' tour, which had been getting great reviews, so I happily accepted Roy's kind invitation.

My seat was alongside the sound and lighting technicians in the middle of the stadium, in a small, enclosed section for around 20 people surrounded by fencing. It was a really fantastic place to sit, with a great view of the spectacular stage set. My favourite memory of the day was when Keith came to the front for the first time to do a solo, at which point a lady called Doris, who was sitting behind me, leant forward and proudly said to me, "That's my son up there."

17: BLUES AND BHAJANS

After Sai Baba's 70th birthday celebrations, I made a point of visiting India every November to see Him. I have always felt that I could 'feel' Him wherever I was in the world and – even though I was usually shattered after a long flight with not enough sleep – the moment He walked into the Sai Kulwant Hall, my heart would swell up with joy. It didn't even matter if He was looking somewhere else, just to see Him was enough for me. With much to learn about myself and the world, going to Puttaparthi meant I could enter a completely different atmosphere, one that involved introspection and inner transformation.

Ever since I had sung at His birthday event, Sai Baba would notice me in the crowd and acknowledge me, and sometimes He would call me over and speak to me. Over the years, I was invited to sing on most of His birthdays, although I missed out on two of them due to illness. If I arrived alone in Puttaparthi, with no musicians, I would sometimes sing to a backing track, and occasionally augmented this with live musicians.

Most years, Sai Baba came over to me in the backstage area before His birthday concert and personally checked me up and down to make sure that I was correctly dressed. One year, He gave me eight saris, and from this, I got the hint that perhaps now was the time to get more feminine and stylish; out went the pyjamas and in came the elegance of a flowing sari. Nowadays, I wear a sari as easily as I would slip into a pair of jeans, though I only dress like this in India.

Usually, when an artist performed for Sai Baba, they would present Him with a rose while kneeling in front of Him, and often they would be allowed to touch His feet or even kiss them. This is called 'Padnamaskar', and it is considered to be a great blessing, a mark of surrender, and a wonderful honour.

My problem with handing Him a rose before a concert was one of practicality. If I got down on my knees, I'd struggle to get up again gracefully because my left knee didn't bend properly, so kneeling was out of the question and I had to think of another option. (That's one more position gone out of my life!) The answer came to me in the form of rose petals, as it was much easier for me to just drop the petals on His feet, which I continued to do before each concert.

By now, I was going to India twice or even three times a year. I like the fact that I could be in the Ashram one week, and then a Blues club or at a Festival the next. It keeps me on my toes, shows me the world from two totally different perspectives, and gives me plenty to think about. Strangely, I tend to write my Indian-style songs when I'm out on the road doing Blues, when the mind can wander while sitting in the back of a van going to a gig. Conversely, in India, where there is usually a lot of sitting around, I often find my mind thinking of ways to write naughty Blues songs. Inspiration about love can come from all directions.

I still like to write raunchy lyrics with double entendres as they are fun to perform and it is – after all – one of the things I'm known for. The 'Hot Stuff' and the 'Blues it up' CDs were really my tribute to the old days when sexual lyrics were very tongue-in-cheek, basically good time music without being crude, and definitely not offensive. If they passed the test of being performed in front of my mother, and she heard them often, then so far as I was concerned, they were fine.

In 1999, it was time for me to record a new Ace album, so I got the band together and produced a CD called 'Experienced'. The musicians, and all the extra people who came in to play on it, were the old friends I'd worked with over the years, which made recording so much easier. The London Blues Band then consisted of Dino Baptiste (piano), Javier Garcia (bass), Matt Schofield (guitar), Evan Jenkins (Drums) and Mike Paice (saxophone/harmonica), but several mates also came in to the studios to contribute. 'Big' Martin Winning and Nick Payn (saxophone), David Malin, Corrinna Greyson and Ian Siegal (all backing vocals), together with Rolf Harris and Shining Bear (didgeridoo) performing on one song called 'One Kiss x 108'. Also playing on two tracks was my old guitarist Sammy Mitchell, whose speciality was bottleneck guitar played on an old battered steel 'machine'. Both he and his instrument looked like they had been through a few wars, and sadly he's now another one up in that ever increasing blues band in the sky.

The album was recorded on two-inch tape, which doesn't seem to exist anymore, as the last factory that made these heavy spools stopped production a number of years ago. I've always stored my old recordings, and boy, do they take up space, but back then I hadn't realised that the tape would perish so fast. Once when I wanted to remix a song 15 years later, I found that the tape was sticking in the machine. When this happens, the only way to save a recording is to literally bake it in a special oven.

The 'Experienced' album was, I felt, the best Blues album I had made to date. Because the Blues is about emotions and experience, I couldn't do justice to it when I was younger; my voice didn't have the edge it needed to convey the emotion, nor did I have the first-hand experience to sing about Blues themes convincingly. Being older, my voice had matured and now had real gravitas to live up to the title of the album.

*

People should never assume that life on Sai Baba's Ashram was all about chanting, singing bhajans, and waiting to see Sai Baba or, even better, getting a private interview with Him. There were often concerts and sports events; even the Harlem Globetrotters played there once, with India's then-president, Abdul Kalam, in the audience. However, the most special sporting event in Puttaparthi took place on Sunday the 30th of December 1997, when a major international cricket match was held featuring all the top stars.

The Hill View Stadium was converted into a perfect cricket pitch, which everyone had said was impossible to do. Then again, they also said that if Baba wills a thing, then it happens. The legendary Indian batsman Sunil Gavaskar, former West Indies Captain Clive Lloyd, and Pakistani legends Hanif Mohammad and Zaheer Abbas, all joined Sai Baba on the dais. Tens of thousands of spectators filled the stadium, and countless more by way of a live TV broadcast, as the two teams, led by Sachin Tendulkar for India and Arjuna Ranatunga for the World XI, led their teams out onto the pitch. To the delight of Sai Baba and the crowd, the Indian team won the match, and the Sri Sathya Sai Unity Cup, with the man of the match – Sachin Tendulkar – collecting the trophy from Clive Lloyd.

Sachin has almost God-like status in India, with huge crowds gathering wherever he goes. Like the lovely Sunil, he is a Sai Baba devotee, and I have seen them both on several occasions. Sunil attended Sai Baba's 70th birthday celebrations, when another famous West Indian cricket, Alvin Kallicharran, was also present. It was Alvin who introduced me to the huge crowd when I sang on the final day.

I have always had a soft spot for cricket and cricketers. It probably dates back to my time at Francis Holland School, when every summer I was taken to Lord's cricket ground to watch the annual Eton v Harrow match. Then again, my main memory of those days was that I used to try to eat all the strawberries.

I was once lucky enough to be staying in the splendid Taj Mahal Palace Hotel in Bombay at the same time as the Indian and Australian cricket teams. Rather confusingly, one of the Australian cricketers was called Jason Gillespie, and the hotel telephone operator kept putting his calls through to my room and my calls through to him. The hotel staff said that this was the first time that they'd had two Gillespies in the hotel at the same time. It was on this trip that I also met the wonderful Bill Frindall, known to cricket fans as "The Bearded Wonder" for seemingly having every cricket fact stored in his head. What a lovely man he was, sadly no longer with us. For many years, he acted as the official statistician on the BBC radio cricket commentaries, and it was Bill that the likes of Brian Johnston, Henry Blofeld, and Jonathan Agnew would ask what often seemed to be the most obscure questions about the game. Brian, who liked to be called "Johnners", originally named Bill as the Bearded Wonder, which he subsequently reduced to "Bearders" in much the same way as he would refer to "Blowers" or "Aggers". No wonder this sport can be called the game for Gentlemen!

*

In the early years of the new decade, I was busy recording my Indian music. Not all of this was in Sanskrit, and my album 'In the Garden of Heavenly Peace' had lyrics in English. It was released in 2001, once again with one of Jorg Huber's weird and wonderfully oriental covers.

For this album, I started working with Tim Cross, who had for several years in the eighties been a member of Mike 'Tubular Bells' Oldfield's touring band. Tim played keyboards, and we ended up doing some co-writes, although I wrote most of the other songs and that included a re-recording of my hit 'Move Your Body Close To Me'. Another song on the album had a melody written by the Indian superstar, Jagjit Singh, called 'Watch Over Me'.

My first meeting with Jagjit was on one of my many trips to Bombay. Pandit Dinesh had given me his name and number, but I only became aware of his massive fame when I asked the telephone receptionist in the hotel to get him on the line, and she nearly passed out just by seeing his name written on the paper I had handed her. Having heard a haunting melody on one of his earlier cassettes, I wrote an English lyric to it but had no idea how to ask for permission from Jagjit himself to use it. When I finally got him on the telephone, he immediately offered to meet, saying he would come and collect me from the Taj Hotel.

Jagjit's house was like any other real musician's place, littered with musical instruments and not obsessively tidy, so I felt rather at home. When I sang him the lyrics I had written to his song, he was so pleased that he gave me permission to write English words for any other songs of his.

'In the Garden of Heavenly Peace' remains one of my favourite CDs to this day, as I was able to sing in my mother tongue but still use a lot of Indian instruments, including the electric violin played by Chandru, and percussion and tablas added at the end by Pandit Dinesh. The parts that Dinesh added to my recordings were always known by me and my colleagues in the studio as the 'fairy dust'; the expression comes from a quote from the Troggs in their famous 'outtakes' bootleg tape that everyone in the music business listened to in the seventies. In-between all the swearing and in-fighting that was secretly being recorded in the studios, Reg Presley suddenly says, "Put some fuckin' fairy dust on it."

They had been in the studios for hours and hours and had come up with nothing, causing all the Troggs to fight among themselves about a song that they just couldn't get right. None of this would have come to light had not a bright tape operator pressed the record button. Back in the seventies, everyone I knew could quote many sentences from the infamous Troggs tape, but these days only the 'fairy dust' quote seems to be remembered.

When my album was finally finished, I got on a flight to India and went to Puttaparthi to present it to Sai Baba. Mercifully, He blessed it and again I was asked to sing for His birthday.

When it comes to love, the feeling of universality has always been important to me, and so I called my fourth Sanskrit CD 'Universal Bhajans'. It was recorded at Arvind Studios in Bangalore, and was also released in 2001. For the first time, I was making an album without being surrounded by my usual musician pals, and found myself very alone.

I had engaged Chandru to make all the musical arrangements, so he was my only contact with the other musicians. English was not spoken much, and as I spoke no Kannada, Marathi, Hindi, or Telegu, I felt isolated. At one point, late at night, I even banged my head against a wall in desperation and burst into tears while trying to record a vocal, as it was still relatively new territory for me to be singing in Sanskrit.

Being a trooper I soldiered on, and somehow the production got done in time, and I flew home to London to get the whole thing mixed, mastered, and printed, again with a Jorg picture on the cover (this time of me sitting in a temple and wearing a red sari). When the final printed CD was in my hand, I flew back to India to present it to Sai Baba, and the moment He blessed it, all the trials and tribulations that I had felt during the production just fell away.

*

Every five years, the birthday celebrations at Puttaparthi took on greater significance and were a huge event, usually attended by dignitaries such as the Prime Minister and President of India, and it would invariably result in a large military presence. If you add to this the thousands and thousands who would arrive for the Big Day on November 23rd, then you can imagine what a massive gathering the birthday was, far bigger than Woodstock or Glastonbury. Visually, it was different to those Western festivals, as the ladies were colourfully dressed in their finery on one side, whilst there would be a sea of white on the men's side.

Sai Baba again invited me to sing for His 75th birthday celebration in 2001, so I asked the London Blues Band if they felt like coming to India. As a bit of an incentive, I told them that there were also a number of Blues gigs organised in Bangalore and Bombay, so they would make some money as well. As a result, the line-up was Dino Baptiste on piano, Matt Schofield on guitar, Javier Garcia on bass, Evan Jenkins on drums, and Mike Paice on saxophone and harmonica.

In addition, as I had decided to do not only Blues but also some songs with a much more Indian style, I recruited Chandru, the virtuoso violinist. Previously I had sung one mantra for his amazing 'Evening of One Hundred Violinists', known collectively as the Bollywood Strings Orchestra, at a special concert at the Festival Hall in London, so I knew that his touch would fit in well with the band. Also part of the team was Shining Bear, the didgeridoo player, and I think it may have been the first time that such an instrument was played on the stage at the vast stadium. The musicians were well-prepared musically as we had rehearsed in London, and Greg Upchurch was there as my assistant to make sure that things ran as smoothly as possible.

As they all headed off for the airport in London, together with Annette and Frankie Miller who had also decided to join us, they were filmed by my first cousin, Sir Crispin Buxton, and Ben Cole, who came along to make a documentary film of the whole trip. I had gone on ahead to India to make sure that everything would be ready, and on arrival in Puttaparthi was immediately called in for a private interview with Sai Baba. He wanted to know exactly which songs I was going to sing and who was playing what, and He even asked that Greg Upchurch should come out on stage and introduce me to the audience. This meant that once Greg arrived, he had to practise how to offer up a rose while getting down and up on his knees, which must have been quite nerve-racking for him, as he had never done such a thing before. It did give the rest of us something to laugh about while he rehearsed his movements.

Sai Baba also assured me that my musicians would be well-fed and housed in good accommodation, and He even sent a bus to pick the band up from Bangalore airport. This was a great weight off my mind, as I knew the guys were not at all interested in the spiritual aspect of the gig, and I had worried in case they all hated

When we finally all returned to London, I put the songs I had performed in India on a CD called 'Songs of Love'.

*

One of the best Blues tours I ever did was around India in 2002 with the London Blues Band, organised by the British Council. By then, I had a French guitarist called 'Fred P.G.' to replace Matt Schofield, and as Dino couldn't do the tour, I quickly had to find someone good enough to replace him. I'd heard about a 20-year-old French whizz-kid pianist living in Bordeaux called Julien Brunetaud who apparently loved (and played like) Otis Spann. That was good enough for me, so I offered him the job without ever hearing him touch the piano.

Everything was so well organised that, whilst travelling between 11 cities and playing 22 concerts, amazingly not one plane was late, not one piece of luggage was lost, and no one got sick. Even better, as the Taj Hotel Group was one of the sponsors, the musicians all got to sleep in five-star luxury.

The Taj Mahal Palace in Mumbai has to be one of my favourite destinations in the world, and if anyone wanted to take me away for a week of fun and games in a first-class establishment, this would be my choice. In 2014, I even appeared in a BBC documentary about it called 'Hotel India', in which I was able to extol its virtues to a wide audience. And as for the city, it really rocks.

The Blues tour went from Goa to Cochin, Bangalore to Bombay, Pune to Hyderabad, Lucknow to Delhi and Calcutta. Each place was such a buzz, giving me a chance to hear Qawali music at the Sufi shrine of Nizamuddin in Delhi, or at the Deva Sharif shrine near Lucknow. As the whole country is so alive with music, colour, smells (both good and bad!), and smiling helpful people, this is – and will always be – the number one choice for me when I actually get time to have a holiday.

Once the main part of the tour was over, I travelled on to Darjeeling for a two-week engagement to sing at the wonderfully old-fashioned Hotel Windemere.

Darjeeling, where the tea grows, is high up in the north of India, and I was booked to sing at the hotel over Christmas and New Year. The audience was quite a straight-laced bunch who were probably expecting songs from West End musicals, and I doubt if any of them had ever heard of the Blues, so I had trouble finding suitable songs to sing. None of this seemed to matter, however, when one looked out over to 'Kanchenchunga', Tiger Mountain. Occasionally, the clouds would be down and you could see very little, and then suddenly the sun would burst through and the mountains, in all their glory, would be revealed.

One day, the hotel asked if I would perform for a group of nuns, which I was happy to do – subject to the usual problem of finding suitable songs to sing. In the end, I was forced to resort to numbers like 'Summertime' and 'It Ain't Necessarily So', but halfway through that song, I realised that I'd soon be singing the chorus which has the words, "The things that you're liable to read in the Bible, it ain't necessarily so."

What those poor nuns thought, I can't imagine. In a big venue, I could have hoped that no one was listening, but this was a room where the audience was two feet from me, and I was nearly sitting on their laps. I hope I didn't cause any offence.

*

Later in 2002, I came to Puttaparthi with Jorg to get Sai Baba's approval for the publication of the 'Mirrors of Love' book. I had also made a CD of the same name with David Malin and Nick Hogarth, on which I had taken many of the Sufi quotations from the book and put them to music. As usual, I was sitting in the crowd, waiting for Sai Baba to walk in my direction, and when He was standing right in front of me, he asked me where my musicians were. I replied that I didn't have any with me, and He smiled and said, "Don't worry, I will send you some of my boys."

To have the opportunity to work with His students was a first for me, and a first for them too. Luckily, the house I stayed in at the Ashram had a back room which was perfect for rehearsals, and the next day the seven boys duly arrived with their instruments, and I got down to showing them how my Western songs should be performed.

In the Ashram, the students and teachers all live together in what might well be described as 'the middle of nowhere', with very few outside distractions; it's a rigid lifestyle with very disciplined hours, and very little contact with the opposite gender. I could have written the words 'opposite sex', but the 'S Word' was most definitely not one that was used there. These boys were are as pure as the driven snow, whilst my old London life made me feel about as pure as driven sludge! However, this is the whole point of an ashram: to find inner peace, discover what really makes us all tick, and to up the Love quota to the point of overflowing.

All of these boys were studying subjects that were way beyond my brain capacity, so music wasn't their main thing at all, more of a hobby. Nevertheless, they all learnt the songs so quickly and seemingly with little effort. I had noticed that some Indian artistes never give their backing musicians a namecheck, so I told them on the first day of our rehearsals that – at the performance – I wanted to introduce each of them by name to the audience. When I suggested this, they all looked horrified and said that I shouldn't do that, and that it would be better if they were just described as "Swami's students".

A few days later, Sai Baba arrived at our practice session, and the first thing He said to me was, "You must introduce each boy to the audience, by name."

This made me smile as I knew it was the right thing to do, but it also showed that Sai Baba had known what I had said to the boys a few days earlier. Looking back, I think that these boys were being taught how to interact with outsiders, and I felt very honoured that they had been entrusted into my care.

We had six days to get the performance together, so this meant rehearsing daily, either in my backroom or in a huge empty auditorium called the Poornachandra Hall. Sai Baba would often peep through the back curtains to watch us, at which point all the boys would put down their instruments and sit with their hands touching, palm to palm, as a mark of respect. If you do this when you meet someone, you'd say 'Namaste' or 'Namaskar', which is the greeting that more or less means 'The spirit within me salutes the spirit within you'.

On one of the days that Sai Baba was out walking at Darshan, He called me over and told me that He would come to our music practice on Thursday. I had to tell the boys, to ensure that they would be dressed in their best clothes, and also had to tell Hima, my wonderful 'heart sister' (as Sai Baba once called her), as she wanted to organise food to be served to Him and about 15 other people.

By the time He arrived at the house, there were about 40 people crammed inside, but somehow they all got fed. The table was laid out with plates of savoury food, and behind each plate was a little bowl of dessert, my all-time favourite in India. It's called kheer in some parts of the country, in others it's called paysam, and it can be made of rice, vermicelli, or sago, and served hot or cold. Whatever it is made from, it's very sweet and delicious, and I guess fattening too, but who cares about that when faced with heaven in a bowl.

As I stood behind Sai Baba while he was serving the food, I was thinking that I wasn't interested in the savoury food, all I *really* wanted was something sweet. Without turning around, Baba just reached forward for a bowl of paysam, gave it a stir, and handed it to me with a beaming smile, after which He went back to serving everyone else the savoury food. I know it's only a small example of Him showing His omnipotence, but I've since met many people who have had experiences far more impressive than just being given a bowl of paysam, such as being cured from cancer or saved from a deadly accident.

This was the year that I performed songs from the 'Mirrors of Love' book, and how my heart soared when, after the concert, Sai Baba said to me, "Divine words!" It had taken me 20 years to handpick all the phrases of love contained in the book and the songs, all of which had been written by a Saint or a Sage and were therefore loaded with wisdom.

*

In 2003, I used almost the same nucleus of musicians for my next Ace CD called 'Staying Power', though Dino Baptiste was back on keyboards. Several of the songs were co-writes with saxophonist 'Big' Martin Winning, but I wrote most of the rest myself, including the song 'I Sigh For You'. There I was, thinking of Sai Baba again, and feeling once more quite chuffed at being able to use the double meaning of 'Sigh' and 'Sai'.

The final track was written by one of the finest singer-songwriters of the seventies – Frankie Miller – a Scotsman who had a voice to die for and who had a big hit in 1978 with a song called 'Darlin'.

He was a great songwriter, and continued to write killer songs until the day that a brain aneurism struck him down. His wife, Annette, arranged for him (attached to tubes and machines) to be flown home from America where it happened, and after a few years of hospital and recovery time, he is still alive thanks to Annette, without whom he would never have made it. Anyway, I thought it would be nice to do one of his songs, called 'You're the Star'.

The album was reviewed by Thom Jurek for AllMusic, who described me as "a powerful vocalist who infuses this sexually loaded material with verve, toughness, and a steamy sensuality", and the songs as "bawdy, rollicking, and at times near raunchy, unapologetically about sex". What a shame the album sales weren't as good as this review.

18: KIMBERLEY, JAGGER, AND MORE MUSTIQUE

As usual, I planned to spend Christmas (this time in 2006) at Bolwick Hall in Norfolk with my mother and stepfather. They had moved into the Hall when they left London in the late 1970s. It is a splendid Grade II listed heritage building, built on the site of a structure which is listed in the Domesday Book, and is surrounded by magnificent gardens and a lake laid out by the famous landscape gardener Humphry Repton.

A few years earlier, Jorg and I had spent Christmas in Leslie's Spanish farmhouse (known as 'the Goatshed') near Ronda, with Leslie and his wife Paca. On Christmas Day, we went climbing up the mountain behind the house, and although the view looking over towards Tangiers was fantastic, I suddenly thought of my mother back home in Bolwick Hall. Knowing just how much Christmas meant to her, I started to cry and felt really bad about leaving her. I could climb mountains any other day of the year, but I resolved never to do such a thing again on Christmas Day. From then on, I always spent Christmas with my mother.

Every year, we would go over to Kimberley Hall, the residence of my aunt and uncle Phyll and Ron Buxton, to join the many Buxton relations for a huge Boxing Day family lunch. The current Hall was built in 1712 for Sir John Wodehouse (an ancestor of the author P.G. Wodehouse) by William Talman, though subsequently extended and enlarged. It sits on top of a slope in a 700-acre park, lake and woodland landscaped by Capability Brown, and overlooks the River Tiffey.

Like other families across the world, our trip to Kimberley Hall was the annual chance to see many relations in one go, and we visited so often that it felt almost like a second home to me. After my stepfather, Tom, died a few years later, my mother decided to sell Bolwick Hall and took a flat around the corner from me in South Kensington, as well as keeping a place in the wing of Kimberley Hall.

Every July, the Buxton Family Party – known to the gossip columnists as 'Toffstock' – was held on the huge Kimberley Hall grounds. It was three days of fun, with bands playing, fireworks

Holding this letter in my hand, I went and sat on my tiger skin cushion, and once again He stopped by me and took the letter. He read it out loud, with a look and voice of horror when He got to the words 'Ladies Choir' in relation to Sathya. Then He broke into a big smile to show He had been shamming His horror, and He told me to go ahead.

The ladies and I had been thinking for days what to call ourselves for the album, and in the end, we came up with 'The Shanti Sisters'. The word Shanti means peace, and that is how the whole production went. The only thing I had to do was to ensure that Sathya should be tucked out of the way in the control room, so that when he played his instrument, he wouldn't see the swaying bodies of the singing ladies.

The album was called 'Sing Out' and was released in 2004 under the name Dana Gillespie and The Shanti Sisters, with another Jorg cover awash with girlie things like roses and pussy cats.

*

Away from India, Mick Jagger was staying on Mustique at the time of the 2005 Blues Festival, and he kindly agreed to perform with The London Blues Band, who were the backing musicians for the festival. When we rehearsed the songs in Felix Dennis's music room, Mick said that he wanted to do the Robert Johnson/Elmore James song 'Dust my Broom' and another one originally done by Freddie King called 'Going Down'. At the time, Mick described it as an Albert King song, but none of the band wanted to tell him he'd got the wrong King!

As the two songs chosen by Mick were Blues standards, my band already knew them, with the result that we'd finished the rehearsal in ten minutes. Mick couldn't believe that the band were able to master the songs so quickly. I guess that when the Stones rehearse a new number it takes longer because they are doing new material, and – rumour has it – they sometimes get distracted.

Word went around the island very quickly that day that Mick was due to appear. Usually, the bar would have a good crowd in the evening, but that night they were packed in like sardines. It was a memorable occasion, and the band were naturally thrilled to be backing the great Mick Jagger. As usual, I recorded the performances for the compilation CD, so can now say that I have recorded and produced two songs with Mick Jagger. He also sang 'Honky Tonk Women', but I didn't include it on the CD because I didn't feel that it was quite the right style for a Blues album. Jorg filmed our performance and you can watch it, and admire the very fetching tiger print pyjama suit I was wearing as Mick's backing vocalist, on YouTube.

On another occasion, when my mother was with me on Mustique, Mick invited us both round to his house for dinner. At the end of the meal, Mick rolled a grass joint, which is – of course – de rigueur in the West Indies, and as there were a few other people there, it got passed around the table. When I had a quick puff, my mother's eyes came out on organ stops; she had never seen me smoking before. Forever afterwards, she called a joint a "Mick Jagger cigarette".

A few years later, Ronnie Wood turned up on Mustique during his honeymoon with his new wife Sally, and as he also got up to perform at the festival I can say that I've produced another song featuring a Rolling Stone. It was lovely to talk to Ronnie again, as I hadn't seen him for many years. He and Sally had arrived from Necker Island, but he told me that they had left after a week because Richard Branson was trying to organise every day for them. According to Ronnie, Branson would tell them, "Nine o'clock breakfast, then down to the beach for some snorkelling, then in the afternoon, it's windsurfing."

You can't tell a Rolling Stone to have breakfast at 9 o'clock! He said it was all far too regimented, and that he much preferred the relaxed atmosphere on Mustique.

I ran the Mustique Blues Festival with Basil for 20 years, and saw it grow from a small event for a few friends to the major event it is now. Making the annual compilation albums was something I loved to do, even though it meant that I never had time to socialise. From the moment the music started, I would either be running around checking the sound, getting the musicians up on stage at their allotted times, or sitting on a barstool by the mixing board. I knew that I had to keep a detailed record of all the songs to identify the best takes, so would listen carefully and make notes like 'great solo', or 'must do an edit in this song'. Everyone else would be roaring drunk and indulging in whatever the island had

My mother also came along on this trip, as she wanted to witness one of these massive events. Initially, she had been a little worried about being in such an enormous crowd, but Sai Baba had said He would make sure she was well looked after and, as ever, He kept His word.

Shortly after our arrival, we were both invited to a private audience with Sai Baba and, as we entered the room, He immediately stepped forward and put His thumb on her eye and held it there for two minutes. Afterwards, she told me that she had been suffering from a pain in her eye, and that the moment He took his thumb away, the pain had gone. She hadn't wanted to say anything to me about the eye before, as she was worried it would spoil the trip.

The weather had been inclement for days, and I kept saying to the organisers that they should erect a tent over the musicians and their instruments in case it rained on the Big Night. No one listened to me until the actual day, when it became obvious that the sun wasn't going to shine at all, so they hastily erected an open-sided ceremonial tent called a shamiana. In fact, it drizzled the whole time, which without the tent would have meant disaster for the musical instruments. It still wasn't ideal, as the shamiana was designed for Indian musicians who always play sitting down cross-legged. As I sing standing up, I had to stand outside the tent, with the result that I got soaking wet. Luckily, I was wearing a sari that Baba had given me several years earlier which, even as He handed it to me, I knew I was meant to wear for His 80th birthday as it just said 'Special Occasion' to me. It was made in rainbow colours and gold, as sparkly as can be, and its shimmering rainbow effect meant that the rain didn't show up on the material as I performed.

Indians have always had rather strange ways of wiring things up, and it's not unusual to see loads of tangled wires above the streets looking like birds' nests. While I was singing, I looked down at my bare feet and saw that I was standing on about 30 wires and cables, and both they and I were getting rained on. This made me think that if I did get 'fried' and died up there on this stage, in front of everyone, at least it would be a spectacular ending! Obviously, I didn't croak, though my mother did get ill from sitting through so many hours in the cold, and it took her weeks to get over it.

The whole evening show went on for a very long time, as many performers overran their timings. As it got later and later, I began to fret as to whether my performance would be cut as I was scheduled to sing at the very end. Sai Baba was sitting on a huge throne-like chair high up in front of the vast crowd, and I saw Him speak to a man dressed in white. A moment later, this person raced through the crowd and up the stairs to get to where the performers were standing, and he came straight to me with a message directly from Baba to say, "Don't worry, Swami says your performance will go ahead as planned." I'm thankful to say it did.

One of the songs in my programme was called 'Rose of My Heart', which was co-written with Tim Cross. Knowing that I wouldn't be able to offer Sai Baba my usual rose petals before the performance, this song was written to offer up the next best equivalent of a rose, in song form.

Once the whole show was over, all the artistes were told that if we assembled at the side of the stage where Sai Baba was still sitting, we'd be able to walk past slowly and offer our respects. I felt so sorry for Him, that He'd had to sit through so many hours of pomp and celebrations, that I wanted to be quick on the walk past so that others would have a chance to get close to Him. However, as I got near, He discreetly lifted up the hem of His orange robe which showed His slightly swollen Feet and I bent down and placed a handful of rose petals on them. Once I had done that, He let the hem of His robe down, gave me the sweetest of smiles, and then went back to attending to the next lot of artistes lined up behind me. It was a small gesture which was over in a moment, but it was of great significance to me as I had wanted to put my usual offering of rose petals on His Feet but never thought I'd get the chance.

The finished CD, which had been recorded especially for this birthday, was called 'Love The Love'. Many of my favourite musicians were involved in the recording sessions, including Tim Renwick on guitar, Sirishkumar on tablas, Dinesh on percussion, and Tim Cross on keyboards.

The closing track on the CD is called 'The Whole Universe', and I almost felt as if I was being 'guided' when I wrote this song, as the words come from one of India's holiest books, the Upanishads, where Krishna is speaking and giving guidance to perform songs for Sai Baba in July. Tim and I also took the 'Mata Mata' tracks with us to India to see if there would be a chance to add some Indian instruments to the recordings in the studios. So, when we weren't rehearsing with the choir, we were in the studios with Sai Prakash on sitar, Yaman on violin, Sivakumar on tablas, Ravi Teja on flute and Aswath, one of the star singers of Puttaparthi, who sang magnificently. We even got some of the UK Boys Choir to do some backing vocals.

Just as it seemed that it couldn't get any better, it did, in the form of India's most famous and talented mandolin player called U. Srinivas, who also happened to be in Puttaparthi to perform for Sai Baba. Someone told me that he had been spotted in the Ashram, and I said that I'd love to have him play on the new production. Having never spoken to him in my life, I had no idea how to contact him, but much to my surprise and delight a friend standing next to me said, "I've got his mobile telephone number, so you can ring him now if you like."

I had first seen him perform as a teenage prodigy in London, at the Bharatya Vidya Bhavan, and he was incredible even then. But now, at the age of 40, he was the absolute King of the Mandolin and I couldn't let such a chance slip. The mandolin is not usually known as an Indian instrument, and U. Srinivas was the first to play it in an Indian style. I phoned him up and, to my happiness, he said that it would be an honour for him to do a couple of tracks with us.

The studio was prepared for his arrival the next day, and there was respectful quiet as he opened his mandolin case, which I was pleased to see had many photographs of Sai Baba stuck on the inside of it. I had told Tim how extraordinary he was as a performer, and – once he started to play – a whole new energy entered the room. Looking at Tim, not usually the most emotional of fellows, I swear I saw a tear of joy run down his cheek. The way that Srinivas' fingers flew over the small fretboard was mind-boggling, and I felt truly honoured to have had him on the recording. Sadly, he was to die soon afterwards, at the way too young age of 45.

In the meantime, over 3,000 pilgrims had arrived from the UK, including the members of the UK Youth Choir. The whole event had been organised magnificently by Rita and Shitu Chudasama, who brought their son Achintya, who is my godson, with them. The women singers all wore shocking pink saris, and the men were all in white, and I was very proud that they performed a number of songs that I had written for Sai Baba. After the show was over, He called me up to his chair on a raised dais in front of the temple to thank me, then twice called Tim and gave him some vibhuti ash. I was touched that Tim was shown so much attention, but with the benefit of hindsight, I realise that Sai Baba knew that Tim would never be coming back to India.

After we got back to England, there were a few overdubs to be done to the recordings, so we called in Jake Zaitz and Tim Renwick on guitars, and David Malin on backing vocals, zither, and percussion.

Tim and I had a very similar outlook on how everything else takes a back seat until a production is finished, and I would often jokingly say to him, when leaving his studio to go home, "Even if I die before the final work is done, can you please make sure you finish it without me."

It wasn't a joke; I meant it, and he knew it. For both of us, the music was the only thing that mattered, and this was what had driven us all our lives.

As we were finishing the 'Mata Mata' CD, Tim got really ill and had to be hospitalised, but the production went on and I finished it without him which felt very odd. At least I was in the safe hands of Dominique Brethes to do the mixing. The end result is good, but I sorely missed my friend Tim in the control room, giving words of encouragement to me when I did the vocal tracks.

Ultimately, Tim was to lose his fight with cancer in 2012. I had first recorded with him in the eighties, and he became so much more to me than a keyboard player. It is said that every woman needs a gay man in their life, and I'm lucky to have quite a few of them, Tim stands out for me as we spent so much time together – usually in his little home studio – where we'd be recording and writing songs.

Tim was short in stature, slightly plump, and my cousin Rudi once said that he looked like an extra from Planet of the Apes. This was due to his somewhat simian facial features, but Rudi was not being

It has been well-documented that many people claim to have seen Him in many places around the world. I've even seen photographs of Him in Switzerland, Kazakhstan, Chicago, Russia, and closer to home in Harrow, with vibhuti ash pouring off them. Sai Baba used to say that this was His calling card, and even the people who denigrated Him, by saying it was faked, would not be able to explain how this 'magician' could do such a 'trick' while sitting thousands of miles away in India.

Singing to Robert Powell in Ken Russell's "Mahler".
Only it isn't my voice!

On location with Robert, in the Lake District.

On the set of Mai Zetterling's film "Scrubbers" — 25 Feb. 1982

Playing Budd the Prison Warder in Mai Zetterling's "Scrubbers". Rather more acting ability required here!

Marsha Hunt 14 March 1982

William Tell T.V. 5 Oct. 88

Marsha Hunt, my co-star in "Catch My Soul" and "Mardi Gras"; "William Tell", another Mai Zetterling production.

Looking nautical for "Seaside Special" in 1978.

With Dudley Moore and Hugh Griffith in
"The Hound Of The Baskervilles".

Elton throws a party for a lot of old friends,
including Kiki Dee and me.

Nick McCann's 2017 painting of me.
He also directed me in the film "Byron's Mine".

Singing in the Sai Kulwant Hall, at two of the many Birthday
celebrations for Sai Baba that I was invited to perform at.

With Jorg in Puttaparthi in 1984, and again
in 2006 for Sai Baba's 80th birthday.

Sally and Ronnie Wood, on honeymoon in Mustique
in 2012, with Jorg, Michael Leiner, and me.

Backed by Donald Fagan of Steely Dan at
the Mustique Blues Festival.

Basil Charles OBE, with whom I co-founded
the Mustique Blues Festival in 1996.

Chilling with Chaka Khan and Bonnie Tyler,
after we all sang at The Gasometer in Vienna.

Performing with The London Blues Band: Dino Baptiste,
Jeff Walker, Jake Zaitz, Evan Jenkins and Mike Paice,
at the 606 Club in London.

Singing with Jake and Artie Zaitz at the 606 Club.

Duetting with Dino Baptiste on "The Organ Grinder Blues"
at The Phoenix Arts Club.

Singing "Funk Me, It's Hot!" with Jake Zaitz.

Albums 1968-1998

Albums 1998-2019

Albums I produced (and performed on) between
1996 and 2015 for the Mustique Blues Festival.
Most of the covers were designed by Jorg Huber.

Look what I found in Portobello Market - one of those "Top of the Pops" albums I did with Elton back in the sixties.

A well-travelled guitar case – with its well-travelled owner.

21: UNDER MY BED

In 2014, I sang six songs on a CD called 'Guilty', with the title track being the old Randy Newman song. The project was very much the brainchild of Joachim Palden, the Viennese boogie pianist that I have worked with since 1980.

As Joachim has his own studios and his own way of working, I never got involved with his productions, I just did the singing and let him do the rest. I must say that the work he did on the CD cover is particularly fetching, as it features a cartoon of a bare-breasted woman, done by the French artist Jacques de Loustal. Whenever I'm asked to sign my name on this CD, I always feel a bit bad about scrawling over her bosom – especially as it wasn't even mine!

*

Many women want to have babies, and are then able to trace back their life's timeline by the ages of their children. This was never a desire in my life and, instead, I have viewed all my albums as my children. This has the added advantage that you can turn them off if you want a bit of silence.

So I can trace my life's history by the music I have made. Indeed, I've always equated making an album to making a baby, as it normally takes me about nine months between song conception and release of the final product. The afterbirth is all the promo that follows, and I'm really happy to do the gigs and interviews, though because I'm a bit of a fossil, I'm not all that involved with the social media action that comes along with it.

When I look back at the work that went into making 'Cat's Meow', which was recorded in 2014 and released on Ace Records in January 2015, I can see that it really started with my love of a furry pussycat that lived in Basil's house on Mustique. Her name was PussPuss, and she must have been the runt of the litter as she was smaller than most tabby cats, but her tiny size didn't stop her from having an exceptionally loud voice. Before we went into the studio to record, I wanted to capture the voice of PussPuss and use it on a song. This meant getting up early and going downstairs to the kitchen with a packet of Whiskas cat food that I had brought specially from England. Proving that bribery and corruption really

Puttaparthi, for the final rehearsals before our performance in the huge and colourful Sai Kulwant Hall.

I was the conductor for this performance, and was really proud of the way that all the participants learnt their parts and sang their hearts out. Of course, I got Jorg to do another great psychedelic CD cover, this time with a heart on the front. He also managed to do another brightly-coloured heart design for the follow-up album which was called 'The Perfection Of Love', but he wasn't in the best of health by then, and I instinctively knew that this would be the last cover he would ever do for me.

*

Obviously, I hadn't deserted the Blues, and I had for some time been thinking about making a record in a very old-fashioned style. In 1980, in Vienna, I had been introduced to the one man who only plays the old-style Blues, everything from the twenties and thirties. This man's name is Al Cook, and I'm happy to say that he's still alive and kicking, and more importantly, he still plays his old style Blues. When it came to doing the next album, he was my obvious choice to work with.

Al has a little cellar studio near his Viennese apartment, and this was where we recorded with his band. The album was inspired by the double entendre songs of the late pre-war era, and featured a mixture of old 'party Blues' and some self-penned numbers in a similar 'dirty' style. So there are songs with titles like 'I Want My Hands On It', 'He's Just My Size', 'My Handy Man', and 'Press My Button, Ring My Bell', together with a song of mine which has become a favourite when performed live, 'FCK Blues', the self-explanatory chorus of which is: "the only thing that's missing is U".

The CD was called 'Take It Off Slowly', and was released by Wolf Records. I'm really happy with the production work that Al Cook did, and it's one of the few times that I have let someone else do the mixing and mastering of one of my albums. Al's sound was so distinctive that I knew he'd stick to the old original style and not muck it about with modern technology.

*

If you have read every page of this book so far, you will not need to be told that I have had problems with my knees for most of my life. So it was with a mixture of hope and trepidation that I finally arranged to go under the knife for knee replacement surgery on my right knee in 2019; the left one having been done a few years previously.

The operation itself went fairly smoothly, but I then had to face several months of 'knee-hab', during which time I was virtually immobile; no walks in the park or to my favourite deli, and no gigs. Bit by bit, the knee began to feel better, partly thanks to my daily visits to the swimming pool every morning, and I'm now once again able to get around without the dreadful pain I had experienced for so long. If you are reading this, I send a big thank you to the doctor, medical team, and knee-hab personnel who helped to make my life worth living again.

Towards the end of 2019, I received the sad news that my old friend Leslie Spitz had died. He used to be known as the 'Bed Man' of Chelsea, thanks to the number of antique brass bed shops he owned in the King's Road. He also had a beautiful little rustic house with no electricity near Ronda, in the hills of southern Spain, and would often disappear there with a van to find antiques to bring back to his shops. Whenever I had a gap between gigs, I would join him there, though in the early days most of our time together was spent with me hobbling about, often in pain. He was always helpful and once – when my knee gave in – he even carried me down a mountain in Spain; no mean feat for a man who was shorter than me.

We also did a lot of travelling together, around Morocco and India, as well as in America during the Mainman years. Later, he and Jorg became good friends, and we'd often take holidays together. He was a really important character in my life story, and I will miss him until the day I start to push up my own daisies.

*

One of the joys of being on the road with a band is when it takes you to uncommon countries, and this was the case when I was asked to perform in Kazakhstan. This was a country I'd visited a few times, for concerts organised by the Sai Centres, but on this occasion I was asked to come with the London Blues band.

The main concert was to be held in the astonishing glass pyramid in Astana, which is a new city and the capital of the country. As do things... I'm already plotting what to do for my next production.

*

Although I have always had a band to sing with, I didn't give them a proper name until about 30 years ago. As a proud Londoner, it made sense to call it the London Blues Band. A sign of a good bandleader is when the same musicians stay together for a long time. In my experience, if you treat people well and play good music, they will stay loyal to you.

One man has been a member of my band longer than any other. For over 35 years, I've had Mike Paice on stage with me, playing saxophone and harmonica. It's pretty rare to have a musician that plays both instruments superbly, but that is definitely the case with him. He was once a member of Jools Holland's band, The Millionaires, and also played with Bryan Ferry.

Paicey is also a mad keen birdwatcher. Whenever we went anywhere in the band bus, Paicey would sit with his binoculars around his neck on the front seat – in what I'd call the crow's nest – and would announce to whoever was awake that an interesting bird was to be seen.

So mad for birds was he that he wrote a book, called 'The Bird Life of Mustique in the Grenadines', which is on sale on the island. Sweetly, he dedicated the book to my mother. He used to take people on birdwatching tours across the island, provided they didn't mind getting up at dawn to go sloshing about in the swamp; he even discovered a new species of lizard.

Paicey once nearly got kicked out of the band. We were playing at a big French Blues festival and had to go on stage punctually, but he missed the start of the concert as he'd lost track of time while out following one of his feathered friends. I was furious with him but, once I had calmed down, how could I sack a man who was just totally involved with his passion? I've always employed a 'three strikes and you're out' rule, and the only time I've ever sacked anyone was due to their performance being affected by excessive alcohol. Although it wasn't at all professional to be late on stage, I couldn't bring myself to sack Paicey because of his love of birds.

Dino Baptiste, who plays piano, is a total workaholic, and it's not unusual to find him playing eight or more gigs a week. We first met just before doing the Bob Dylan tour in 1997, when I needed someone pretty good to fill the shoes of Dave Rowberry. Understanding that most boogie pianists are from German-speaking countries, I knew I might have a problem finding a piano man who would fit in with the band and who also lived in London. Someone gave me Dino's number, so I called him up and asked him over to my place.

After he'd played for about 30 seconds, I told him to stop; it was clear he was the right man for the job. Just as he was leaving, I spontaneously asked him when his birthday was, and blow me down, it was the same as mine... March 30th. That sealed it as far as I was concerned, and he's been with the band ever since.

We also share our birthdays with Eric Clapton, Celine Dion, Rolf Harris, Robbie Coltrane, Norah Jones, Warren Beatty, Vincent van Gogh and Goya. Quite an eclectic group!

My current guitarist is Jake Zaitz, who's been in the band since Matt Schofield left to live in America. Jake is Polish-born but has lived in England for many years. If anyone was the party animal, it used to be Jake – the wild one of the group – although he has calmed down a lot since marrying Anastasiia.

The rest of the band usually features the phenomenal Evan Jenkins on drums, and Jake's son – Artie Zaitz – on bass. Artie is a brilliant multi-instrumentalist who has stood in on both keyboards and guitar when the regular guy couldn't make it; he could probably sing all my songs too!

In my (totally unbiased) opinion, the London Blues Band is one of the best on the circuit, and these boys are very dear to my heart. As we have aged together, the hijinks have diminished, but we certainly had some crazy times in the past.

One happened on the big last night at the Festival in Mustique. At the very end of the evening, I was doing the finale on stage, announcing all the performers' names so they could step forward and take a bow. When I got to one particular musician, I said his name and turned around to find that there was a gap where he should have been standing. Maybe no one else noticed as it was

INDEX

PHOTO CREDITS

Arranged by insert page and image number. Dana Gillespie, or Unknown, unless otherwise listed. Front Cover Gered Mankowitz/©Bowstir Ltd/2020/mankowitz.com; 3[3] Fono Roma; 5[1] Disc and Record Echo; 5[2] New Musical Express; 6[1] Gered Mankowitz/©Bowstir Ltd/2020/mankowitz.com; 7[1] Gered Mankowitz/©Bowstir Ltd/2020/mankowitz.com; 7[2] Clive Arrowsmith/MMtek/Mainman Archive; 8[1,2] TCD/Prod.DB/Alamy Stock Photo; 9[1,2,3,4] Michael Stroud/MMtek/Mainman Archive; 10[1] Gered Mankowitz/©Bowstir Ltd/2020/mankowitz.com; 10[2] Leee Black Childers/MMtek/Mainman Archive; 11[1,2,3] Gered Mankowitz/©Bowstir Ltd/2020/mankowitz.com; 12[1],13[2] Sandra Wood; 14[2] MMtek/Mainman Archive; 17[3] Leslie Spitz; 18[1] Donald Cooper/Photostage; 20[1] Mick Rock/MMtek/Mainman Archive; 20[2] Joe Stevens/MMtek/Mainman Archive; 20[3] Terry O'Neill/MMtek/ Mainman Archive; 21[1,2] MMtek/Mainman Archive; 23[6] Angie Bowie; 24[4] Robin Sylvester; 25[1,2] MMtek/Mainman Archive; 25[3] Clive Arrowsmith/MMtek/Mainman Archive; 25[4] Terry O'Neill/MMtek/ Mainman; 26[1] Clive Arrowsmith/MMtek/Mainman Archive; 26[2,3] Joseph Stevens/MMtek/Mainman Archive; 26[4] MMtek/Mainman Archive; 27[1] Richard Bernstein, based on a photo by Terry O'Neill; 28[1] Leslie Spitz; 28[2] Gered Mankowitz/©Bowstir Ltd/2020/ mankowitz.com; 28[3] Phill Brown; 29[1,2] Gered Mankowitz/©Bowstir Ltd/2020/mankowitz.com; 30[1,2] Leslie Spitz; 30[3] John Porter; 31[1] Terry O'Neill/MMtek/Mainman Archive; 32 PA Images/Alamy Stock Photo; 32[2] Nick McCann; 32[3] Frank Hodge; 33[2] Photo 12/Alamy Stock Photo; 34[1,2] Everett Collection Inc/Alamy Stock Photo; 35[1] Keystone Press/Alamy Stock Photo; 35[2] Greg Dark; 35[3] Moviestore Collection Ltd/Alamy Stock Photo; 36[1,2,4] Mai Zetterling; 37[2] AF archive/Alamy Stock Photo; 38[2] Leslie Spitz, 40[1]-41[2] Jorg Huber; 44[1,2] Mike Hewitson; 45 Nick McCann; 46[1]-48[2] Jorg Huber; 49[1] Anne Gillespie; 50[1,2,3] Rudi Dolezal; 51[1]-52[2] Jorg Huber; 53[1] Milica Theessink; 53[2]-55[1] Jorg Huber; 55[2] Leslie Spitz; 56[1] Tatiana Gorilovsky; 56[2]-57[2],61[1]-62[1] David Shasha; 62[2] Tris Penna; 62[3] Rose Ann Liener; 63[1] David Shasha; 63[2] Marcus Shields; 64 Jake Zaitz; Back Cover Anastasiia Zaitz; Dust Jacket Flap Front Gered Mankowitz/©Bowstir Ltd/2020/mankowitz.com; Dust Jacket Flap Back Maciek Shasha

OTHER MUSIC BOOKS
FROM THE PUBLISHER

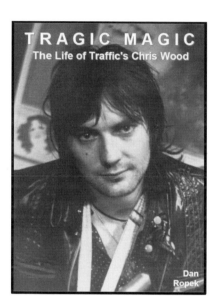

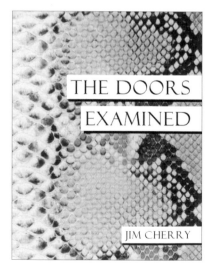

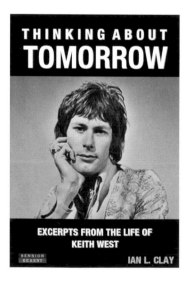